New Perspectives on African Literature
Ayi Kwei Armah's Africa

New Perspectives on African Literature

General Editor:
Eldred Jones
Emeritus Professor of English
Fourah Bay College, University of Sierra Leone
Freetown, Sierra Leone

No. 1: Ayi Kwei Armah's Africa:
The Sources of His Fiction   DEREK WRIGHT

Ayi Kwei Armah's Africa
The Sources of His Fiction

DEREK WRIGHT
Lecturer in English
Northern Territory University
Darwin, Australia

HANS ZELL PUBLISHERS
London · Munich · New York · 1989

PR
9379.9
A7
Z98
1989

© Copyright Derek Wright 1989
Hans Zell Publishers
An imprint of the K.G. Saur division of Butterworths
Shropshire House, 2–10 Capper Street, London WC1E 6JA. England

British Library Cataloguing in Publication Data
Wright, Derek.
    Ayi Kwei Armah's Africa: the sources of his fiction.–(New
    perspectives in African literature; no. 1)
    1. Fiction in English. Ghanaian writers.
    Armah, Ayi Kwei, 1939–. Critical studies
    I. Title   II. Series
    823

ISBN 0–905450–95–7

Typeset by DMD, St. Clements, Oxford
Printed and bound in Great Britain
by Unwin Brothers Limited, The Gresham Press
Old Woking, Surrey.

Contents

Preface

In this book the predominantly African backgrounds to and influences upon Armah's fiction are traced by situating it in its proper ritual, mythological, political and literary contexts. For background information of a purely biographical or historical nature, the reader should look elsewhere. The spadework in the latter area, and in basic thematic analysis of the novels, has been done by Robert Fraser in his valuable critical introduction, *The Novels of Ayi Kwei Armah: A Study in Polemical Fiction* (1980). My own work, designed to suit the specialized needs of scholars and students of African literature as well as the interests of the general reader, carries the fiction into a broader cultural and anthropological ambience and considers it in terms of a more complex series of determinants. I have also assumed a greater familiarity with the texts of the novels than is assumed by Fraser's book.

Armah's early novels form the focus of this book. I am aware of the possible objection that the attention paid to Fanon and the indigenous ritual and mythological currents underlying the narratives of the first two books has not been extended to the literary and intellectual mentors — African griots, Chancellor Williams, Cheikh Anta Diop — of the last two. This did not happen because to the present writer the latter influences seem, like the novels themselves, to be more transparent and so less inviting of complex analysis than the earlier ones. The indebtedness to an African heritage and world-view which I have discerned in the allusive, labyrinthine prose of *The Beautyful Ones Are Not Yet Born* and *Fragments* is a rich, subtextual one: as such, it has provided more substantial critical fare than the mannered experimentation with simulated orality in *Two Thousand Seasons* and the simplistic historical vision of *The Healers*. Much work remains to be done on the sources of Armah's histories, but my feeling is that it would be better left to someone who holds them in higher esteem that I do and I had no wish to make a long book even longer.

I would like to thank the editors of the following journals and presses for allowing me to reproduce some material contained, and presented in a different form, in articles originally published by them: *Ariel* and the University of Calgary Press; *English Studies in Africa* and the Witwatersrand University Press; *The Journal of Commonwealth Literature* and Hans Zell Publishers; *Research in African Literatures* and the University of Texas Press; *World Literature Today* and the University of Oklahoma Press. I am grateful to Robert Fraser and Heinemann Educational Books Ltd for permission to quote from *The Novels of Ayi Kwei Armah*. Acknowledgements are also due to the following: Heinemann Educational Books Ltd for Armah's five novels, *African Religions and Philosophy* by John S.Mbiti, and *Messages: Poems from Ghana*, eds.Kofi Awoonor and G.Adali-Mortty; Grove Press, Inc. for *The Wretched of the Earth* by Frantz Fanon; Century Hutchinson Ltd for *The Autobiography of Malcolm X*; Jonathan Cape Ltd and Random House, Inc. for *Black Power* by Stokely Carmichael and Charles V.Hamilton; Michael Joseph Ltd for *The Fire Next Time* by James Baldwin; and Oxford University Press for *The Fabulators* by Robert Scholes. Finally, special thanks are due to the following individuals: Renate Mohrbach-Wright for her translations of foreign language articles; Anna Akermann of the University College Library, Darwin, for her swift rounding up of Armah's recent journalism; and Professor Ken Goodwin of the University of Queensland for his supervision of my

post-graduate work on African literature, which provided
the germ of this book.

Darwin 1988

I

Introduction

Ayi Kwei Armah is an African author and his Africanness is the main subject of this work. That such a truism, in the mouth of a Western critic, should sound contentious to the reader of African fiction and even have a provoking ring of controversy in the ears of some African writers and academics is understandable but is also cause for critical concern. Armah's early departure and lengthy absences from his native Ghana, together with his setting of his early novels in an unashamedly modern, urban and Westernized Africa, have helped to create the impression that his writing reveals little real knowledge of or interest in traditional African culture. The novelist's spurning, in his polemical essays, of what he deems to be a romantic and mystifying idealization of that culture by Negritude and Pan-Africanism, has probably deepened these doubts. It is hoped that the following critical explorations will go some way towards correcting these misapprehensions and rehabilitating some of the more distinctively African qualities which inform the work of this author — an author who has always eschewed the notion of exile and whose lengthiest periods of residence abroad have not, in fact, been spent in the United States and Europe but in other parts of Africa (Algeria, Tanzania, Lesotho and, most recently, Senegal).

In the light of Armah's African background and American education, the question of the literary and political influences upon his fiction has always been a vexed one. The idea that the vision and techniques of the early novels are foreign-derived or at least foreign-inspired has become a commonplace in the criticism of African fiction, and Western commentators who have tracked Armah's route into contemporary Ghana via specific European models such as Sartre, Kafka, Beckett, Céline, and Robbe-Grillet are legion. It is not proposed in this work to deny the reality of Western influence on Armah's thought and style, or to disentangle the African and European influences in the seamless web of his fiction, especially since there are areas of his writing, such as the treatment of time in the first novel, where Western stylistics and ideas drawn from African oral cultures go happily hand in hand and are mutually reinforcing. It is simply proposed that attention be paid to some of those African influences which have hitherto been neglected or ignored. Neither has any attempt been made to obscure or diminish the significance of the dominant non-African political allegiances and influences, notably those of Fanon and the black American revolution, which are as evident in Armah's work as white literary influence. In the political arena, however, the novelist's peculiar debts to Fanon's analysis of post-colonial society clearly reveal that analysis to be African in its reference if not in its origin, even if Fanon's personal experience of Ghana is left out of account. The polarized racial vision of *Why Are We So Blest?* obviously draws upon Armah's experience of America during those years of racial confrontation which saw a marked shift from integrationist to black separatist politics. Yet it is the extrication of Africa from Europe, not the separation of the black from the white race with which it is sometimes confused in this unevenly-executed novel, or the peculiarly American race-situation, that is his primary concern.

It is perhaps less obvious that the modern malaise of Armah's alienated been-to is not merely a foreign literary imposition, either of existential angst or absurdist ennui, which upholds an un-African view of the universe. For the historically-minded novelist trained as a social scientist, this Western-induced paralysis is transparently the product of an exploitative politico-economic process by which Europe has not only exported its psychological maladies to its colonized subjects but continues to bequeath to Independent Africa problems that are only a modified version of those borne by colonial Africa: problems that arise from a stultifying Western interference in and indirect control of African affairs. Armah delves deeper than the personal disenchantment of his protagonists to the historical determinants identified by Fanon and the search leads him back, finally, to a pre-modern Africa. His small body of fiction reveals a deepening suspicion of all conceptual systems derived from Europe and this is ultimately extended to their concomitant literary styles and techniques, even when discernible — as they clearly are in the first three novels — in his own work. In the exclusively literary zone of influence there are, no doubt, vestiges of the French *nouveau roman* in the descriptive tableaux of *The Beautyful Ones Are Not Yet Born*: Armah was employed as a translator in Paris and Algiers during the writing of the book and there are certainly francophone leanings in all his early work which are unusual in an anglophone African author. As my discussion of the first novel demonstrates, however, the stylistic excesses are often made to serve peculiarly ritualistic and traditionally African concepts.

The divergence of Armah's visionary, symbolic modes from the plodding realism of mainstream African fiction led initially to the censure of his language and social vision (along with his portrait of Nkrumah's Ghana) as "inauthentic", or only incidentally African, by a kind of un-African Activities Committee of the literary imagination, originally chaired by Chinua Achebe and stacked by his academic disciples. The school of critics spawned by this narrowly "Africanist" line of thinking alleged a number of specific and general shortcomings: a rejection of the extended family system's "familial warmth" by a private, Westernized sensibility;[1] an abject failure to realize Ghanaian settings and even to differentiate between different kinds of Ghanaian speech;[2] an impaired vision, depicting a falsified, unrecognizable Ghana and betraying a long-expatriated author's failing insight into the drama of the Nkrumah political experiment;[3] and a predilection for "one-sided realities" that explain African political failure in terms of the personalities of leaders instead of "the complex process of history".[4] American commentators were not slow to add their voices to this chorus of critical irrelevance.[5]

In the matter of the family system, I have tried to show in my examination of the first two novels that Armah does not condone but exposes and excoriates that very same Westernized corruption of traditional family values (a process not initiated by himself) — values which, undermined by a perverted individualism, are no longer an expression of a communal ethic. Most of the other charges can be answered at their own level of banality. It is easy enough, for example, to refute one critic's claim that the first novel

> has nothing essentially Ghanaian about it: no specifically Ghanaian mannerisms or special brand of politics, no language in the local idiom of the people . . . and the major events in the novel never take place in any well-known geographical or political centre in Ghana.[6]

Events take place at the Esikafo Aba Estates, the Sekondi-Takoradi wharves and the Kansawora Railway Office, where the man passes a third of the novel. The supposed movement of the book from the ill-defined and allegoric to the particular and historical has been much exaggerated: in fact, we are explicitly in Ghana from the messenger's win in the Ghana lottery in the second chapter. It is perhaps worth mentioning at the outset that there are a number of features which Armah's early work has in common with more conventional African novels. As regards language, for example, the local idiom of proverb is used in the first book by the boatman, who falls back upon "the ancient dignity of formal speech" in his ironic welcoming of the fugitive Koomson,[7] and Ghanaian pidgin is used sporadically in the course of the novel by a number of characters from Koomson down to the watchman. Thus it cannot be convincingly maintained that Armah confines pidgin to latrine graffiti on the assumption, made by another critic, that he "probably regards pidgin as unworthy of literary record".[8] The first two novels are, moreover, imbued with a variety of debased rituals, purificatory and sacrificial ceremonial motifs, local mythologies, residual ancestral beliefs and the vestiges of religious practices, all of which have their roots in traditional African society.

The picture of Nkrumah's Ghana in the first book is, of course, stark and selective. Trimmed to fit Fanonian theory, it records the speed and waste, the abortive plans and false public utilities, and leaves out the industry. But allowance for Armah's polemically heightened mode of realism should not divert attention from the fact that there is much in the historical reality of Nkrumah's Ghana that invites the dystopian treatment it receives in the novel: it has not, in the novelist's visionary reconstruction, been so subjectivized as to become historically unrecognizable. There are references to specific historical events of the Nkrumah era, such as the investigation into the regime's corruption led by Legon's Professor Abraham, whose findings were largely suppressed by C.P.P. officials.[9] Furthermore, the post-war upheaval and national demoralization from which Nkrumah's movement emerged are harrowingly documented in the long flashback at the centre of the novel. Kofi Busia's researches into the system of "pilot boys" steering incoming seamen towards Takoradi's wharfside prostitutes, who "could earn what was then a princely wage of eight to fifteen pounds a month",[10] are reflected, for instance, in Armah's savage picture of wharf-life between the War and Independence: "The wharves turned men into gulls and vultures, sharp waiters for the weird foreign appetites to satisfy, pilots of the hungry alien seeking human flesh."[11]

Allegations of a "one-sided reality" are less swiftly dealt with. It is true that Armah's novels do tend to reduce "the complex process of history" to the suspiciously perfect symmetry of cyclical patterns. Neo-colonialism rein-carnates colonial and pre-colonial evils that were never really expelled: the first novel piles up the vast accumulated filth of Africa's history for the man, in mock-ritual manner, to carry out to sea. Certainly, Armah seems to have less interest in the peculiarities of the Nkrumah regime than in what it can be made to represent, in mytho-symbolic form, for Africa, in its passage through the neo-colonial phase. Although selected personnel are needed for the vision to acquire any power of historical relevance, pattern and process are more important than particulars, and the political personalities through which historical processes are filtered are essentially cartoon constructions. This was unsatisfying to some African critics who appeared to be looking for the documentary realism of social history; for whom anything that was not concretely embodied either in historical or in geographical actuality was liable to be dismissed as "foreign metaphor";[12] by whom the distillation of contemporary history into myth was frowned upon as something tendentiously European. It is not my intention at this point to resurrect a dead and largely deadlocked debate about what constitutes "Africanness" and "African" writing, with a view to trying to isolate some unique and pristine "African" quality from all the other influences at work upon a piece of fiction.

Suffice it to say that even if Armah himself, in his devastating reply to Charles Larson, [13] had not vigorously denied many of the foregoing imputations about his work, it would still be luminously apparent from the novels themselves that the "Africanness" of his imagination, if we can use such a term, is an elusive quality that reveals itself to a correspondingly subtle and probing critical approach, not a shallow property that can be substantiated or refuted by reference to sociological accuracy, setting or narrative realism. What Armah seems to have been attempting from his first novel onwards is a systematic and visionary reformulation of the given "reality", in which both metaphor and myth are of crucial importance. Running counter to the despairing conclusions of the psychological narrative, an important network of images in the first novel's metaphoric structure takes the first steps towards the negotiatory polemicism of *Why Are We So Blest?* and the histories, abandoning a transcriptive for a prescriptive style. These metaphors proclaim their own proprietorship of reality in a methodical counter-attack which, in its respective methods and aims, both reflects and refutes psycho-linguistic constructs inherited from colonialism, particularly those that polarize colours and images to promote white racist supremacy. In this novel the gleam of material power and success is obsessively linked with whiteness: white hotels, bungalows, fences, uniforms. Things get brighter and whiter as they get closer to the command-centres (Koomson's house glitters with silver) and thus closer to the invisible white powers that lie behind them. White-washed power and prosperity are able, from their special positions, to keep themselves immune to dirt and defilement (pure water flows from the Hill Stations) and even extend their ownership-powers to the "bleaching" of language: words like "clean" and "pure" are linked with white superiority. The black regime's language of definition is much the same as that of the former white one. But the whiteness of the gleam is a filth-producing whiteness. Its cleanness has "more rottenness in it than the slime at the bottom of a garbage dump".[14] The cleanness of the dammed-up water in the little stream soon becomes tainted by the mud of its beginnings and the gleaming white municipal bin signs are covered over with the refuse of white-modelled consumerism. The white uniforms of neo-colonial stewards connect them with servitude and slavery and the clean water flowing from the high places of white colonial power is used by lepers, "catching its cleanness before it reached the mud".[15] In the novel's post-colonial black society, whiteness is something that everyone from politician to street-seller is drawn into: it imposes itself as pervasively and contagiously as the white desert which, in *Two Thousand Seasons*, gives nothing but takes everything into itself. The colour-scheme has not yet polarized into an absolute black-white reversal of colonial constructs, but there are incipient signs of the later sharpening of whiteness into one of the key characteristics of evil, in *Why Are We So Blest?*, and into the very epitome of evil in *Two Thousand Seasons*, where everything that is not black automatically becomes anti-black (and anti-good) and therefore white (and evil), Arabs and Europeans alike.

The first novel's indictments of contemporary Ghana make a virtue out of one-sidedness, their aim being to redress the lopsidedness of a vast edifice of colonial literature and the parallel imbalance in the value structures of imitation-white societies. Armah's hyperbole of whiteness and filth, his dystopian vision of a world piled high with excrement and constituting a version, or perversion, of white values was surely calculated to horrify Western audiences, although for some African critics the effort to shock the oppressor almost killed off the victim. Others were more perceptive. Ama Ata Aidoo saw that it is "quite misleading to approach the book as though it is just a novel in any 'traditional' sense of the word"[16] and Sunday Anozie, arguing in structuralist terms for a new kind of realism in the African novel, noted "a structural genetic rapport between the internal socio-political crises of Africa . . . and the types of characters and plots of novels".[17] Plot, characterization and symbolism were seen to grow out of and to be governed by the long crisis of neo-colonial manipulation and failing national confidence which had become the norm and paradigm for much of Independent Africa. Though worried initially that its near "metaphysical dimensions" might not be consistent with the awakening of revolutionary anxiety, Wole Soyinka conceded that "the vision is there, nevertheless, and is perhaps more subtly subversive than in his latter explicit work, *Two Thousand Seasons*".[18] The sheer volume of attention given to the ritualistic-cum-fatalistic dimensions of the novel's metaphors to the neglect of the polemical ones, in my own account, should not detract from its polemical thrust towards that divesting the mind of colonial structures that is necessary for the writer to enter Fanon's "fighting phase", towards getting the beautiful ones born. The reader is invited to take sides and make choices which are heavily pre-empted by the superior attractiveness of one of the options, irrespective of the "disturbing ambiguities" and multi-layered complexities of the symbolic structure as a whole. *The Beautyful Ones Are Not Yet Born* was never meant to be a piece of "objective realism".

The driving polemical harangue that continues through Armah's entire *oeuvre* does not, however, make the world of his novels a simple affair. Armah's Africa is a complicated amalgam of vanishing but unvanquished pasts and bleakly futureless presents, a rich interplay of contemporary life not so much with the not yet born as with the not yet dead. Herein lies the crux of his complexity and the essentially African origins of his inspiration. In the first two novels, traditional West African cultures are vestigially but nonetheless powerfully present, both in their superior ethical imperatives and their inherent deficiencies. The cyclical narrative and metaphoric structures of the first book are worked out against an intricate backcloth of indigenous ritual motifs and myths which act as the vehicles of peculiarly African ideas about pollution and purification, time and communality. In the next novel, *Fragments*, a ritualistic subtext draws more specifically upon arcane areas of Akan custom and religion to rehabilitate a dead order of value as a living presence in the novel. Armah's investigation of debased ritual practices in both of these novels establishes a complex and problematic continuity between a traditional past and a corruptly modern present: in this fictional realm, straddling two worlds, traditionally-honoured ancestors are starved of libations by drunken modern priests and the few remaining gods have been driven from almost deserted groves by a self-worshipping materialism. Racked by a self-distrust which reflects a national failure of confidence in the constructive potential of indigenous culture, the contemporary cognates of griots, chanters and sculptors have gone overseas in search of foreign approval. Local folk myths have been tampered with by television technocrats fishing for foreign foundation grants. Yet in spite of this degenerative process, and perhaps partly in determined resistance to it, the past in the early novels contrives to be dormant rather than dead and its interplay with the present in which it has a vestigial existence draws upon Armah's imaginative possession of old West African coastal mythologies and ritual forms and the religious beliefs and values which inform them. My discussion of this area of reference in the chapters on the main fiction has involved investigations of the alternative time concepts behind the first novel, the Akan theology of *Fragments*, and the pattern of the purification ritual which forms a haunting ironic backcloth to the action of the first book and hovers over the twin narrative of Baako and Juana in the second. The analysis of this complex of ideas gives some indication of Armah's unexpected common ground with literature from which his own writing might be thought far removed, such as the tradition-oriented plays of the early Soyinka, and with the work of writers who have adopted a hostile critical stance towards him, such as Awoonor: in the latter's opinion, only misguided Western critics regard Armah as "the most authentic artistic voice in African fiction".[19] Other African commentators, with a more catholic and hospitable concept of traditionalism, have drawn attention to the first novel's indebtedness to African fable[20] and the graphic personification of the oral tradition, [21] and to the last novel's striking simulation of the oracular and editing devices of oral narrative.[22] These additional fruitful areas of enquiry are, however, beyond the scope of my argument, which is sited principally in ritual and mythology.

One possible misapprehension should be anticipated and dispelled at the outset. It is not the intention of this work to present the author's continuing awareness of the past and the delimited value of traditional culture as a ripening progress which achieves its final florescence in the vision of the histories. On the contrary, my brief chapters on the later novels highlight the decline in performance and the damage done to form as a result of Armah's moving away from these earlier values. Whatever continuities exist, the historical outlook of the last two books is essentially different from that of the early ones. The subtextual "Africanness" of the latter has graduated, in the histories, into something more explicit and insistent, something formulated and schematized, unambiguously, into ideology, and Armah's choice of an alternative genre is, inevitably, marked by a corresponding loss of subtlety and complexity in both symbolism and characterization. The past itself, which assumes many different guises in the first two books, is endowed with a new singleness and simplicity by the dogma of "the Way". The continuity of the main fiction is a disputed issue and my interpretation places what has become, in much recent criticism, an unfashionable emphasis on the discontinuity of Armah's literary career. It is designed to do justice, of a very specific and detailed kind, to the versatility of a novelist who never does the same thing twice, a tireless experimenter who has a genius for finding new mediums for old messages. Armah's obsessive vision of an Africa whose only hope for the future lies in breaking free from the paralysing grip of Western values and controls is embodied in five entirely different, independent fictional modes: the classical-cum-allegorical, the semi-autobiographical *Bildungsroman*, the political polemic, the epic and the historical novel. A narrow monothematic interpretation that highlights questionable continuities at the expense of these palpable formal differences stands always in danger of reading Armah's *oeuvre* as if it were really a single novel — rather as E. M. W. Tillyard, for example, in his account of Shakespeare's second historical tetralogy leaves the impression that one has been reading about a single play.[23] It is perhaps significant that some of the weakest moments in critical endeavours to cover the whole span of Armah's fiction are to be found in the forging of spurious continuities between individual novels, a phenomenon which is particularly marked in what is, to date, the only book on Armah. Apparently at a loss for a more organic connection, Robert Fraser unconvincingly bridges the leap from the first to the second, and from the third to the fourth novel by the somewhat gratuitous introduction into his perorating comments on *The Beautyful Ones Are Not Yet Born* and *Why Are We So Blest?* of, respectively, the suppressed "cult of the artist" and the suddenly urgent need for a communal vision and plural voice. [24] Even less convincing in Fraser's otherwise perceptive monograph is the rationalization through hindsight of Armah's image patterns:

> Suffice it here to note that there are certain symbols which transcend the divisions between the books, recurring in such a way as to amount to motifs pervading the whole of Armah's writing. The most obvious of these is the stream which surfaces in the third chapter of *The Beautyful Ones* and, in its meandering imperilled progress to the sea, runs through most of the novels to date. Wherever it occurs the connotation would seem to be of an indigenous, prehistoric sense of integrity attempting to force its way through the accumulated moral pollution of the centuries. [25]

The forcing of ways here is accomplished not so much by the image and its author as by the critic who is determined to squeeze the novels into an unspectacular metaphoric landscape bordered on one side by the blocked stream of the first novel and on the other by the rushing seabound rivers of the fourth. Fraser's reading of the image is a correct one: the metaphor of passages clogged by ancient accumulations of pollution is pervasive in the first novel and establishes important links with its view of history and its figurative employment of a traditional purification rite. What is suspect is the retrospective imposition of the stream-river-sea image complex of the histories onto the symbolism of the early novels and the attempt to make it retroactive. In fact, the stream itself makes only one brief appearance in the first book and is almost wholly absent from the next two. Naana's "circular way", in *Fragments*, is river-like but, except for one among a kaleidoscopic medley of metaphors for ancestral voices that envisages them as "something rushing and breathless like a young river", [26] she uses no river images and does not translate the abstract concept of her cyclical journey into this particular form. The stream image is stamped upon the first page of *Why Are We So Blest?* with the arbitrariness of the personal insignia which it appears to have become in Armah's writing and, having served as epigraph to the novel's theme of diverted energies, plays no further part in the narrative.

It would be more correct to say that it is the intellectual shape of Armah's symbols which is recurrent, rather than the symbols themselves. For example, the idea of the cycle, either with its regenerative connotations or with its darker hints of vicious circles of entrapment, underlies theme and structure throughout the fiction, from the early stories to the latest novel. But within the limits of this very loose pattern of consistency, each novel starts again with a new metaphoric pattern and is structured around its own independent symbolic centre, which makes no reference beyond the work at hand. In each book the commanding metaphor is quite different, in fact: the ingestion-evacuation circuit in the first; fragmentation, coupled with selective blindness and returning ghosts, in the second; Promethean deliverance in the third; the ongoing, cyclical course of water and the seasons, in opposition to the changeless blank of the desert, in the fourth; the restorative healing of wounds — personal, national and racial — in the fifth.

A pattern of evolution is certainly traceable in Armah's work, impelling him in the direction of political commitment, and this is evident in the shifting identities of the recurring and conflicting "two communities" in the novels: from the individual and the family, in *The Beautyful Ones Are Not Yet Born*, to the family and Ghanaian society, in *Fragments*, and thence to Africa and America, in *Why Are We So Blest?* and to Africa and the whole non-black world, in *Two Thousand Seasons*. But to run together the themes and symbols of each book with a dovetailed precision is to risk oversight of the unique and separate phases of this process. To return to Fraser:

> Thus we can see that, right at the imagistic heart of these books there is the constant visualisation of a conflict essential to Armah's vision of history: the struggle between the native genius of a people trying to assert its cultural integrity, and the forces, usually internalised, which would divert it into alien channels.[27]

This is more true of the later novels than the earlier ones, the "native genius" of Armah's Ghanaians being slow to emerge. In *Fragments* it has gone underground and has to be smuggled back into the text in almost occult fashion through allusions to the traditional wisdoms enshrined in defunct rituals and mythologies. In *The Beautyful Ones Are Not Yet Born* the new mass-culture of materialism seems to have almost obliterated it. In *Why Are We So Blest?* the African cultural integrities mobilized by political revolution are easily diverted into the alien channels of compromising Western comforts.

Such errors of judgement are the price of a too-ambitious generalization. I have attempted to consider each novel on its own terms and have limited discussion of their common ground to a consideration of ritual structures. The aim here has been to analyse, not to schematize; to break down, not to link up; to determine the intrinsic character of each book, not to locate its position in some intellectual sequence or pattern governing the whole work. A preoccupation with fidelity to Armah's densely and intricately textured prose has resulted in a certain amount of close criticism, particularly of *The Beautyful Ones Are Not Yet Born* which, of all the early novels, is most richly endowed with the special kind of "Africanness" that I am concerned to demonstrate. Brief space has been granted to two hitherto neglected or overlooked areas of Armah's writing, the short stories and essays which anticipate some of the themes of the main fiction. It is hoped that this critical close-up, however inconclusive, will make clear the numerous ways in which this author draws upon his African heritage and will leave no doubts about the rightful place in a tradition of African writing that is due to a body of work already too much beclouded by misunderstanding.

II

The Short Stories

All of Armah's apprenticeship fiction was written in the 1960s, the decade of post-Independence disenchantment which also saw the publication of his polemical essays on African socialism, Fanon and the political "mystification" of Independence; and it is best read in conjunction with these essays. Yet, with the exception of "An African Fable", the early stories are not merely didactic parables and the subtle and ironic diversity of their adopted voices ill-prepares the reader for the more monolithic narratives and polemical harangues of the novels. Armah's familiar themes are often submerged in these sketches under the cover of narrative personae who are unusually distanced from the writer's own viewpoint, and subjects which will later be the ground of partisan commitment are removed from contention by an adroit neutrality.

"Asemka", Armah's first story with an African setting, delicately balances traditional communal values against the Western model of the nuclear family and the withdrawn, alienated lives of Westernized clerks.[1] The narrator, a gregarious elderly woman living in a rooming-house, is scandalized by the aloof, uncommunicative behaviour of a reclusive widower, Mr Ainoo, and, when she importunately suggests that his daughter Essie should not live in the same household as his new young wife, he dismisses her with a few curt, cynical remarks about the naturalness and inevitability of familial conflict. Resolving not to trouble his peace further, she subsequently disobeys her natural instincts by neglecting to tell him of his daughter's seduction and desertion by a drifter,

Mr Mensah. The pregnant girl is packed off in disgrace to a hospital, which her proud father refuses to visit.

Far from being recommended to the reader, the woman's views irrelevantly parrot custom-bound axioms and she casts doubts on the purity of her motives by her own evident sexual designs on Ainoo. She seeks to remove or stifle possible sources of conflict instead of learning how to live with them and trusts blindly to the conservative dogma of traditional culture about the sagacity of elders: Essie is advised to stay with a "wise elder" such as her grandmother. Yet her instincts prove to be at least partly right. The daughter does quarrel with her stepmother and, as foreseen, takes refuge at her grandmother's house although this, far from ensuring her safety, then provides the alibi for her sexual liaison with Mensah. Ainoo's desire for solitude makes him insensitive to his daughter's predicament and his impenitently proud adoption of supposedly more enlightened Western views of family relations has disastrous consequences. But the woman's decision not to act on her knowledge gives her a hollow victory. Following the precedent set by his foreign code of privacy, she abrogates her communal responsibility by keeping silent and is in turn drawn into the infectious circle of Ainoo's self-defeating pride and Westernized aloofness, which isolate good-will and frustrate fraternal impulses. Ainoo, who has come too far to return to African ways, only deepens his dependency on the Western habits he has cultivated and strengthens his isolation whilst the woman, left with an empty triumph, is saddened by this "new pride" which "has come into our men, that they want to be alone and hard".[2] The narrator's garrulous dogmatizing becomes an unlikely vehicle for Armah's first exposure of the "strange disease" of loneliness in those who cut themselves off from community. Suffering ensues when the connectedness of human beings is denied and no one is allowed to take responsibility for anyone else. At the same time, the story expresses reservations about communal values in modern urban contexts which are interesting in the light of the treatment in the first two novels of the extended family and the suffocating familial warmth of the tyrannical loved ones.

"Yaw Manu's Charm",[3] a more substantial story, is a disturbing study of the far-reaching effects of neo-colonial psychology. The eponymous subject is a humbler version of those alienated Africans who consent to their uprooting from their own cultures by foreign scholarships and, in the words of Modin in the third novel, have swallowed the wish for their own destruction. A clerk of limited intelligence but deep integrity and piety, Manu has lived apart from his immediate African centre from an early age, obsessed with the ambition to study in England and advance himself into the "been-to" elite. After being forced to leave the Catholic school which taught him that "only faith could bring success", he continues to retake and fail the Cambridge Certificate examination whilst working in the British Bank of West Africa, all the while pouring money, borrowed at heavy rates of interest from a local money-lender, into expensive and dubious correspondence courses, brain-pills and "secret-of-success" magazines purchased from England. Convinced that he can succeed by faith without intelligence, he finally buys a charm from a Muslim *maalam* who tells him that it will make him invisible and, in a fantasy of magical power, bizarrely tries to rob the bank in which he works. He is imprisoned and sent to a mental asylum.

Armah again employs an unreliable narrator who screens the truth behind a fog of prejudices. Yaw's plight is recounted in a rambling, cliché-ridden narrative by a shallow former schoolmate and fellow bank clerk who radiates artificial bonhomie and pompous respectability. It is like looking at the world of the man in the first novel

through the eyes of the corrupt, pretentious senior civil
servants, whose forced sycophantic laughter in the presence of the white man is again much in evidence.
A Sunday Christian and vociferous conformist, he is
embarrassed by Yaw's intense piety and silent withdrawn
industry. The totally corrupt universe of the first novel is
here in conception, and the narrator's social insight is
shrewd enough to see through the hypocrisy of honesty in
a corrupt society: "After all, everybody knows that it is
impossible for an honest man to become rich, and yet the
rich are respected."[4] But he is so blinded by his
Europeanized snobberies that he fails to notice any
inconsistency between the incredulous contempt which
he pours on charm-selling *maalams* and his nostalgic
affection for the superstitious Catholic rituals of his
schooldays, and the ironic echo of the priest's mountain-
moving claims for faith in the *maalam's* "You fit do anytin"
is too painfully sharp for his obtuse hearing. The story's
finale has him running to the police to serve as chief
witness in the prosecution of the *maalam's* native
imposture whilst its more pernicious foreign counterpart
goes unchallenged.

The Catholic Church, which is really Yaw Manu's fatal
charm, is seen to compound social and political hypocrisies inherited from the colonial system. The exclusive
Catholic schools train the chosen few for elite status while
dispensing simplistic formulae, to the effect that "Saint
Joseph was only a poor carpenter", to assure the failures
that privilege is really neither important nor desirable.
They evade or deny the social divisions which they help to
create and depend upon. When their own kind of magic
fails Manu he tries to realize the "invisibility" which, in
social terms, they have trained him for, by other magical
means. The Church's role in Yaw's destruction is evident
in its wasting of his study-time at the altar of the school
chapel, the mystical trance-like states of his adult life in

which he talks "distantly, like a priest or catechist", and his behaviour during the bank robbery when, though under the spell of a juju charm, he is "silent and serene, like a priest when he is walking towards the altar".[5] The narrator insists that "priests and witch doctors never ate from the same bowl, so to speak",[6] but the story of Yaw Manu gives them a baleful continuity. Black magic finishes what white magic has started, and neither of these profits the simple, pious man in an elitist system that does not reward honesty or faith.

Yaw Manu is innocent of his slave-psychology: too deeply enslaved to be aware of it, he is unable to divest himself of the dreams it has instilled in him. In Yaw's hapless search for status and his squandering of African money on doubtful European products in pursuit of a European education that would, as Baako and Modin discover, implant in him only a sense of his own inferiority and the deepened enslavement of his people, Armah has constructed a comic-pathetic paradigm of the unchanged patterns of economic flow and psychological dependency under African Independence. The tale demonstrates how, even at the lowest levels of aspiration, African resources are absorbed into the service of an exploitative European structure, represented here by the parasitic elites of church and state who operate as factors in the employ of the imperial command-centres of foreign political and economic powers. "Yaw Manu's Charm" is somewhat weakened by the exotic episode of the *maalam* and the heavy-handed satiric portrait of the colonial bank manager, but these are minor flaws on the surface of an accomplished exercise in incisive and compassionate irony.

These two stories achieve a technical finesse at the price of a thinness of characterization and descriptive texture. Their experiments with narrative technique generate ironies which disengage the reader from their subjects and a similar thinness and distance, though coming from a quite different source, mark the style of Armah's first novel. The man's indiscriminate, almost pathological compassion for the poor and oppressed, extending even to those who neither seek nor invite it, serves to impersonalize, rather than intensify, the facts of suffering. It is part of an abstract pattern of ritualized empathy which remotely collectivizes the sufferers as objects instead of individualizing them as people. The people waiting at the bus stop at the start of chapter 4 of *The Beautyful Ones Are Not Yet Born*, for example, appear as a static tableau or frieze of itemized sculpted figures. It will be demonstrated in my discussion of the novel that the man's anonymity is essential to his ritual function and is not inconsistent with his individuality, but the parallel anonymity of the community he serves does at times reduce it to a collection of figures in a pattern, woven with an almost allegorical sparseness of texture. The impersonal presence of ritual process, implying an ordained and fatalistic order that often seems to be at odds with the idea of revolutionary change urged by the novel's polemics, adds to this impression of sculptured permanence and formality.

Armah's next American-published story, which appeared in the same year as the first novel, cuts across the neutralizing narrative devices of the first two African-set stories and the classic formality of the novel's ritual mode, however, and focuses with an angry sharpness on individual cruelty and injustice. The author has argued in his political essay on the "mystification" of African Independence that the conscript labour that was part of the colonial system is not fundamentally different from the servitude which "nationalist leadership in independent Africa has had the genius to dish out . . . to their liberated countrymen, urging not just acceptance but exaltation".[7] The harrowing third-person narrative of "The Offal Kind" follows the viewpoint of Araba from her being farmed out as a very young girl to an important "Lady", who sadistically works, beats and starves her almost to death, through her passage into vagrancy and Remand Home internment, to her eventual fate as a prostitute.[8] Armah has deliberately conceived this story after the pattern of Victorian England at the peak of its colonial power. From a rural family-system that can no longer take care of its children, girls are farmed out to self-styled aristocrats in whose employ they regress from household servants to the status of medieval serfs. Affecting a nineteenth-century remoteness from the masses, doubtless learned from the colonial cadres on which they model themselves, this Victorianized elite mentally reduces the abandoned of the city to the human refuse of the title. For those who work in this living museum of English Victorianism, there is nothing in life except work: Araba has no free time and the Remand Home's night-watchman, an earlier version of the un-sleeping office sweeper in the first novel, is tired from his other jobs during the day and falls asleep at his post. Driven penniless from the house of the society-woman and into vagrancy, Araba is kept from returning to her family home by a Victorian sense of shame and takes refuge with the market women, who first have to sell themselves as prostitutes in order to raise the capital for the selling of food-stuffs. At the end of the story Araba receives her first customer: "Briefly, the concrete posts of the Remand Home passed before the girl's eyes."[9] The choice is grimly clear: prison or prostitution. The vagrant girls go round and round in a vicious circle, serving the exploitative interests of an affluent Westernized elite which has carefully cultivated the legacy of Victorian imperialism in the post-Independence period. Araba is not merely a counter in a political parable, however: she is, much more than Yaw Manu, realized as an individual, with her sufferings sharply registered, and Armah's decision to dispense with the obstructive narrator allows for a vividly poetic rendering of sensuous detail as part of the character's unarticulated psychological impressions. Araba's reflections on the effects of the rains on the coastal town produce some haunting, elegiac lyrical passages that anticipate the stylistic richness of the first two novels: a richness that is most in evidence in Armah's work either when the authorial voice is directly employed or when the character-viewpoint is made to coincide nearly with the author's own. These techniques feature effectively in the intricate and intense "An African Fable" and his first-published and, arguably, his finest short story, "Contact".

The subject of "Contact" is Kobina, a lonely young African studying in America in the early 1960s.[10] The returning warmth of spring provokes in him a sudden renewal of the desire for "meaningful human contact" and takes him out of the "desiccated heat" and "artificial warmth" of his room, which he has come to associate with white America, to a party given by an aggressive sex-obsessed Afro-American called Lowell. Warming to the subject of Africa's supposed superior sexual wisdom, Lowell forces the embarrassed African into a reluctant drum duo, in which the two men enact musically a somewhat one-sided sexual climax, the American taking the powerful "masculine" beat and the African the softer "feminine" rhythm. Lowell then proceeds to lecture Kobina and Carin, a white girl Kobina has befriended, on the passive complicity of the black race with its rape by "white erect phallic cultures" and the penetration of racial mythology into the corners of private relationships, particularly through sexual manipulation. Implicitly warning Kobina against Carin, Lowell aligns himself with the separatist politics of black revolution: "But we can keep fighting on a personal level. So they raped us collectively. We don't have to let them rape us individually too."[11] Left mistrustful of their own motives at Lowell's departure, the couple nevertheless retire to Kobina's room to attempt the "real meeting" of races, the "simultaneous letting go" which, according to Kobina, "happens to one couple in a thousand".[12] The sexual exchange is a failure and, though Carin reassures him that they have at least made "a beginning", the African retreats into his self-disgust. In a local café along a "considerably chillier" street they run into Lowell who, chorus-like, leaves hanging over the ending the vexed question: "Just as a talking point, who used whom tonight?"[13]

The story contains in miniature the ingredients of *Why Are We So Blest?*, notably the racial manipulation of sex, and the triangle of characters looks like a trial sketch of Modin, Aimée and Solo. In the later novel Armah will construe the stultified sensibility's bored, sensation-devouring quest for excitement in the acting out of inauthentic fantasy roles as a symptom of white America's emotional and sexual illness, and this deadened condition, apparently the result of the exhausting colonial violence of the white race, is consistent with the tale's symbolically enervating, insensitizing cold, which muffles humanity in clothes too thick to allow contact. Carin, whose name associates naturally with Aimée's, has according to Lowell, "exhausted the pleasures of being privileged and white" and now wants "a taste of the pain of being black".[14] But the sexual roles of Modin and Aimée are, in fact, reversed here: instead of the African undertaking therapy of the frigid white woman and having his loving kindness murderously exploited, it is the sensitive white girl who takes charge of the sexual education of the over-impetuous African. In the story it is Lowell, the mouther of the glib formulae of black revolution, who is the morally suspect character and the principal "user" of people. Casting the African in the role of expert on "authentic drum rhythm", he treats him as a kind of performing animal and appoints himself as ringmaster in a

cross-cultural sexual experiment. His pruriently negritudinous view of Africa as "hot and spicy" and instinctively wise in the flesh is, ominously, the myth-muddled
white colonial view of Africa pandered to by Pan-
Africanists and certain francophone African poets. Lowell
has, on the one hand, assimilated and interiorized
perniciously romantic white fantasies of Africa whilst, on
the other, imbibing the white American insensitivity of
which his race is a victim.

The miniature epiphany of the drum crystallizes these
paradoxes. Superficially, the symbolism contrasts the
aggressively "masculine" pattern of black America's political and sexual revolution with Africa's "feminine"
submission to the rape of colonialism, simply "lying there,
open and greased, inviting the aggression of some erect
phallic culture".[15] Afro-America's male energy, "hard and
straight and aggressive", gives "female" Africa the "completion" she needs to be herself. But beneath these
oppositions there are uncomfortable continuities. There is
a euphoric moment of communion in which the two men
are "engrossed in the rhythms coming out of their
common drum", but then Lowell's frantic harder beats
drown Kobina's softer notes and the male rhythm reaches
its solitary climax, "ending with two muffled, satisfied
notes, leaving Kobina's feminine rhythm going on underneath, softly as before",[16] like Carin's continuing,
independent motion after Kobina's premature orgasm.
The spurious ritual communion of the drum has Lowell
taking the white role in a symbolic re-enactment of the
"Rape of Africa" of which he speaks so much. Insofar as
its ideas of black Africa are absorbed into the institutional-
ized white ones, black America collaborates with this
repeated rape: the black American does to the African
what the white man has done to both of them, leaving no
loophole for breaking the cycle. It is also significant that
the violation of the partner takes place at the merely

gestural level of ritual and power-fantasy. Lowell's tire-
some sexual gaucherie, Carin observes, only isolates him
further from sexual contact. As the unilateral condition of
the compromised African leaders and expatriates in *Why
Are We So Blest?* indicates, assimilation into a desiccated
white culture entails an instinctual sacrifice which, in
Armah's writing, finds its peculiar mark of distinction in
an actual or symbolic impotence. Lowell, like the bogus
black revolutionary professor Earl Lynch in the novel, is
given away by his name. He is more American than Afro,
bearing the prestigious white wasp-name of the American
aristocracy, a Mayflowerman. Of the characters in the tale,
he is the least able to experience Kobina's common
humanity, the least capable of contact.

The sexual encounter itself is also ambiguously
described. Carin's perfunctory attempt at orgasm reads
like a self-absorbed rite of penance and sacrifice, in which
racial guilt part-identifies with and part-expiates the
suffering of the traditionally used black victim (Carin has a
negrophiliac interest in what Lowell calls the "self-pitying
blues"). There are disturbing hints that, in merely allowing herself to be used sexually, Carin is herself the
psychological manipulator, using the African as a reluctant instrument of punishment on herself in a fantasy of
racial rape-revenge. Kobina, in his impatient lust, is only
in appearance the dominant, active "male" partner: even
in this quasi-rape he is still playing the passive, compliant,
"female" role of the drum ritual. Physically unable to give
pleasure and psychologically unable merely to take it, he
reaches an "apologetic climax" and is immediately consumed by a shame which has been partly engineered by
Carin's deliberate passivity. Kobina has told her earlier
that sex "is only the physical expression of what happens
on every level", and it would seem from the tale's
conclusion that Lowell is right — that the corrosive legacy
of racial history runs too deep for private remedies — were

it not for the fact that the couple's sexual failure is located in the inexperienced Kobina's disabling and defeatist idealism. He is, in Carin's verdict, "unrealistic", an "erotic perfectionist" who "wants the moon every time": failing to get it, he takes refuge in his "one-couple-in-a-thousand" cynicism. Racked by self-mistrust, they try for a relationship in defiance of racial determinants, but their tense consciousness of the race-context so inhibits the endeavour it promotes that it makes spontaneous expression impossible, forcing partners into pre-established roles. Armah's more liberal vision at the start of his writing career envisages an interracial relationship temporarily damaged by compromise with historical stereotypes, but there is no endorsement of the Lowell-Solo view that the historical pattern of exploitation and servitude must be the key to all black-white relations. What rescues the story from the morbid racial determinism of *Why Are We So Blest?* is the ability of Kobina and Carin (unlike Modin and Aimée) to fight their way out of the programmatic frame set for them by the third member of the triangle. Her rite of racial penance over, Carin hopes to build something more natural and constructive upon it. As she insists, "a beginning" has been made.

"An African Fable" is more grimly prophetic of the main fiction and directly anticipates the first novel's philosophy of perception.[17] In *The Beautyful Ones Are Not Yet Born* the involuntary perceptions of the passive consciousness broaden the man's vision, carrying fleeting intimations both of community and a deeper ritual perspective of meaning. But they can also lead to self-deluding infatuation, as in the case of the gleam-worshipper's merely "beholding" or "unconnected eye". This latter organ, because it cannot see beyond externals and is not guided by any moral precepts, falls an easy prey to the gleam's belligerent materialism. D.S.Izevbaye has defined the gleam's lurid attraction as "an active, external beauty whose power makes the beholder's eye a mere receiver of impressions"[18] and the behaviour of Estella Koomson's dress, which "seemed to catch each individual ray of light and aim it straight into the beholding eye",[19] appears to support this idea of aggressive materiality and passive perceivers who cannot see or act other than as they do (the Teacher, using the analogy of Plato's cave-dwellers, observes that the new mass psychology of materialism imposes totalitarian definitions not only on what is desirable and possible but also on what is perceivable and conceivable). In "An African Fable" Armah deals with these purely negative qualities of the passive consciousness, weaving them into a parable of neo-colonialism and taking the first steps towards the phenomenology which pervades the first novel and will later be programmed into the black aesthetics of the histories.

The warrior who, at the start of the fable, finds the woman waiting on the shore for someone to liberate her from the endless rape of her body is conceived after the lone questor of the grail in European mythology. Outside his fragmented, "unconnected" state lies the eternal, infinite connectedness of Africa, "before which even the foolish cannot help but have a momentary vision of the infinity of ends and beginnings that join to create freshening cycles".[20] But the "unconnected eye" of the warrior perceives only unconnectedness, not trusting to the wisdom of deeper intuitions. Because they are un-monitored by any controlling moral intelligence, the impressions of this merely "beholding eye" fail to grasp the woman's deeper ideal beauty and its cyclical permanence, which call for the more penetrating discernment of the "watching" or "connected eye". The warrior responds instead to "a different beauty, one which comes out on the way and makes of the beholder, in a sense only, a receiver of impressions already too strong to be missed".[21] Passive perception is here tantamount to non-perception, and the result is that the beholder becomes obsessed with the woman's decaying external beauty, to the extent of believing that only her decay and destruction are renewable. The woman herself partly conspires with this fatalism and extends a merely cynical welcome to her latest liberator: anticipating the been-to of the second and third novels, she is unable to break out in a new direction but is driven inward upon herself in a circle of exploitation, "caught revolving inside the interminable tunnels of the too-long deceived mind, interminably asking this question that always seemed to swallow itself: 'Again?'".[22] The warrior feels himself drawn "not indeed against his will but as if his will itself had always been a willing part of this thing whose dwelling place was outside himself".[23] Thus is he implicated in the confusion of personal will with Africa's needs, a besetting vice of Armah's messianic politicians, and the imposition is seen to repeat white perception of Africa: the black rapist who is soon to take over from the white one fragments her beauty into "parts" in a way that is characteristic of "white perception" in the novels. Solo claims, in *Why Are We So Blest?*, that the Western artist can "find relief in discrete beauty" and is "blest with that atrophy of vision that can see beauty in deliberately broken-off pieces of a world sickened with oppression's ugliness".[24]

The political dimensions of the parable now move into focus. The warrior's white-influenced vision notes only atomized externals, mistaking the visible form of the thing for the thing itself. Armah has written elsewhere of "rhetoric taken for fact" in post-colonial Africa and of victims of demagogues who are persuaded "more from a fascination with forms than from any appreciation of realisable content".[25] "African politicians love flashy scenes and highfalutin words" and operate "in a make-believe situation", in which their view of the people they rule is as fogged as that of the white colonial one.[26]

Unsure whether the rape he witnesses is not really "an act of love" and the woman's cry "a call of salvation or a call to possession", the warrior in the fable mistakes that cry for the beat of his own heart and, even at the moment of her liberation and the murder of her oppressor, continues to mistake the historical cycle of Africa's exploitation for a pre-ordained process, unalterable as the seasons: "one marvellous drop in the endless cycle of waters that never end and are always beginning . . . the woman was still dripping with the teary moistness of her ordained rape."[27]

Under the heading of the apathetic and fatalistic "beholding eye" Armah congregates the shibboleths and mystifications of Independent Africa: the fascination with form in an insidiously beautiful rhetoric, taken for reality; intoxicating liberation myths and *Osagyefo* mystiques; the flashy, glamorized materialism of politicians. Behind these fronts, the newly-unleashed brutal power of Independent rule mixes "love and desire" for the woman Africa with a "contempt and repulsion" identical to those felt by the white violator. Incapable of piercing Africa's hidden spiritual power, the deliverer contents himself with the physical penetration of her merely "beheld" beauty, deeming this to be all: "And this baffling beauty of the woman's self, the night-like beauty that seemed to urge the beholder to pierce it in order to perceive it, of itself was deepening, not assuaging, the Warrior's confusion."[28] Power to protect slips into power to exploit as a result of incorrect perception of what is being defended. The woman Africa is subjected to a humiliating repetition of her history which brings no political regeneration into harmony with her seasonal cycles of renewal: "And in her mind there was no separation between now and then, nothing at all between the present and the depths of ages that should long have been forgotten."[29]

Her timeless rape is described, significantly, as "a voyage through the little cycle· that was not only a part of the whole, but the amazing mimic of the whole itself".[30] It would perhaps be over-ambitious to make the microcosm of the little cycle serve as an image for the relationship between the early stories and the major fiction, especially since Armah's grasp of his main themes is as yet unsure in these pieces and the performance is uneven, a failing most particularly marked in the lush verbal extravagance of the fable itself. Yet the germ of the main work is present in the themes of the stories: Africa's continuing oppression under the mystique of Independence and helpless entrapment in a cycle of neo-colonial dependency; the failure of human reciprocity and connectedness under the pressures of the manipulatory system of relationships which results; the renewal of disillusionment and despair in place of the awaited political and spiritual regeneration of the post-colonial world. These themes are also present in Armah's only published poem, "Aftermath", in which an intimately personal situation of betrayed love spirals out to incorporate the larger, cyclical themes of national and racial betrayal. The female speaker of the poem has been abandoned with child by a Westernized, isolation-seeking artist and her hopes for an independent and freely-reciprocated love with this white-surrogate have been betrayed into the familiar pattern of exploitative service and dependency which, in Armah's work, is the distinctive mark of Africa's relationship with the West:

> I have felt the fear
> Of chains that bind
> And anchors that hold
> And people who cling
> In loving dependence.[31]

Armah's early fondness for the grand syncretic image, perfected later in the symbol of the cannibalized fish in the first novel and Modin's climactic death in the third, leads to the simultaneous expression of personal sexual betrayal, the solitary artist's fragmentation from the African community, and neo-colonialism's betrayal of "an ideal Independent love". At the end of the poem, as at the end of all but one of the stories, a new birth is promised as the bitter fruit of a destroyed or unsatisfactory sexual relationship: it is an illusory hope, a false spring, a creature of negation like the symbolic death-child in the sixth chapter of the first novel.

> Go create your great works of art
> For which you need this desperate freedom.
> I shall not be the last
> To try alone
> That other kind of creation
> Which you have thrust on me.[32]

"The whole world is covered over with the hell of Europe", Modin will write in his notebook in Armah's third novel, and the white imperial inheritance weighs as heavily upon the episodes of the early writings as upon those of the novels to follow. The African and the white American girl in "Contact" find the legacy of racial history pressing inescapably in upon them, forcing them to repeat predetermined roles, whilst Yaw Manu and Araba are trapped in vicious circles which result, directly or indirectly, from Africa's historical dependence upon the West. In Armah's stories white ownership of reality has spread itself into the ambitions and sexual lives of indigenous and expatriate Africans, cut off family life from communal traditions, and created a race of Victorianized Afro-English as aloof as their colonial predecessors. The idea of an unchanging cycle of exploitative and frustrating dependency is repeated in Yaw Manu's futile retaking of his exam, Araba's circular round of prison and prostitution, Kobina's springtime return to the thousandth try for contact with the oppressor, the woman's repeated rape, and the residual, unwanted births — the sterile issue of casual seduction, rape, prostitution — which offer no promise for the future. Araba's new life is the living death of the child prostitute; Essie's child fails to re-unite her estranged family; Carin's "beginning" comes with a false spring; the raped woman Africa foresees only more of the same. These fruitless dependencies will unfold onto the larger canvasses of the novels in a series of brilliantly resonant, compulsive images, seen here in embryonic form, and the idea of preordained cyclic repetition will coalesce with Armah's preoccupation with ritual motifs and modes of expression. Scenes such as the blindly loving, lurid rape of the woman Africa and the symbolic realism of the drum ritual provide glimpses of the imagination behind the murderous fellation-castration of Modin and the ambiguous births of the ritual-suffused first novel. The seeds of Armah's mature style, pre-possessing themes and characteristic poetic exuberance are at least present in the stories, ready to be opened up by the wider vistas of the main fiction, and most especially in evidence is the ability to suddenly charge the prose with a syncretic, grand crystallizing image — the cannibalized fish in the first novel, the dog-slaying in the second, Modin's climactic death in the third — which, in a single movement, pulls together many threads of meaning. An early specimen of such symbolism is Yaw Manu at the close of his tale, hidden only in the invisibility of the social leper and the culturally inauthentic frustrated évolué as he tries to rob the alien economic control source and nerve centre of his puppet psychology. His bizarre hypnosis gathers in an unforgettable image the symptoms of the trance of neo-colonialism which Armah's small corpus of fiction will set out to break.

III

Breaking the Cycle: The Fanonian Vision

Fanon was not himself an African and Armah's Africa, even in the purely political arena, is not identical with Fanon's. Nevertheless, Fanon's analysis of Third World colonies has a dominantly African, albeit peculiarly Algerian, focus and his influence, as much stylistic as ideological, is as implicit in Armah's fiction as it is explicit in his essays. The prophet's arsenal supplies the novelist's polemic with much of its rhetorical weaponry and the fiction's metaphoric landscape and lurid theology of suffering — its Blest of the Euro-American Olympus and its Damned of the Earth — come straight from Fanon.[1] For Armah, as for Fanon, the sloganeering rhetoric of African politicians outpaces deeds and disguises mild reform as revolution,[2] yet is analysed as if it corresponded to reality instead of obscuring it,[3] and Fanon's political cartoon of the national bourgeoisie's shameless opportunism and economic stagnation in the post-colonial era reads like a résumé of *The Beautyful Ones Are Not Yet Born*:

> Privileges multiply and corruption triumphs, while morality declines. The strength of the police force and power of the army are proportionate to the stagnation in which the rest of the nation is sunk . . . Scandals are numerous, ministers grow rich, their wives doll themselves up, the members of parliament feather their nests and there is not a soul down to the simple policeman or the customs officer who does not join the great procession of corruption . . . This bourgeoisie . . . appears to be afflicted with precocious senility.[4]

The underdeveloped, uninventive middle class elites who walk Fanon's pages step with ease into the shoes of Armah's drunken attorney-generals, brazen ministerial buffoons, crass television technocrats and self-worshipping artistic dilettantes. Here in plenty is the useless bourgeoisie which, in *The Wretched of the Earth*, indolently allows the economy to rot and is content to serve as a neo-imperial agent, protecting and profiting from the investments of the Western prototype which it caricatures.[5] This class, argue Armah's essays, "has no real ascertainable function beyond its identity and its privileges"[6] and subscribes to "an ethic that has everything to do with consumption and notoriously little to do with production of any sort".[7] The senior civil servants of the first two novels do nothing except occupy their sinecures and Akosua Russell's state-subsidized soirées enable her to get eight years' mileage out of a solitary wretched poem. Naana laments "this great haste to consume things we have taken no care nor trouble to produce"[8] and Ocran tells Baako that Ghana "is run by this so-called elite of pompous asses trained to do nothing. Nothing works".[9]

Lacking the initiative and expertise to set up factories, this ruling elite, in Fanon's model, chooses instead to bestow a "chauvinistic tenderness" upon a modestly productive and lucrative artisan class, and the embryonic urban proletariat quickly slips into line: the collected forces of the craftsmen, unskilled and unemployed "line up behind this nationalistic attitude" and dutifully "follow in the steps of their bourgeoisie", from which solidarity-inviting benefits accrue.[10] Likewise, mass subscription to middle-class materialism in Armah's early novels produces a socio-cultural monolith, in which the bourgeoisie, instead of provoking into existence an antagonistic proletarian counter-culture, absorbs into itself with a near-Marcusian one-dimensionality what proves to be a wholly emulative, sycophantic and bureaucratized working class.

The drivers and conductors, the workmen whose chatter fills the man's hungry lunch-hour, the clerks and potentially ministerial dockers, and the officious nurse who, in *Fragments*, turns Araba away from the V.I.P. ward, all acquire from their single-minded infatuation with the materialism of their masters a monotonous equality which transcends their social differences. Moreover, Armah's urban sociology demonstrates how "vertical" divisions of family, kinship and ethnic groups cut asymmetrically across "horizontal" class divisions, so that the values of the "big men" in the family — Koomson and Brempong — infiltrate and compromise those of their poor relations. The result is the totalitarian mentality of a single-class culture.

Fanon gave short shrift to Independent Africa's besotted urban proletariat and to the Marxist myth of its revolutionary destiny, which he saw as a safety-valve or opiate imported with the European class structure which gave it existence. The European Left's repeated betrayal of revolutionary causes in the Third World shook any lingering faith in international and interracial class solidarity, and impatience with Western ideological models led him to the contemptuous dismissal of orthodox Marxism as the inverted handmaiden of colonialism. Armah is not far behind his mentor. In *Why Are We So Blest?*, Earl Lynch's capitulation to Marxism is seen as the ultimate racial sellout, the black man's final deluded entrapment of himself in the circle of white culture: "His captivity he calls rebellion . . . Caught in the white net of minds he had sought a break for his spirit and found the whitest of philosophies, Marxism."[11] Of Fanon's contenders for the role of revolutionary class — a Bakunin-like *lumpenproletariat* of migrants, delinquents and criminals, and the African peasantry — Armah has little to say, however, and less to hope. The former materializes briefly in the victim-violence of the first book's returning soldiers, the dog-slayers in *Fragments*, the migrant girls in "The Offal Kind", and the Afrasian beggars who haunt Solo's walks in Laccreyville, but declares its powerlessness in each instance, and the latter, at the periphery of Juana's vision in *Fragments*, are truly damned — not merely wretched or pitiful but beyond hope, too lost for revolutionary recall. In the contemporary settings of the early novels "the people" have been reduced to being the repository of interesting myths which the middle class elites subvert for reactionary purposes, as in Akosua Russell's technologizing of the Mammy Water myth, and it cannot be said that the urbanized and expatriated narrative viewpoints of these books provide a more precise focus. But neither do Fanon's polemics. Fanon's programme for revolution, more a series of moral imperatives than practical strategies, did not progress far beyond a vague faith in the "upward thrust of the people" and alliances between the masses and selected principled intellectuals, "a small number of honest intellectuals, who have no very precise ideas about politics, but who instinctively distrust the race for positions and pensions".[12] Armah's fiction, ritually complex but politically simplistic, ventures into the same territory of lone intellectual champions and benighted masses awaiting deliverance, and his political essays speak with a like vagueness about the education of the masses and the growing "consciousness of connections between socio-economic inequalities and the structures of the social order" that will serve as a revolutionary fuse.[13]

Armah's critical intelligence is alert, however, to many of Fanon's simplifications and his reservations assert themselves in three main areas: decolonization, tribalism and Algerian Independence. The essay on African Independence is quick to make the vital distinction between administrative and settler colonies which finds no place on the scheme of Fanon's monochromatic canvas. The indigenous Ghanaian is more sensitive than the uprooted Martinican and adopted Algerian to the ancientness of the political dialogue between the colonial powers and a long-established, propertied West African bourgeoisie, which was not suddenly created in the panic rush of decolonization and for which violent revolution was neither possible nor desirable. The sociological sketch of the transposition of bourgeois traditions to Africa in Armah's essay on African Socialism testifies to the rooted tenacity of this class as his first two novels do to its enduring presence. Fanonian theory, arguing always from the revolutionary model of Algeria, tended to behave as if all decolonization started from the same point. Secondly, Armah resists the strong tendencies in Fanon to regard the formation of tribal divisions and social classes purely as the conjurings of colonialism and to deny the pre-colonial status of tribal and social violence.[14] The two historical novels argue for the existence of strongly stratified, hierarchical social structures and indigenous colonial practice within pre-colonial societies, and, although Armah's attack on "communalist" naiveties in the African Socialism essay mentions Fanon only in an absolving afterthought, the latter's Algerian-based attribution of almost all internal rivalries to colonial machinations ironically gives some credence to converse myths of a classless or "communalist" pre-colonial Africa: fabrications exploited by the largely bogus socialisms of Senghor, Nkrumah and Nyerere, and ridiculed in Armah's essay. The mystifications of the communalist-socialist syndrome, alleges the essay, permit the new nationalist leaders to plead traditional African society's social and political homogeneity in defence of the abolition of opposition parties; fantasies of pre-tribal, pre-class unity entrench the modern totalitarian monoliths and bourgeois dictatorships that Fanon so deplored.[15]

Thirdly, Fanon's prophetic exemption of Algeria's hard-won independence from the fate of sub-Saharan decolonization is heavily qualified. Fanon had leapt from the realization that peaceful succession does not authentically decolonize to the fallacy that violent revolution would. But the crippling effect of the war left Algeria dependent upon a continuing French economic and technical presence and, as Armah's essay on African Independence illustrates, she continued to supply raw materials within the structure of an essentially colonial economy whose economic flow pattern was unchanged.[16] The Afrasian sections of *Why Are We So Blest?*, which grew out of the author's stay in Algiers in 1963, constitute Armah's epilogue to the revolution and epitaph to Fanon's hopes. His Afrasia is a war-ruined nation of beggars ruled from ex-colonial mansions by privileged managerial cadres. Fanon's fuse for firing the struggle — the *lumpenproletariat* of beggars, drifters, unemployed — is here the burnt-out residue of a revolution which has left their lot fundamentally unaltered. Fanon's observations of Africa's false decolonization processes — for example, that new nationalist administrations have always excluded from power the militants who have been the essence of the revolution[17] — are transferred by Armah to Fanon's own Algeria. "Who won?" asks the old *moudjahid* at the beginning of the novel. "Afterwards, who gains? . . . It is not the militants!"[18] Punning on the meanings of "essence", Solo explains grimly that the militants serve as sacrificial fuel for the revolution, carrying the political opportunists to power on their backs. The political consciousness stimulated by the revolution gave a temporary equality to bourgeois and *fellah*, male and female, Moslem and infidel, but did not permanently dissolve social, sexual and religious divisions (in Armah's novel the sexual attitudes of the new managerial elites mix a reactionary, colonial-style hunting mentality with the traditionally exclusive and protectionist machismo of Islam).[19] Fanon had mistaken temporary for permanent phenomena, a national for a social revolution. Neither is there much in the behaviour of the Congherian revolutionary leaders in Afrasian exile to support Fanon's propagandizing hopes for a community of interests between sub-Saharan Africa and the Mahgrib and for the new national consciousness as the springboard that would launch Africa towards continental unity.[20] The decadent Portuguese-colonized Congherians in Afrasian exile carry away little inspiration from their limited rapport with their North African hosts and, in fact, their will to action seems to have been sapped and their power emasculated by the luxuries of Western- ized exile in the midst of a revolution very much in decline. In the wake of the growing isolation of Algeria and other Mahgrib nations from the African continent, it is perhaps significant that some West African writers, notably Ouologuem in *Bound to Violence* and Armah himself in *Two Thousand Seasons*, opted for a hostile, separatist vision of the North and for an imperial tradition of the Arabs as pre-European colonizers and destroyers in preference to the cooperative one of Moslem and Negro working together to build magnificent sub-Saharan states that Europe destroyed.

Armah's real debts are not so much to Fanon's political analysis as to his psychology of neo-colonialism and his psychopathology of blackness, which expand beyond a strictly African frame of reference to take in the whole black world, and his interest is as much in the shape and style of Fanon's ideas, in their metaphoric and meta- physical dimensions, as in the ideas themselves. Fanon saw the black man as fighting from within the prison house of white racial concepts, political myths and national boundaries: no matter which way he turned to divest his psychic geography of colonial structures he was led deeper into whiteness. "We have taken everything from the other side, and the other side gives us nothing

. . .Taking means in nearly every case being taken."[21] These futile symmetries inform both the fatalistic cyclical structures of the first three novels and the polemics against neo-colonialism in the essays. Fanon's conclusion that the colonial mentality is neither reasonable nor accommodating — "Colonialism is not a thinking machine, nor a body endowed with reasoning faculties. It is violence in its natural state . . ."[22] — is reflected in Armah's argument that race-prejudiced Western scholarship, working blindly in the interests of the West and intent upon the militant recolonization of African literature, is similarly endowed with limited and obtuse reasoning faculties: "The skilful interpreter functions in close tune with the allergies, aspirations, ideals, manias, philias, phobias, and prejudices — above all the prejudices — of his audience . . . Operating almost by instinct, he censors information before he transmits it."[23] In Fanon's political theory, white structuring of reality ensures that everything is defined in response to itself and leads back to the fulfilment of white purposes; in his racial psychopathology, all the black man's efforts are aimed at achieving a white existence, even to the extent of interiorizing, along with white social values, the archetypal colour-myths of the European collective unconscious.[24] Negritude, for example, is viewed as a white-sponsored phenomenon, pandering to the white man's idea of "the Negro" and tied up with dependency complexes which urge the emulation of the white man and the purchase of his approval.[25] Thus all black ideas are seen to take their shape manichaeistically, either from opposition to white aggression or compliance with it: colonialism, Fanon contended, could not "accept the fact that things happen without its control, without its direction".[26] Maran's assimilated Jean Veneuse (Fanon's example in *Black Skin, White Masks*) is informed by his white patrons that he is no longer black, as is Modin by Mike the Fascist: "But you're here with us. You belong."[27] But patronizing strings are attached to honorary whiteness, directing the expatriate African (set apart by his "special intelligence") back into colonized inferiority. "At the end of the treasure hunt through the colonial school system to the metropole itself," warns Armah, "comes the traumatic shock of identity": the discovery that "all the credits and distinctions do not really suffice as a passport to the Paradise of the white man's myth system, complete acceptance as an individual".[28]

Fanon furnishes Armah's fiction with two key images: the all-pervasive, saturative white monolith, and the doomed cycle which causes all energy and movement towards liberation to run itself into a circle of frustration and to enslaved dependence upon it. "When people like me, they tell me it is in spite of my colour," wrote the young Fanon. "When they dislike me, they point out that it is not because of my colour. Either way, I am locked into the infernal cycle."[29] Faced with Oppenhardt's obdurate racism in *Why Are We So Blest?*, Modin feels "exactly as if we were repeating our first conversations" and that his life in America "has run in cycles of loneliness and destructive involvement".[30] The factor-cycle of the second and third novels explores the processes by which indigenes are drawn into this whirlpool of whiteness and converted into agent-oppressors. "Individually, a few of us can break out, go through the educational systems of our oppressors, emerging with a ridiculous illusion that we are free . . . but what is success for a slave when the system rewards us for using the best in us to deepen the slavery of our people and ourselves?"[31] Solo, the Europeanized African artist, finds himself assuming the Western writer's fragmented sensibility and assesses Modin's hopelessness: "The African absorbed into Europe, trying to escape death, eager to shed privilege, not knowing how deep the destruction has eaten into himself, hoping to achieve a healing juncture with his destroyed people."[32] This cycle of psychological dependency is reflected in the unchanged economic flow patterns persisting between African states and Europe. Fanon argued that the young independent nation, initially obliged to use the economic channels created by the colonial regime, quickly fell under the sway of an African client-bourgeoisie which served as a Western business agent in its operation of a transmission line between the nation and Western capitalism. Protected foreign investments and technical aid, heavily qualified by commercial and political conditions which the ex-colonial powers took fewer and fewer pains to conceal, combined to ensure that these economic channels sank back, inevitably, into neo-colonialist lines.[33] Armah notes in his essay on African Independence that lines of colonial commercial access, running from cash-crop area to metropole, changed hardly at all and that post-colonial Africanization programmes more often entailed the elevation, rather than the disappearance, of metropolitan personnel.[34] The economic and moral bankruptcy of the new nation, his argument follows Fanon's, is masked by the Cult of the Leader, who mystifies the masses by shifts in the logomachy, not the economy, and so, like the colonial settlers before him, persuades them to identify the gains of the privileged few as their own.[35]

In a bold imaginative synthesis Armah links the plight of the post-colonial economy with that of the recolonized African writer. The white critic is suspected of being a sinister foreign controller, distorting African truths to fit Western prejudices "just as much as any other Western expert hustling Africa, be he a business man, an economic adviser or a mercenary wardog".[36] As the independent economy is really only an appendage of the imperial economy, so African literature, as annexed by American criticism, becomes merely an appendage of Western literature, existing at a low point on the literary hierarchy's evolutionary scale and worthy of praise only insofar as it accommodates itself to Western literary values and traditions. "Colonialism wants everything to come from itself," wrote Fanon, and Armah extends this egocentric arrogance to "neo-colonial" criticism as represented by the work of Charles Larson, whose chief aim seems to be to Americanize the novelist and claim him for the West. This is achieved in a number of ways: by insinuations that an expatriated African author could forget his own "inferior" language and substitute for it the "superior" one of the country of his sojourn; by patronizing slurs on the intelligence and receptivity of African readers in order to valorize notions of Western refuge and long-awaited acclaim by a properly appreciative American audience; and by a variety of Westernizing biographical falsifications, "de-Africanizing" textual misreadings, and myopic allegations of indebtedness to European authors such as Joyce. Compulsively, Larson's innocent racist assumptions discover Western sources for everything. America is credited with a magical monopoly of superior "universal values" and original creativity, as if all genius were really Western under the skin and all successful writers honorary Americans. Larson has effectively reduced African creativity to a mere stage in the development of white civilization, an earlier phase still aspiring to Euro-American excellence. By the same complacent evolutionism, Fanon's hypothetical white historian, in *Black Skin, White Masks,* diminished African religion into an exhausted, outmoded property, and Sartre reduced Negritude to a minor term in the progression of a European Hegelian dialectic. Both left Fanon feeling that he was merely "repeating a cycle. My originality had been torn out of me".[37] "As African Literature develops, the best of it must become less African, more Western," runs Armah's sardonic summary of "Larsony". "The very best of it won't even be African at all. Africa, because it is inherently inferior . . . will of course reject the work of the best African writers." These genuine artists, according to such logic, will reinforce this rejection of themselves and will "quite naturally, go into exile in Europe and America, in the West, where their genius will find its natural home swimming in the mainstream of Western values".[38] The been-to-into-agent syndrome is a cultural and literary phenomenon as well as a political and economic one. The African writer and intellectual is drawn inevitably into the familiar patronizing and inferiorizing circle of whitening Westernization charted in Fanon's first book and turned to powerful effect in Armah's third novel.

Of course, the work of Fanon and Armah themselves has not escaped this fate. At the end of *The Wretched of the Earth* Fanon urged the total abjuration of Europe but, if he had turned his back on Europe, at least one eye looked over his shoulder, trained on the treacherous French Left which seems to have been the main target of his shock therapy. Moreover, the book in which Europe was written off was sent, of necessity, to a Parisian publisher and prefaced by a French philosopher whose claim that the Third World "finds itself" and "speaks to itself" through Fanon's voice now sounds odd in the light of Fanon's minimal influence on African political thought. Armah notes that, to the African leaders who have turned their backs on him, Fanon's books "make bizarre, incomprehensible, menacing reading",[39] and it has become a commonplace of Western political commentary that Fanon's Bakunin-like promotion of revolutionary sub-proletariats made his books the gospels of urban riot and terrorism among the radicals and racially repressed slum-dwellers of Europe and the United States, not the inhabitants of African shanty-towns and South American favelas. It is arguable that Armah's work has not fared much better. In his essay on Fanon he is alert to the luxurious taste for self-torture in Western culture which demands the packaging of black suffering for white consumption,[40] and to what has been called Fanon's "ability to evoke shame and pain in the bosoms of white middle class masochists".[41] Fanon argued that the colonial powers actually encouraged these modes of expression and made their existence possible: "Stinging denunciations, the exposing of distressing conditions and passions which find their outlet in expression are in fact assimilated by the occupying power in a cathartic process."[42] *Why Are We So Blest?* is, self-consciously, such a "stinging denunciation", contained by its publication in a "colonial edition" and instantly disarmed by its own subject and target: a racist white patronage sufficiently entrenched and hospitable to withstand any assault upon its sensibility and render it harmless. Larson's enormities stumble upon at least one hard truth: that, until his patient search for an African publisher for *Two Thousand Seasons* (in which resistance to oppression is still more cathartic than constructive), Armah's principal audience was the white American fiction-reading middle class. Meanwhile, at the level of political action, both men offered a few limited pointers to the way out of the impasse. Fanon habitually projected a vigorously inventive revolutionary consciousness in opposition to a lethargic white-imitative middle class one. His answer to the great deception of neo-colonial leadership was to open up the mass mind to the reality "that everything depends on them" and "that there is no such thing as a demiurge, that there is no famous man who will take the responsibility for everything",[43] a warning against messianic mystification echoed in Armah's essay on the Biafran War.[44] Fanon was sure that the greatest danger that threatened Africa was the absence of ideology and that only the invention of an original, non-Western ideology could break the grip of Europe's influence and prevent the inevitable slipping back into intellectual dependency.[45] Armah, however, in his essay on African

Socialism, had already charted the failing course of Africa's search for ideological alternatives. Impatience with both colonial capitalism and its Marxist counter-creations, together with the need to be original and the reluctance to be seen borrowing foreign conceptual tools, had driven Africa's new political leaders back upon dubiously-derived African socialisms which were really neither African nor socialist. These experiments led neither outward into a new stage of political history nor genuinely inward into traditional African thought, and took Independent Africa nowhere except into deeper dependency upon the West.[46]

It is, perhaps, in the cultivation of cultural and racial consciousness rather than political consciousness, however, that Fanon offers Armah a strategy for breaking the cycle. Fanon wrote in his last book:

> This passionate search for a national culture which existed before the colonial era finds its legitimate reason in the anxiety shared by native intellectuals to shrink away from that Western culture in which they all risk being swamped . . . It was with the greatest delight that they discovered that there was nothing to be ashamed of in the past, but rather dignity, glory . . . The native intellectual who decides to give battle to colonial lies fights on the field of the whole continent. The past is given back its value.[47]

In the passage of Fanon's thought from *Black Skin, White Masks* to *The Wretched of the Earth* the black intellectual's pursuit of a new, integrated black identity in a white world gave way to an embittered and desperate decontamination of himself from that world and all its goods. Negritude, for Fanon, continued to be a mystifying irrelevance and he remained as alert as ever to the pernicious glorification of the African past, by Senghor and Nkrumah, as an opiate to divert attention from the troubles of the present. The intellectual retrieval of a usable past and alternative cultural histories, though speeding up Africa's extrication from the corrupting swamp of Western culture, could not be part of the physical struggle to alleviate suffering. Nevertheless, the rehabilitation of a "future national culture" was now deemed to be politically worthwhile.

Armah's progress as a writer, as a number of commentators have observed,[48] loosely parallels Fanon's passage between these poles and can be aligned with Fanon's tripartite scheme for the decolonized writer. His first and most Westernized novel comes closest to the assimilation phase which is dominated by the literary techniques of the mother country and notably by symbolists and surrealists, though in Armah's case the debt is mainly a stylistic one.[49] Armah, in Fanonian mood, is on record as deploring his first novel because of its lack of "an absolutely African focus . . . and address",[50] a judgement which my own examination of the novel will question and qualify. The next two novels fit roughly into Fanon's second phase of disturbance and painful liberation, in which the uprooted and expatriated writer tries unsuccessfully, in the fashion of Baako and Modin, to recross the immense distance which has grown between himself and the African community which he wishes to serve. The last two novels clearly subscribe to the militant posture of Fanon's "fighting phase", in which the writer, seeking out only the functional potential of the past, devises a future-oriented revolutionary literature to address and awaken his own people. The gradual shift of emphasis in Armah's writing is away from the grim portrayal of a pre-colonial past of despotic privilege and greed, expressed directly in the essays and through the panoramic historical retrospections of the early novels: those rapid, almost subliminally brief allusions to slave-chiefs, factors and colonial landlords as prototypes for contemporary figures which stress the continuity of past and present. The development is not a simple and unbroken one. Even Armah's late essay on Mofolo's *Chaka*, which ostensibly belongs to the "fighting phase" of his own writing, is not averse to discovering in Chaka's case-history a psycho-pathological blueprint for the modern African dictator and a more accurate model for post-colonial Africa than for the retrieval of pristine or pre-colonial African genius.[51] Nevertheless, the shift is steadily towards what Soyinka has called" the visionary reconstruction of the past for the purposes of a social direction".[52] Fanon specifically recommended as a way out of the neo-colonial impasse a "literature of combat" which would enliven in modernized form "the stories, epics and songs of the people" as they exist in the oral tradition and which, though national in its origins, was to be continental in its aspirations.[53] The cumulative effect of the monotonous racism in *Two Thousand Seasons* is perhaps more negative than com-bative, but its climactic detribalized, denationalized vision clearly derives its impetus from Fanon's pan-Africanized combative phase, as does its sentimental pluralism and vituperative gloating over defeated colonial enemies.[54]

The movement is, inevitably, from the specific to the general. As the pressing concerns of the political activist carried Fanon away from the particulars of psychiatric case-studies to the generic phantasms of the Algerian people, national culture and African unity, so the felt need for a more explicitly African focus impelled Armah's retreat from the social specifics of the first two novels to the nebulous, polarized abstractions of whiteness and the Way. The Fanonian influence on Armah's work, especially in its florescence in the histories, is, on the whole, a reductive one which increases the fiction's polemical thrust as it dilutes its artistic power and results in a thinning of the rich and intricate texture of the early novels. Most of what follows will concern itself with the peculiar but undeniably African focus of those early works.

IV

The Ritual Background to the Novels

Fanonian psychological complexes are not the only things in Armah's novels which travel in circles. "Each thing that goes away returns and nothing in the end is lost," Naana opens the second novel, *Fragments*. "That is the way everything goes and turns around".[1] Almost everything in the novels moves in circles. In *The Beautyful Ones Are Not Yet Born* the courses through which political regimes rise and fall shrink satirically to the dimensions of the physiological circuit's daily cycle of ingestion and evacuation, and then spiral through further cycles — weekly and monthly, artificial and natural — to the climactic calendrical evacuation of the nation at the end of the novel. In *Fragments* wheels move within wheels through a web of simultaneous cycles. The religious idea of a continuous circuit of passage through a world of ancestor-spirits, into which this world's dying are reborn and from which outgoing spirits become the material world's new births, is given a warped parody in the ritual death, spiritualization and ghostly return of the cargo-bringer: "The main export to the other world is people," runs Baako's cargo-theory. "The true dead going back to the ancestors, the ritual dead."[2] A little closer to its original spirit, the religious circuit receives more traditional, albeit partly ironic, treatment in the regenerated return of the singer from the sea in the Mammy Water myth which features in both of these novels. In the third novel, *Why Are We So Blest?*, a figurative theology of neo-colonialism borrowed from

Fanon transforms the familiar circular passage into the carefully monitored voyage of intellectual "factors" between the lands of the blest and the damned, Olympus and Tartarus, the centre and periphery, the sacred and profane worlds.

In each of these cases the cyclical journey is placed in the context of calendrical ritual. The decline of the Nkrumah regime is played off against an end-of-year purification rite, the birth and death of Araba's child hinge on the autumnal equinox which marks the changing of the Akan agricultural year, and Modin's death, following his twelfth diary entry, chimes with the start of the twelve-day changeover from the old to the new year on the Western Christian calendar. My discussion of the motif of the carrier will demonstrate that the ambiguity surrounding the endings of these novels is ritually limited, but this ambiguity can be taken to reflect loosely the numinous period of transition in calendrical and general rites of passage: a period when ends and beginnings are confused and ritual observances mark the closeness of the old and the dead to the newly born.[3] The ritual metaphors of the novels hold out the respective prospects of purification, sacrificial regeneration and Promethean deliverance, but always against a foreground of purely negative or destructive action, and the religious and mythological motifs which are woven around these key metaphors compound the ambiguities. The anonymous man returns from his purifying sea journey to an unredeemed world where corrupt regimes continue to come and go, and both the carrier's purgative sea passage and Mammy Water's regenerative sea-cycle are measured against Maanan's terminal decline into madness. Naana's despair of this world and resigned retreat into the next are held in balance with Baako's continuing despair in the world and his escape into madness. The worthwhile but inevitably punished Promethean endeavour with which the myth structure dignifies Modin's death is checked by Solo's verdict of "useless, unregenerative destruction".[4]

The symmetries of Armah's ritual design are also evident in his numerological structures. In *The Beautyful Ones Are Not Yet Born* the seven years of the progeric manchild's passage from life to death match the insane rush of the first Independent government through an accelerated life in which too much happens for its significance to be properly understood and remembered. But this illusory phenomenon is partly corrected by Maanan — here an inverted Mammy Water — for whom the same seven years measure out the painful path to madness, paved by bitter disillusionment with her messiah and the loss of her political faith. In the next novel the healing figure of Mammy Water, who sends her visionary and restored lovers back from the sea after seven years, is represented by the Puerto Rican psychiatrist Juana, who comes from across the sea to Ghana in the seventh year of her failing marriage and, after making love in Mammy Water's element, listens with Baako to the fisherboy's "seven separate songs" which rhythmize the sea's giving up of its nourishment. More central to the ritual fabric of *Fragments* is the custom of outdooring the newly born only after seven complete days have passed, whereupon the child may be admitted, or initiated, into its full life cycle on the earth. The completed cycle of one week represents the life cycle in microcosm, and beyond that, the whole cycle of birth and death since the newly born are understood as being on loan from the other world, to which they will return along their "circular way" sooner or later. During the course of this perilous initiatory cycle the child is a thing of two worlds: it is, in Naana's words, "only a traveler between the world of spirits and this one of heavy flesh" and is still "in the keeping of the spirits".[5] The guardian spirits who, in traditional belief, accompany the child will not retreat to the other world and abandon it to earthly care until this trial period comes to an end with the completion of the seventh day of life. "The seventh night, deep deep night of the black black land of gods and deities they will come out . . . If they insist then I shall die the death of blood," says Amamu of their Ewe counterparts in Kofi Awoonor's novel *This Earth, My Brother*. . .[6] Seven as the number of healing regeneration, fertility and continuing life seems also to be bound up with the West African belief that spirit-children — variously called *abiku*, *ogbanje* and *amomawu* — are contracted to the spirit world to come and go to the same mother a total of seven times before being persuaded to resume a normal life-cycle.[7] The behaviour of Araba and Efua in *Fragments* seems least likely to persuade the reluctant child to remain in this world. Allowing the pay-cycle to override the ordained weekly cycle, the family departs from traditional practice by bringing the outdooring ceremony forward by two days and thus commuting the hallowed seven into an ominous five — ominous because the already premature baby finally arrived after five miscarriages and because its coming is linked by the mother with the parallel home-coming, after five years abroad in the "other world" of America, of her brother Baako, who is himself Efua's fifth child. There is more at stake here than mere numerological sanctities, however, and there is more than the ritual order's traditional alliance of religious feeling with practical common sense: "They have lost all belief in the wisdom of those gone before, but what new power has made them forget that a child too soon exposed is bound to die?" asks Naana.[8] There are more far-reaching theological implications. In the unbroken eschatological cycle of traditional beliefs like Naana's, the newly born are watched over by the ancestors from whose spirit world they have just arrived and may even reincarnate some of their characteristics; the children will later repay the debt by guaranteeing to elders who are about to become ancestors a "personal immortality" in their own living memories.[9] The inability of Araba's child to get born until after the fifth attempt is proportionate to the exclusion from the family of the grandmother. The refusal of a dignified, revered old age and death to Naana implies also the denial of her personal immortality since she is forgotten even before her death. The neglect of one end of the continuum interferes with developments at the other: the circle of death and birth, the ancestors and the unborn, is abruptly broken, the wheel on which "everything goes and turns around" halted. The five years of Araba's miscarrying children, one for each year of Baako's exile, are also the five years in which Naana's position in the family is allowed to deteriorate from that of a family elder who retains the authority to assert her superior rights at a libation ceremony (at Baako's departure) to that of one who, now blind and ignored, has no rights at all (Naana at Baako's return). The traditional function of ritual is to hold in place the walls of a sacred cycle of being. It ensures the contiguity of the cycle's interdependent phases of birth, growth and death, arrival and departure, childhood and spirithood, in the light of the belief that a going in one world is always a coming in another. The different meanings of the word *Naana* in Akan — grandparent, grandchild or ancestor — establish a verbal continuum between elders, dead and children (Naana, the spirits and Baako in the novel) that reflects their actual interconnectedness in the cycle. The custom by which mothers ask the ancestors to intercede for them in their prayers for fertility testifies to the power of the dead over birth and, proportionately, of outgoing over incoming lives.[10] The not-yet-born turn in a wheel of dependency with the not-yet-dead and the undisturbed continuity of the cycle is of paramount importance.

The twofold nature of Armah's ritual cycle, its ability to operate in two mutually exclusive orders, underlies the ambivalent vision of the early fiction. Whenever rituality and cyclicality converge in a religious or metaphysical context, as in the case of Naana's beliefs, their evaluation is nearly always positive; when the meeting occurs in an unrepentantly material context, the evaluation is negative. In *The Beautyful Ones Are Not Yet Born* the secondary resonances from a species of nature-metaphysics work in redemptive opposition to primary material senses, with the result that ritual hope is played off against the material negation of event. At the end of the novel the man carries to sea the corruption of the fallen regime in the form of Koomson. In the wake of this definitive purification ritual and in the presence of the sea's creative-destructive cycle, the man comes to a confirmation of an almost mystical perception of nature, which has been growing steadily, or is at least intermittently present, throughout the novel. In nature's ongoing regenerative process, corruption is seen not as an absolute evil but as a necessary part in a dynamic continuity, out of which grow new flowerings from dung, new seeds from rotten fruit, new life from death and decomposition. The disconnective purification in a rite of separation and expulsion is itself a stage in an unbroken cycle, a part of the interconnectedness of all things. At the psychological level, however, this metaphysical mysticism is merely another stage in the man's inner debate, another round of moral musings which need have no final value. In fact, the novel provides no final endorsement of this view of the cycle of corruption. For example, at one point in the narrative the man appears to ponder over the possibility of children benefiting innocently from parental corruption, like new life analogically deriving from "seeds feeding on their own rotten fruit". The man asks rhetorically if it is only the "monstrous fruit . . . that could find the end of its life in the struggle against sweetness and corruption?"[11] One important feature of the novel's cyclical imagery of growth and decay is, as

Joan Solomon has observed, the man's use of the "concept of natural physical process to judge human behaviour, attempting, through it, to get moral issues into focus".[12] Some critics have been made uneasy by this implicit use of physical ripening and rotting as a yardstick to measure moral behaviour, seeing it as a dangerous norm. Henry Chakava wonders if it is "correct to analogise human weaknesses to natural processes" and, following the implications of the analogy, claims that "since Armah has established corruption as an innate natural process, the man cannot be an exception to this rule".[13] Indeed, were the analogies to be literalized into absolutes, the man's own moral position would be "unnatural". But, the nature-metaphysics notwithstanding, there is no clear evidence that any such absolute has been established. In the first novel things tend to create their own norms, and like the old manchild, operate according to their own highly peculiar natures. Even time moves in different ways and there are no universal criteria for all types and rates of change. The truly "monstrous fruit" of the novel, the Nkrumah government, offers no struggle against but succumbs to sweetness and corruption at the end of its life, and the *Osagyefo* himself is pictured as feeding monstrously from the parental tree of the nation, to the point of killing it, and imposing his own personal death-cycle upon the nation's life.[14]

In an abnormal world of monstrous redefinitions, "monstrous" itself acquires new meanings. The first Independence government's accelerated life-cycle sets the model for speedy social climbing, quick money and patterns of consumption that lead to the rapid exhaustion of resources and equally rapid decay. To do otherwise — to end one's life in the struggle *against* the sweets of corruption — immediately becomes monstrous and abnormal. Premature decay also has its own special nature and pleasures: the corrupt conductor of the symbolic social bus, held together by too much rust to stop it from falling completely apart, takes extreme delight in the ancient rotten smell of a brand new cedi note. But even he is not so immersed in the totalitarian order of corruption that he feels no guilt in the presence of the imagined "watcher". His shame, unnecessary fears, and violent abuse of the man have as much to do with the guilty pleasure taken in accelerated decay as with the detection of his cheating. The paradoxes of the "unnatural natural" and the "abnormal normal" are tied up with that central ambivalence in Armah's treatment of the complex phenomenon of corruption which entwines different and opposed orders of experience: the human and non-human, the moral and physical, the metaphysical and material, the literal and metaphoric. A process of "corruption" which is quite "natural" or "normal" in one of these contexts will not necessarily be so in the other, and if some critics have used the word "corruption" as if it had a single self-evident meaning and universal application,[15] then Armah's blurring of the different contexts is partly to blame.

For example, at the start of chapter 5 the man's thoughts pass swiftly from the natural waste, filth and decay in the gutters to "corruption" in the sense of moral deterioration through the fraudulent acquisition of material wealth and thence, in the example of Rama Krishna, to "corruption" in the narrower sense of sheer physiological disintegration.[16] In the novel as a whole, the corruption metaphor is perfectly logical and integrated: put at its simplest, moral corruption in government and corrupt consumer habits produce waste and decay in the environment and, since those who produce the refuse also steal the money intended for its disposal, their corruption is aptly symbolized by it. But here the logic has given way to vague association. Rama Krishna is in no way related to the corrupt heroes of the gleam or even to the man's toying with temptation but, although he has deliberately placed himself, as far as is humanly possible, outside the consumer-cycle, he dies, ironically, of consumption, his heart and lungs eaten up by worms. The point seems to be that in a totalitarian environment there is no escape and those who refuse to consume are themselves consumed, but the manipulation of the metaphors results in some moral confusion. Purely on the level of the man's psychology, each round of metaphorical speculations is merely another turning point in his developing search for a strategy to deal with a corrupt world, a quest which is temporarily halted but not resolved by the coup. On this level, the passage about the "monstrous fruit" might be read as a futile attempt at self-persuasion through a false analogy (true for trees but not for people). More plausibly, it reads like a self-consciously ironic exploration of the growth-decay image, in which the man plays devil's advocate, after the cynical manner of the Teacher, to tempt himself with easy options. In this reading, he sees through his own metaphor and the mock-measuring principle only reasserts his moral stubbornness by making clear to him all the attitudes of compromise, the facile excuses and comfortable compliance with corruption. The problem is that the man's mind moves in and out of metaphor with such agile facility that the absorption of incident into image, the passing of fact into figure, and the subsequent dominance of metaphoric reality over narrative action make it easy to forget that the man does not act upon his discovery, any more than he acts upon the Teacher's "good" advice. We have to be reminded that the "sweetness and corruption" referred to are not immediately of the human kind: they are poetic ideas of growth and decay taken from plant life, not innate human conditions. The novel's ritualization as cyclical recurrence of the growth and treatment of "corruption" — moral, physical, natural — ambivalently conflates these two independent orders of experience as it insists upon their separate and disparate natures.

The next novel presents a more unified vision. In *Fragments*, where Naana's beliefs are of a more specifically religious nature and their value more definite if not more absolute than the man's, the cycle is an explicitly theological one and its unbrokenness is maintained by the performance of precise ritual acts such as libation, prayer, sacrifice and thanks-offerings. To honour the dead is to safeguard the living. Only by the flawless observance of these rites — which means balking Foli when he tries to cheat the ancestors of their due — can the cycle of death and rebirth, departure and safe return, be kept whole and in motion: "Nothing at all was left out. The uncle called upon the nephew the protection of the old ones gone before. The circle was not broken. The departed one will return."[17] Thus, although Efua, of the modern generation, fears that Baako may never return from the United States, Naana adheres to a traditional faith in ritual efficacy. In the contemporary world into which Naana has survived, however, the circle has already been irreparably broken by the incursions of the West and its metaphysics undermined by materialism. Naana's lament at this development suggests a fracturing linearization of the original circularly-conceived wholeness:

> The larger meaning which lent sense to every small thing and every momentary happening years and years ago has shattered into a thousand and thirty useless pieces. Things have passed which I have never seen whole, only broken and twisted against themselves.[18]

Ritual is emptied of value in this process of fragmentation by a separation of meaning from form which steers attention away from the inherent power resident within ritual properties and occasions to their outward show. Hence the novel's strangely disembodied descriptive style, the obsessive lingering on hard shiny surfaces, the awe of language in the presence of material objects. The furniture of festivals and ceremonies is turned into a succession of spiritless objects — the kente cloth trampled by Brempong's champagne-washed feet, the ancestral libations which Foli and Korankye pour down their own throats — all of which are greedily exploited to procure more of the same. Ritual performances become discrete things: they are deprived of their traditional place in a wider religious cycle of events and are connected instead to a cargo circuit of commodities. But the fragmentation, as Daniéle Stewart has noted, leads to an unenergetic degradation of ritual patterns, not to their destruction and disappearance; to an unimaginative and often absurd redeployment to meet the demands of a consumer society, rather than a replacement.[19] Doubtless, there is a pragmatist somewhere in Armah who would prefer these ancient customs, along with traditional myths, to disappear altogether instead of lingering on to lend a spurious legitimacy to evil modern practices. In the first novel gifts of kola are perverted from being honourable tokens of respect and hospitality into shameless bribes and traditional proverbs are twisted out of their customary meanings to defend the practice. The lengthy funeral rites of ancient village custom become the pretext by which a corrupt urban clerk endlessly extends his holidays. In *Fragments* libation is an excuse for Foli's bibulous indulgence, Korankye's sacrifice of the ram to mark the reception of the child is desecrated by an irreverence more appropriate to a drunken feast, and the Mammy Water myth survives the assault of the modern media only in the form of Akosua Russell's execrable piece of propaganda on the electrification of Amosema village.

In the course of these modern degradations there is no departure from the psychology of cyclical process, only an impatient acceleration of that process in its diversion to profit-making purposes. The first week of the child's life is truncated by a third of its length, following an already accelerated gestation period: its poetic corollary is the rapid circular motion of the icy electric fan that scatters the collection money at the five-day outdooring and dispatches the child to the other world from which it has barely arrived. The misplaced emphasis on Baako's beneficial return even before his departure has the same effect of blasphemously accelerating the circular process of the outward and return passage, evidently with a view to speeding the cargo-bringing son back into the African world as quickly as his infant namesake will be propelled out of it. Naana discerns, in retrospect, the "hot desire impatient at his departure for his return".[20] The impatient, acquisitive haste to telescope departure and return, death and birth, implosively shrinks the time-cycle until its stages are indistinguishable, and produces matching explosions in the lives of those who, like Bukari and Skido, cannot keep the pace and are unable to get the goods home quickly enough. The fragile Baako also fragments and disintegrates at speed. Taken too quickly, things fly apart in giddy atomization: the whirling bank-notes at the outdooring, Bukari's splintered whiskey glass, the shattered television screens in the stampede at Ghanavision, the "snapped fractions" of builder's rubble around Efua's prematurely-laid house foundations.

The higher cyclicalism of the spirit occupies minority space in the novels: the man's nature-metaphysics, Naana's religious beliefs, the mystical concept of return to an African "Way" when two thousand seasons have gone round in Armah's historical fantasy. Its peripheral passage is always the life-giving one towards release, restoration or regeneration, and deaths and endings are not final but processes of translation to a different and usually a higher level. Naana's belief in the conservation of value, that "nothing in the end is lost", implies progress or at least a salvaging, holding action: a cyclicalist view which finds its most extreme expression in J.B. Danquah's concept of evolutionary reincarnation.[21] In its metaphysical form the circle is, traditionally (in Africa and the West), a symbol of perfection, completion, fulfilment. The ritual observances that sustain it have positive associations: for Naana "the traveler's drink of ceremony" is a hallowed property and the "perfect words" of the libation ceremony somehow survive their desecration and retain their intrinsic beauty even in the mouth of the drunken Foli. "Even Foli felt their presence."[22] There is a subdued idealistic, perhaps even sentimental element in Armah's vision that prevents these modern desecrations from diminishing entirely the traditional value and importance of custom. In *Fragments*, a work saturated in Akan ritual and mythology, a weight of almost "objective" worth protects hallowed forms, preserves vestiges of their pre-perverted conditions, and outlasts their violation by an impatient modern materialism. The elegant, dirge-like solemnity of the words of the libation, surrounded by Naana's poetic reverie, recaptures some of the dignity and wisdom of ancient beliefs about the importance of ancestors in the eternal cycle of being, and Naana manages to convey enough of the spiritual meaning and practical wisdom of the original outdooring ritual to convince her grandson, who understands too little to share her anger, that he should listen to her more often.

In the material counterpart of the spiritual passage the cycle, in contrast, signifies only futile repetition and recurrence. Even "renewal" is a misleading word for this process because what is renewed is the old order which was there before, so that, as the first novel oppressively insists, "nothing changes". The metaphysical spiral of expansive release is here countered by an inward motion of narrowing entrapment. The former's conservation of recycled energy is matched by the modern materialistic ritual's conspicuous waste, as in the squandering of expensive foreign drinks at Brempong's reception ceremony at the airport and the gratuitous exhibition of wealth at the outdooring. In the material context the circle has a merely negative form: the circle of impending doom closing in upon Baako and the mad dog; the circle of the abandoned, oppressed by the privileged square in Baako's screenplay; the circle of frustrated, self-enclosed art suggested by Ocran's ring of statues; the "senseless cycles" of the poor and the "horrible cycles of the powerless" in the first novel; the vast circumference of the "periphery" magnetized to the oppressive "centre" in Modin's paradigm of neo-colonialism in the third. The deflection back upon itself of the passage from captivity towards liberation is a recurring motif in the novels. In *Two Thousand Seasons* the return of the escapees from the slave boat to a society which has been entirely enslaved during their absence repeats fictionally, and anticipates historically, the fate of the been-to who returns from America to an Africa that is more Western than the West. It is the manipulative foreign control of these circular operations, notably the system of educational "factorship" which takes intellectual slaves abroad and programmes them for an eventual return as Westernized oppressors, which earns for the words ritual, ceremony, and cycle their darkest and most derogatory connotations in Armah's work. An indigenous equivalent is ceremonialized in Baako's screenplay "The Brand". In this work the periodic isolation and absorption of potential deliverers of the enslaved circle by the privileged of the square is calculated to frustrate any energies directed towards change. The predictable success of this project is crowned with "a repeated ritual of congratulation and sustained praise".[23]

Armah often gives to the word ritual its ordinarily negative implications: a mechanical, meaningless ceremonial, thoughtlessly gone through; an unprofitably repeated observance, granting an excessive, undue importance to a fossilized form; something merely procedural or gestural, token-like or symbolic, unreal rather than vital with magical potency. The manufactured rite of Brempong's reception is wholly illusion, "an invitation into a pretended world, happily given, happily taken, so completely accepted that there had hardly been any of the pretenders to whom it could have seemed unreal". In reality little has happened: "A man had gone away, spent time elsewhere, grown months and years, and then returned. Those he had left behind had spent time too, grown along their different waves, waiting to welcome their traveler."[24] The ritual is designed to conceal from fêted and fêters alike their real powerlessness and emptiness. Nevertheless, it is resonant with the special relationship that ritual has with time in traditional society. "The ceremony you ought to understand," Naana tells Baako at the outdooring, "or where do you get the meaning of it, even if it is done right?"[25] Performed correctly and in a meaningful context, ritual practices mark off especially significant moments and periods on the event calendar and usually involve, by their temporary suspension of normal activity, a more intense apprehension of time's passage. Ritual processes in traditional contexts are closely aligned with natural time processes and the proper experience of time, and it is significant that the blind Naana, the novel's repository of ritual values, loses her sense of time when it is upset by the tyranny of artificial pay-cycles and modern technology's reversal of night and day.[26] J.S. Mbiti writes of African birth rites:

> His birth is a slow process which is finalised long after the person has been physically born. In many societies, a person is not considered a full human being until he has gone through the whole process of physical birth, naming ceremonies, puberty and initiation rites, and finally marriage (or even

procreation). Then he is fully "born", he is a complete person.[27]

In such matters as birth, the metaphysics of ritual have direct implications for morality in the material world. The failure of Armah's stagnant consumer society to progress beyond an infantile materialism to full maturity is expressed in the greedy acceleration of the outdooring ceremony which speeds Araba's child in and out of the world before it has completed the first phase of its "birth". This profanity against natural time-process is multiplied by Foli's cargoist eagerness that Baako should no sooner go than return laden with gifts, and by Efua's impetuous commencement on Baako's house even before he has returned. Naana compares the sacrifice of the child with the eating of unripe fruit by people "who have forgotten that fruit is not a gathered gift of the instant but seed hidden in the earth and tended and waited for and allowed to grow".[28] No one in the early novels is willing to take sufficient time and care over the process of getting things properly "born", a gradual process valorized by ritual, and the result is that they quickly die. Araba's child is premature, Oyo's in the first novel is "dragged out of its mother's womb".[29] In *The Beautyful Ones Are Not Yet Born* the newly born Independent state of Ghana is given the symbolic form of a progeric child: like the real child in *Fragments*, this creature is exposed too soon to a stultifying Western materialism unchecked by any moral vision, with the result that its deathly birth is followed by a rapid decline into age. The landscapes of *Why Are We So Blest?* are blasted with a sterility which matches the impotence of the characters. At the end of the first novel, the man's patient fulfilment of his ritualized role of deliverer entitles him to his rebirth from the sea and the limited personal awakening which it brings. But for Koomson, who has not taken time over anything and so has it run out on him, and who has not gone through the full cycle of human maturation, there is only the excretory mock-rebirth, through the latrine hole, into renewed corruption elsewhere — a circular passage which marks his incorrigible failure to develop. The Koomson kind are, ritually and humanly, incomplete. They cannot be among "the beautyful ones" because, in the special moral sense conferred by ritual, they "are not yet born".

Why Are We So Blest? adds a new dimension to rituality in Armah's fiction. In this novel rituals are not merely empty, defunct or of limited and vestigial meaning, but are menacing and malign things, in both their real and figurative forms. In Modin's notebook meditations the word ritual hammers obsessively at the attention. Here, for example, is his account of the Western educational system which leaves the African student inferiorized, exploited and dependent:

> I should have stopped going to lectures long ago. They all form a part of a ritual celebrating a tradition called great because it is European, Western, white. The triumphant assumption of a superior community underlies them all, an assumption designed to reduce us to invisibility while magnifying whiteness. My participation in this kind of ritual made me not just lonely, not just one person unsupported by a larger whole, but less than one person: a person split, fractured because of my participation in alien communal rituals designed to break me and my kind.[30]

The "invisibility" taken on by the liminar in this Western-manufactured ritual is not something in process: it is meant to be permanent and to fracture his links with the "larger whole". Since such rituals are intended to isolate and exclude the African, their communality is alien. In this novel "rituals" are actively evil, grotesquely artificial arrangements purposefully "designed" to do harm and Modin's ritualized murder by whites in the desert is the culminating point in a conspiratorial cult-practice. Armah draws upon the word's more sinister associations of occult secrecy and superstition, cabalistic obscurantism and mystification: "In the imperial situation the education process is turned into an elitist ritual for selecting slave traders . . . In the system the factor is a link that must be hidden . . . his functioning is secret. Thick walls, the elaborate rituals of our education . . . Instead of justification, the rites of secrecy, mystification."[31] The occult ritualization of the educational cycle by Western powers releases associations of such horror in Baako in the earlier novel that, after his return from America, he is unable to conceive the idea of return, even in memory, without experiencing panic and nausea. The sight of the outgoing students at Ocran's school fills him not with nostalgia but with "a semblance of panic, as if time could absorb him into itself and drive him along the edge of some endless, vertiginous cycle over and over again".[32] Even the presence of Araba's child is able to evoke a terror of the educational passage: "Babyhood, infancy, going to school . . . the thought of a person having to go through the whole cycle again brought back his nausea . . ."[33] In the first half of *Why Are We So Blest?* the sickening oscillation of Modin's monologues between his departure for and departure from the United States, moving alternately backwards and forwards in time, arouses the same debilitating sensation of entrapment within a closed circle.

The cycle in its metaphysical conception is something which the man and Naana, in their different ways, can find comfort in, become resigned to and retreat into. But its materialization into a pernicious neo-colonial form in the economics and educational politics practised by the West is a phenomenon which can only be challenged and resisted. In the case of the former, the most important thing is for ritual to keep unbroken the cycle it inaugurates; in its latter Fanonian manifestation the cycle must be broken at all costs if Africa is to be released from its eternal roundabout of dependency and exploitation. The ritual forms which Naana alone still prizes are survivals from a traditional Africa, but those which haunt contemporary Ghana's new hearths and altars — the airports and hotel lounges — appear rather as alien forms imposed upon Africa from outside. Baako explains to his horrified grandmother that the outdooring, a wholly Europeanized affair conducted by men in tuxedos and waistcoats, is "a new festival", only distantly related to the traditional rite which marked the child's entry into the material world and offered thanks to the ancestors. Brempong's reception ceremony, though it carries faint echoes of tribal panegyric and the outdooring of chiefs, is also an essentially new form, catering in its own ridiculous way for the dislocated worshipping impulses left behind by a forsaken religion.

Because of the shifting significance of Armah's cyclical structures, one should be wary of translating their idiosyncratic rituality, except perhaps in ironic ways, into the terms of conventional rites of passage. A note of caution needs to be sounded here as ritual models devised by structural anthropologists in their studies of traditional African societies, notably those of Victor Turner, have attracted a certain amount of attention in critical writing on Armah.[34] Turner's structural models focus on the concept of liminality, which refers to the transitional phase of the rite of passage that carries neophytes across the threshold, or limen, at the boundaries of structures, and during which they belong neither to one clearly defined state nor to another but are anarchically caught, in Turner's phrase, "betwixt and between". Turner opposes the regenerative chaos of the liminal group's "communitas", which is "spontaneous, immediate, concrete", to the "norm-governed, institutionalised, abstract nature of social structure", and postulates a dialectical process which permits participation in the twin modalities of a prized but imperfect structure, on the one hand, and the dynamic communitas of a binarily opposed threshold or liminal group on the other.[35]

A glance at *The Beautyful Ones Are Not Yet Born* reveals many superficial and beguiling resemblances between, in the first case, the marginal liminar and Armah's man, and, in the second, Teacher's wee-smoking fringe fraternity and the liminal communitas group. The man has the metaphoric invisibility of the neophyte who, in the liminal phase of the rite of passage, is unclassified and without clear identity. As someone who has died out of one stable state and is not yet born into another, the liminal persona is surrounded by a symbolism of death and decomposition, faecal and menstrual waste, to which the man is no stranger. If Mary Douglas's equation of the unclear with the unclean, the ambiguous with the dangerously pollutive, is correct, the man's obsessive purification rituals in bath, shower and sea are consistent with his statusless state.[36] His other qualifications for the role of ritual liminar would seem to include anonymity and silence, a lack of possessions, a susceptibility to insult and humiliation, and his apparent strength from positions of weakness, instanced in the moral force of his merely sleeping presence on the bus and his ability to embarrass the Koomsons, for whom he has a taboo-like status. Teacher's wee-group has something of the communitas-model's anarchic, undifferentiated energy, its disturbance potential, and its quick of human interrelatedness which is able to transcend the structure-bound rigidities and crippling neuroses of family life. It is also possible to see Armah's Ghana as permanently marooned in the liminal phase of a national rite of passage between colonialism and true independence. The recharging energy that should carry the neophytic nation through its figurative initiation is halted by the stagnation of the Nkrumah regime, with the result that the new body politic cannot get properly born into its next phase and retains the incomplete rite's liminal lack of definition. The "not-boy-not-man" category in puberty rites is suggested by the symbolic manchild, the boy-man in the latrine, the old-young lawyer and the aged new leaders.[37] Correspondences at this tenuous level of abstraction could be proliferated indefinitely.

Clearly, the revitalizing, cyclical interflow of two mutually determinative forms, which is the key to Turner's model, does not take place in the moribund structure of Armah's Ghana. The wee-group, for example, brings nothing back to the society it has temporarily left. Far from invigorating and diversifying society, as in the structural model, its anarchic power is sucked into the monolithic, totalitarian social structure in the one-way action of energy into entropy. Armah's communitas-group is a substitute for a lost organic community, not something integral to an existing one. Its ritualized moments owe their social and time consciousnesses to a traditional past but there is no traditional ritual process at work in the present to bind the group as a force to recharge society, to which they in fact return in the haphazard despair of isolated individuals. The group's communal conviviality, or communitas, has a merely theoretical opposition to and ideological complementarity with the social structure, but there is no interaction or modifying reciprocity.

Armah has written in one of his essays of the been-to's pseudo-rite of passage which "includes the heroic initiation drama of the crossing of that geographical gulf separating metropolitan centres from the provincial outlands".[38] This ritualized process may, however, take the "initiate" out of the cycle altogether and leave him liminally stranded between his phase of passage and the society to which he is unable to make a reverse-crossing (Baako and Modin, but also Teacher, an indigenous been-to whose marginality has become a permanent condition). Alternatively, as in the more customary case of Brempong, he is returned to the community not to re-energize it from within but to deepen its oppression from without. Modin's entrapment in a cycle of isolation and frustrating contact is entirely destructive, not liberative, and the horrifying parody-rite of pubertal circumcision at the end of the novel marks the passage into a senseless death, not a new phase of life. Historically, the been-to has a limited and diminishing value as a ritual passenger, the main reason being that he is not in any radical sense changed by his experience and shows little inclination to change the society he returns to. He is not a force for regeneration, to which his society is not, in any case, susceptible. The liminal death awarded the outgoing been-to in Armah's second and third novels is an empty ceremony which corresponds to nothing in reality since the ritualized passage entails no turmoil or tribulation except for a few sensitive souls: Baako undergoes the mental death of breakdown and madness, Modin the trauma of isolation and then actual death. For the average half-Westernized, urbanized African youth of the post-Independence period, residence abroad is no longer the purgatorial process, the vicious cycle of inferiorization described in *Black Skin, White Masks*. For the mundane majority, the been-*to* experience is not an ordeal they have been *through*. The nearest Armah gets to the collective chaos of a revolutionary return is the case of the traumatized soldiers in the first novel: these are sent back altered from the white war to spread new fashions, demands and forms of violence which send shock waves through the colonial society. But the Brempongs and Asante-Smiths of the 1960s return full of the materialistic pomp and power which Africa sent them forth to acquire and they conform to expectations by feeding back into their societies more of what keeps them stagnant, unproductive and dependent. Apart from the Baakos and Modins who are isolated by their exceptional status, Armah's been-to cycle is a complacently monolithic continuum which is nothing like the transitional upheaval and regenerative chaos undergone by the liminal neophyte of Turner's structural model.

Using the latter model to illuminating effect, Richard Priebe has done most of the groundwork on ritual structures in Armah's first three novels and my own findings build upon his general research at the same time as they dissent from some of its particulars.[39] I have given a full answer elsewhere to Priebe's claim that, in the African context, "the tacit assumption of society . . . is that the ritual process enacted by the hero is the only way society can be rejuvenated."[40] Suffice it here to point out that the traditional ritual powers of weakness and humility which Priebe has attributed to the man in the first novel are as lacking in efficacy as the supposedly regenerative ones of the been-to in the next two books. These exist only in a condition of thwarted potentiality, and at the level of "ritual" in the pejorative sense — something unrealized as action in the world, something merely symbolic or token-like, gestural or theoretical — rather than with the positive connotations of superior authenticity or supernatural efficacy. There is no indication of a return to strength from a position of temporary inferiority and a levelling susceptibility to insult endured by one on the threshold of power, as in royal rites of passage in traditional African societies. Neither is there an understood, unwritten tolerance of the jester's or praise-singer's liminal privilege of playing the fool and embarrassing the guilty: the corrupt conductor quickly rectifies his error and throws the "seer", who is actually asleep, off the bus; the timber trader Amankwa simply goes elsewhere with his bribe money; the Koomsons endure his disturbing company only for as long as they can exploit him in the matter of the fraudulent boat deal; his wife, convinced at the fall of Koomson of the man's rightness, is nevertheless not converted by him and has no praise for his honesty, only surprised relief that it has paid off. The fact is that Armah's contemporary urban Accra is closer to the modern technological model of society than to the tradition-oriented ones from which Priebe derives his ritual contexts of meaning, and the ritual forms that still haunt the urban scene are no more than vestigial survivals, specifically located in the subtexts of the novels and in no way a cushion against or an alternative to actual revolution. The failure of the ritual processes to express any regenerative interaction between marginal figures and social structures, let alone effect a revolutionary recharging of the system, gives to the fatalistic ritual patterns of the fiction a predominantly ironic presence.[41] In the early novels ritual backcloths are used guardedly by an author who is constantly suspicious of their relevance, and their ironic patternings establish what is in effect a series of oppositions between ritual and reality. It is inadvisable, therefore, to look in the more ironic design of Armah's work for the kind of mystical identification between personal and communal redemption, liminal communitas and central structure, which is discernible in Kofi Awoonor's *This Earth, My Brother . . .* Necessary though it is to consider the ritual behaviour of Armah's protagonists under the abstract concept of *rites de passage* if only to mark his points of departure from conventional forms, this should be done preferably with a view to investigating exactly the author's specific choice of ritual motif and the narrow limits of its efficacy.

A number of critics have noticed the purification motif in the first novel, though none have identified it,[42] and I shall suggest in the next chapter that it probably has something to do with the annual West African purification rite of the carrier, who cleanses the community by carrying its sins and subsequent misfortunes into the wilderness in the form of a miniature wooden boat.[43] In van Gennep's scheme of ritual classification, this purifica-

tion would fall into the category of "pre-transitional rite"
or "preliminal rite of separation".[44] The carrier rite
discharges, does not recharge; its removal of impurities
enables the new year to go forward by the merely
negative, cathartic evacuation of the old one's pollutive
waste, not by any positive reinfusion of energy; it
prepares for but does not enact transition. Here would lie
the crucial difference from the liminar in Turner's model,
for the carrier does not benefit from "an absorption of
powers which will become active after his social status has
been redefined",[45] but suffers rather a waning of strength.
The ritual action, caught in the creative-destructive cycle
of the ingestion-evacuation circuit which is also the
master-metaphor of Armah's first novel, can only clear the
way for creation by a purgation or excretion, during which
the powers of the ritual performer atrophy like the year
and its transported ills: their entropy is internalized into
his own psychology and physiology.[46] Thus Armah may
have chosen a ritual form more consistent with the all-
consuming nature of his totalitarian power structure,
which transmits its own loss of energy to its liminars. In
the works of other writers who have used the carrier motif,
notably Soyinka and Awoonor, the ritual protagonist
either dies or goes mad, unable to survive for long
the anguish of his enervating task, whilst the society,
uninvigorated and largely unreformed, simply goes on.[47]
This would be consistent with the emphasis in Armah's
early fiction which, the first book's ambiguous title
notwithstanding, falls not upon renewal but upon old
worlds running down and ending, and upon the failure of
new ones to be born. The topography of forsaken public
utilities traversed by the man, the "aborted town" full of
unfinished buildings and unfulfilled people which Juana
drives through in the second novel, and the blighted
Saharan landscapes of the third, each belongs to the same
waste-land world, awaiting deliverance and rejuvenation.

It remains to consider the effect of ritual concepts upon Armah's characterization. A distinguishing feature of the first three novels is their polarized opposition of two complex subjectivities who serve as the novels' central interpretative consciousnesses (man and Teacher, Baako and Juana, Modin and Solo) to a largely undifferentiated "community" unilaterally characterized, respectively, by corruption, materialism and political cynicism. Other narrative viewpoints tend to triangularize this pattern but Naana and Aimée are relatively abstract and thinly-drawn figures whose interference with these polarities is minimal. The criticism and, implicitly, the salvation of the monolith- ically perceived community are the exclusive preserves of the interpretative consciousnesses, and the passage of most of the novels' action through them not only affords them their centrality but also gives the impression that they exist at a higher level of intensity and awareness, an impression that would appear to be at odds with the ordinariness and typicality required of them by their ritual identities as carriers.[48] In Baako's case, a chemical imbalance actually produces a "consciousness expansion effect" that enables him to generate his own "expansion toxins".[49] This super-perceptiveness would, however, along with the protagonist's miraculous freedom from taint, be a usual prerequisite for the performance of quasi- ritualistic tasks on the communal behalf, so that what places these consciousnesses above and outside the community also provides a bridge to it. The carrier in the original rite, although a representative member of the community, acquires a kind of outsider status and special value from his preritual seclusion and, more especially, from the social estrangement and stigmatization as a dangerously pollutive, contagious figure which follow from his lingering association with atrophy, disease and madness.[50] In the various recastings and miscastings, in West African literature, of the carrier as visionary healer, teacher, artist or expatriated intellectual, most of which endow the carrier-consciousness with an alienated artistic sensibility, the power to heal or redeem the society is paradoxically dependent upon differentness and estrangement from it: upon the absence and distance of the carrier from the community which sharpen awareness and foster a fresh energy and objectivity in the confrontation of its ills and bearing the burden of its conscience. In *The Strong Breed*, Soyinka's dramatization of an actual carrier rite, the outsider Eman becomes the conscience of the evil community which makes him its victim, and in Awoonor's figurative treatment of the carrier, in *This Earth, My Brother . . .*, the distanced empathy with the oppressed of the lawyer Amamu, who carries on his conscience his society's unprosecuted crimes and unexpiated guilt, corresponds with the ritual introjection of the year's ills into the carrier's effigy.[51] Neither of these saving missions translates into social action, however. Eman's martyrdom offers no more than a glimmer of redemption to the village that sacrifices him and the contemplative Amamu, in his mental breakdown, merely takes over the maddening mental burden of Africa's sufferings and evil legacies.

In these literal and metaphoric uses of the carrier there is a tendency to place communal salvation ineffectually with the sacrificial heroism of solitary individuals, after the models of Western tragedy, and much has been made of the apparently similar placing of the discovery of the communal will, and of society's relief or redemption, at the hands of isolated figures in Armah's early novels.[52] But the man, as my account of the first novel will make clear, is not conceived after the pattern of the Western hero, visionary though his consciousness may often be: the fulfilment of a communal service by an estranged outsider in a ritual performance which paradoxically marks the limited efficacy and concrete relevance of all ritual process is, in fact, a very African form and, in the West African context of the carrier, is perfectly consistent with the phenomenon of individuals in some way championing communities. Moreover, the practical and domestic dimensions of the man's communal role should not be lost sight of. Never a lone questing hero but always embattled, caught in the crossfire between family and gleam, the man does, under sufferance, provide a recipe for living in a corrupt world on terms that are not entirely dishonourable and represent a more realistic experience of human community than is offered by Teacher's over-simplifications. The man, unlike Teacher, has to live in the world and his actions speak of a more positive and pragmatic approach to co-existence with corruption, which weighs against his idealism: for example, the enforced maintenance of the Koomson connection, his patient endurance of a boat deal he cannot prevent, and his honest confession that he is not even sure that he hates the new materialism.

At the same time, it must be conceded that the primary focal sensibilities of the first three novels (the man, Baako and Modin) are necessarily stiffened by a ritual formality and simplicity which are often at odds with their owners' psychological complexities and which correspond to a matching superficiality in the construction of those characters who are the targets of their concentrated vision. First in this fictional territory outside the protagonal consciousness are the elites and their parasites, whose behaviour is sufficiently standardized for the characters to be interchangeable. There is little to choose, from the information provided, between Akosua Russell and Asante-Smith or between a principal secretary and his junior assistant. Brempong is a younger Koomson, Efua an older Oyo, and though the treatment of the mother is more sympathetic than that of the wife, there is nothing approaching an inside view. Secondly, at the margins of this privileged domain — the "square" of Baako's screenplay — and aesthetically distanced by the estranged interpreting consciousness, is the remote outer community, variously characterized as "the people" (in Teacher's fantasy of fraternity with the masses), "the damned", "the lost", or "the doomed circle" (in Baako's cinematics). The spectral, anonymous inhabitants of this realm are the universally rejected and oppressed who await the miracle of some saving relief action: the sweepers and latrine men, the sick and maimed villagers on Baako's country tour, the mutilated soldiers and begging orphans of the Afrasian revolution. These exist, primarily, to be saved.

In *Why Are We So Blest?* the African community, now more remote than ever at the distance of Modin's transatlantic expatriation, is mythicized into the beneficiary of deliverance by a Promethean "reverse-crossover", an idea scoffed at by Mike the Fascist: "I know nobody goes through the struggle to get here so they can fall back into that communal dirt."[53] Meanwhile, in the foreground of the novel's action, the community's would-be revolutionary saviours are revealed as paralysed and emasculated by the luxuries of Western exile. The ritual design is less insistent here but it is still in evidence and follows the usual ironic format. Modin's murderous initiation into the cause of the African revolution, following his liminal-like emergence from the living death of his American exile, is given the form of an emasculatory mock-circumcision rite exactly twelve days from the death of the old year: it is, by implication, the changeover period of recreative chaos during which, according to Mircea Eliade, initiatory rites of passage mark the abolition of time and the destruction and resurrection of the world.[54] But Modin, one of those Africans who have "swallowed the wish for their own destruction", carries only his own death within him, not the life of a new age or the sacrificial hope of a redeemed Africa. His final ritual immolation in an unregenerative desert is merely self-destructive, a futile offering on the altar of Aimée's sensational egoism which is as ineffectual as the Afrasian antics of Congheria's bogus revolutionary saviours.

With the radical shift to pluralized and panoramic visions in Armah's two historical novels comes a spirited effort to enliven the African communities of the past into something more than the collection of conformist subscribers to mass materialism and abject cargoist millenarianism which constitutes his version of the modern community. In the histories a careful weighing of individual fates against a communal destiny replaces the ritualized opposition, albeit ironic, of superior messianic individuals to benighted collectivities which prevails in the early novels. The carrier theme now resurfaces in a new form, not negated by irony or parody, and finally shorn of any earlier associations with the hero-concepts of European tragedy. In *Two Thousand Seasons* the slaves turned-guerrillas become the collective carriers of the Akan, and ultimately the African, historical conscience. In *The Healers* the outlawed and persecuted Densu returns to his community as only one of the novel's eponymous healers in what is a collective, organized mission to minister to the wounded Akan spirit, torn from its true course by the incursions of colonialism.

Armah's organization of ritual motifs, and most particularly that of the carrier, finds its most coherent and subtly suggestive form, however, in *The Beautyful Ones Are Not Yet Born*, and it is to that remarkable first novel that we must now turn.

V

Senseless Cycles: Time and Ritual in *The Beautyful Ones Are Not Yet Born*

Early criticism of *The Beautyful Ones Are Not Yet Born*,[1] both African and non-African, expended a great deal of energy in tracing the novel's inspiration to European and Western sources, and, though my intention in this chapter is to locate and define influence in all its manifestations, not to discount or deny it, my analysis will go some way towards the redressing of an imbalance which is long overdue.

The novel's scatology, as a starting example, is at least marginally indebted to the American vernacular. Filth and shit, which have a way of finding out fraud and guilt and bringing the powerful back to the squalor out of which they have corruptly carved a niche of cleanness and prosperity, function as levelling metaphors which put down pretension, expose false gentility and attack corrupt leadership. But the imagery of consumer waste and excreta is pushed to extremities which are not accounted for by the belief, expressed by one critic, that "of all man's works and creations his excrement is most disgusting" and so "appropriate to represent man's corruption".[2] Neither is it instructive to speak, as did another critic, of "Ibsenian-type analogies, where the filth is meant to reflect the political, social and moral decay of his people".[3] Armah's metaphors participate in their realities in a

manner both more urgent and more intimate than is to be
found in the more distanced medium of analogy: their
vividness, concrete immediacy, and very precise kind of
integration, as will presently be made clear, owe more to
African oral tradition and ritual symbolism than to the
techniques of Western allegory. The equation of the daily
corruption with the daily food cycle, making bribery as
common as the eating which is its metaphor, goes far
beyond the loose emotive association of moral corruption
with the filth and waste of consumer materialism or the
idea that corruption is morally unclean and therefore
vaguely related to excrement. In the scheme of Armah's
exuberant and meticulous symbolism, the intemperate
over-eating of the country's resources by the ruling elite
without their performing any productive work in return
leads to a physiological imbalance, caught splendidly in
Koomson's growling entrails and thundering flatulence,
and to mountains of ancient, undisposed-of shit and dirt
in the environment: the fantastic metaphors, which touch
importantly upon both African pollution concepts and
time-consciousness, are as much influenced by the graphic
and grotesque hyperbole of the traditional griot as
by the extravagances of Western expressionism and
surrealism. Far from the irrationalism of the latter, these
features are the threads of a formidably logical and
symmetrical network of correspondences between the
human ingestion-evacuation cycle and the respective
conditions of the body politic and the Ghanaian environment, and this system of parallels hinges crucially on an
image based firmly in African tradition: the image of
"eating".

This appropriately all-consuming, all-pervasive metaphor takes in everyone in the novel, from the fat-bellied
timber trader Amankwa and the bribe-seeking policeman
to the new leaders "grown fat and cynical from eating
centuries of power" (p. 81) and the bus conductor who

sniffs the rank cedi note as if it were some exotic spicy food. The metaphor has its humble origins in the giving of *kola* in traditional African society, either as a mark of hospitality to an important and influential guest or to someone from whom a favour was expected. In its translation to the larger scale of nation-state capitalism, however, this practice of local ingratiation is perverted into a system of wholesale bribery, in which the vast scale of the "eating" — the jockeying for position through bribery and influence — produces "fatter" (that is, wealthier and more corrupt) politicians who grow increasingly remote from the mass of the population, and only those members of society who have a "big man" in the family are able to feed from the new prosperity. Since *kola* has now been replaced by bribe money, a corrupt equation of money with eating comes into being and the daily bribe is identified with the daily meal, or *kola*, which it provides: the corrupt policeman points to his teeth to indicate that he wants to "eat" and the man expects to hear the words "even *kola* nuts can say thanks" (p. 182). Armah's metaphorical equation aligns eating, digestion and excretion, on the one hand, with bribery (taking *kola* money), corruption and exploitation ("shitting in the people's faces"), on the other. People in the novel consume food, power, money, time and sex: they "eat" to survive, to devour communal resources, to pollute the environment, to oppress and degrade others, to prosper corruptly or to allow others to do so. Much of this activity follows Western patterns of consumption but it operates through a peculiarly African medium and is energized from peculiarly African beginnings. It is, unfortunately, a norm for the novel that such survivals from traditional African life either lose their value altogether in the transposition to contemporary urban and national contexts or function only in perverted forms. The group economics of the extended family system have become a facade for parasitic dependence and what has survived of the ironic praise-singer in the subversive humour of Etse (pp. 83–4) passes to the "praise-singing seller" of bread who lauds Koomson as "my white man" and to the Party sycophants who grow "greasy and fat singing the praises of their chiefs" (pp. 37, 162). Like *kola* offerings, the proper meanings of ancient proverbs are twisted to suit the personal needs and profits of politicians and the boatman's "ancient dignity of formal speech" is but another debased ritual form, seeking in the customary gift of the traveller the expected bribe of the escapee (p. 174). The fraudulent clerk who extends his holidays by the fiction of an eternally dying clan of relatives blasphemously exploits traditional time values which still govern the village funeral, namely the special provision within the cycle of human growth and decay of a certain period for the dead man to rejoin his ancestors. The traditional cyclic conceptualization of time still features in contemporary experience but — as in the case of old proverbs, praise-songs and libations — chiefly at the level of cynical manipulation and at the satiric distance of the acquisitive city-dweller.

This perversion of African traditions in the general sell-out to Western values is balanced, albeit unevenly, by the paradoxical promotion of more traditionally African and communal values by Armah's outsider heroes. From the first novel's returning soldiers, forced by colonialism to fight against the interests of the ones they should protect, to the educated been-to of the next two books who finds himself pressed into the role of modern "factor" to further oppress the people he would serve, and the slaves-turned-guerillas of the histories, the overriding preoccupation of Armah's protagonists is the same: to place a meaningful social vision at the disposal of an increasingly fragmented or absent community. With the pernicious growth of a system which returns the been-to's Western cargo to the false communities of selected "loved ones", at the expense of the larger community, the communally-minded become the most isolated individuals. The ironic result is that an intolerant self-seeking individualism becomes the new communal faith and anyone with a surviving spirit of community is cut off from the body which his beliefs are intended to serve.

The aspiration of the protagonist to lift the community out of its moral and material degradation is reinforced by the narrative experiments at the centre of the first novel. The communal vision implied by them is not an easy achievement. As it progresses, the interlocking dual narrative of Teacher and the man increasingly interconnects only to register the disconnection or divergence of viewpoints, and the very sharp, lyrical rendering of individual sensations in the ostensibly typifying orchard-raiding episode makes for a rather artificial notation of collective identity: it is really the intense experience of one boy — now the man — generalized into three, not the experience of three and, by implication, the whole of African boyhood, compressed into one. The narratives, oscillating between defeatist pessimism and guarded hope, expand at one point to embrace the whole community but only to contract again to the vision of two isolated men. Nevertheless, the narrative continuity and stylistic monotony of the two voices contrive to create the impression of a collective autobiography of the childhood and youth of the new nation and its failed hopes. The outcome is finally satisfactory neither as a single nor a plural vision and its communal potential is realized chiefly at the level of the image-patterns which identify the private with the public realm and human physiology with the body politic. But it is the closest that the author can get, at this stage of his writing, to the idea of a "communal view".

Most importantly, *The Beautyful Ones Are Not Yet Born* is surprisingly rich in indigenous time concepts and much of what follows will be concerned, in a general way, with the survival of traditional ideas about time into, and their complex interplay with, the Westernized world of modern urban Africa. The man, for example, moves daily through a Western chronometric context in his capacity as urban clerk but sleeps and wakes according to a less arbitrary, more organic mode of time, "as if there were an inner system, alerting him with his own anxiety, making him wake even without the mechanical help of the clock" (p. 101). Amid the chaos of the coup, his inner "quietness" enables him to apprehend synchronically different moments of his past, a feat quite at odds with the diachronic order of historical change raging about him, and the sea is envisaged by him not only as an accumulation of dead time but, after a more African fashion, as an ongoing regenerative continuum, "fresh in a special organic way that has in it traces of living things from their beginnings to their endings" (pp. 159, 40). A susceptibility to a more traditional time-consciousness is also revealed by his response to vestigial survivors of the village community such as Koomson's tribal-scarred gardener with his innate organic harmony and slow dignified rhythms now up-rooted and bending like a reed before the pressures of high-speed Africa in the form of Koomson's blue-jeaned daughter (pp. 143–44). Even in the modern Ghana of lost connections, of commuters travelling in pockets of isolation and morse-tapping solitaries "opening up their sores" in anonymous messages crossing the void of the modern state, the African world-view has not been entirely eclipsed. In addition to those places in the novel where a properly ritualistic design breaks through surface realism, there are a number of momentary experiences or "sea-changes", since each takes place in the presence of the sea's self-renewing continuum — the episodes of the radio-song at Teacher's house, the wee-smoking and the man's seashore epiphanies — which might be termed "ritualistic" insofar as they are reminiscent of traditional rites of passage: the ordinary consciousness and social identity are temporarily suspended; there is an instinctual release of personality into a larger regenerative harmony, either of group communion or elemental contact with nature and cosmos; and the deferment of or removal from the normal time order allows the experience of a more intense time consciousness. At a more specific level than the foregoing examples, the following analysis is designed to show how a particular view of history — as the hoarded accumulation of unpurged ills in a cycle of consumption, waste and disposal, inclusive and transcendent of Western interludes — has been ritualized into a visionary and peculiarly African form.

   Arguing from the premise of a cyclical continuum, some anthropologists have suggested that traditional African societies view the passage of time, in the Western sense of advancing non-repetitive change, as deleterious and therefore seek, through rituals of annulment and the refusal of printed memory, to conceal from themselves the fact of alteration.[4] This idea finds its most crudely exaggerated expression in Mircea Eliade's theory that ritual acts perform archetypal gestures which aim at the abolition of history through the repeated, re-enactive return to an initial cosmogenic act.[5] Such acts have the effect of endowing time with spatial contours in order that it may more easily be ritually carried away and symbolically cancelled at an annual or periodic ceremony and, visualizing time in traditional Africa in similarly spatial terms, John S.Mbiti conceives its passage as a backward motion from a dynamic *sasa* dimension, consisting of the present and the immediately possible future, into a static and terminal *zamani* dimension, a final storehouse of past events beyond which time cannot go[6] — definitions which Sunday Anozie restates in terms of diachrony and synchrony.[7] Recent African fiction, as D.S. Izevbaye has demonstrated,[8] has been an area of fruitful interaction between such traditional time concepts and Western notions, cyclicality and linearity, and synchrony and diachrony: *The Beautyful Ones Are Not Yet Born*, in carrying vestigial ritual patterns from traditional Africa over into a contemporary urban setting, touches upon each of these ideas at some time and its tripartite structure gives an initial indication of its broad repertoire of time concepts. In the first part the somnambulistic pace of the narrative and the pages of static description maintain the illusion of an unbroken temporal sequence and convey an impression of time as heavy and slow-moving: this covers the futile cycle of the man's working day and dwindles to a standstill with his arrival, in the evening, at Teacher's house. Here, from a point of narrative suspension, the post-war upheaval and the frenzied power-cycle of the first Independence government are recalled and events are seen to move at an insane speed, reflecting Koomson's order of rapid change, fast cars and quick money. The diachronic order of historical change is most frighteningly in evidence here at the novel's whirling centre, in the nightmarish sixth-chapter retrospection to the chaos unleashed upon post-war Ghana. In this period of violent and desperate novelty, in which meaning runs "irretrievably away with every day that goes" (p. 76), time is an agent of irreversible damage and irrecoverable loss, marked by murder, theft, infidelity, and the collapse of the traditional community under the pressures of the new wealth and fashions which the soldiers bring home from the white war. At the end of this long flashback, the cycle of the single day is completed and the narrative moves into the mode of abridged time, stretching over an indefinite number of weeks and ending with the coup and Koomson's escape, after which the man returns to the cycle of things that do not change: "Oyo, the eyes of the children after six o'clock, the office . . ." (p. 183). In the course of these modulations, time is conceived not only as Western linear change and diachronic energy, on the one hand, and as cyclic continuum, on the other, but also as a ritual property, in which the past — envisaged not as process but as state or place, not as motion but as object — acquires the entropized permanence of Mbiti's *zamani*.

The novel's two distinct temporal orders are, however, roughly equivalent to the Western linear-diachronic and the African cyclical-synchronic models. For the elite's "big men", whose goal is the gleam of material prosperity, "progress" is defined entirely in terms of personal advancement, or "getting ahead", and time is conceived as non-repetitive change, subject to transience and rapid obsolescence: it is construed as a commodity to be consumed, and which can be spent or wasted, kept or lost, and can, irreversibly, run out. Conversely, Koomson's class habitually measures consumption in terms of time: palaces and cars are acquired in "a matter of months", women "fucked and changed like pants", and, at the Winneba training centre where "everybody who wants speed" goes, dockers turned into ministers overnight (p. 89). But for the novel's dwarf-men, trapped like insects in "endless pools" and unable to run away, time is experienced chiefly as duration, being mainly empty, eventless and spent in waiting, and is characterized either as an enormous weight dragged painfully around or as an elastic entity which has to be stretched out like the filing-clerk's hour of daily work, an expandable envelope into which things can be allocated and extended (p. 155). The man's work in the business of Time-Allocation provides time with physical contours which suit well the slow, "endless round" of the poor, for whom time's movement is repetitive, in a horizontal round of non-achievement, and is marked by the durability of goods and the dust gathering on their unvisited houses (p. 118). For members of this lower circle to break out of their "horrible cycle of the powerless" into the higher "factor-cycle" of western-aspiring elites, a strenuous vertical motion, a "soaring upward", is necessary (p. 119). The man is able to pass occasionally and temporarily from one timescape to another and, significantly, "exchanges time" with another clerk at the office to purchase expensive foreign drinks for Koomson's visit, surrendering to "the foolish happiness of the moment" which implicates him in the short-term hedonism of Koomson's time ethic (p. 115). The man spends most of the novel, however, agonizing over a choice of time modes and concomitant moral values for himself and his children. He can either doom them to the motionless time of the poor, to the repetition of "senseless cycles" that leave everything the same, or choose, after concepts of linear progression, to sacrifice the moral health of his "brief self" in the present to invest in a changed future for them, assuming that they will not know or care "about ways that were rotten in the days of disappeared parents" (p. 145). Only at the end of the novel, when Koomson's recklessly consumed time reaches a point of linear expiration and a reverse crossing brings him into the man's senseless round and the latrine man's circuit of life, is the man's choice apparently vindicated.

The novel devises complex parallels and causal connections between these two interdependent orders. In Ghanaian economics accelerated consumption is matched by productive inertia. The taxi driver who speeds Oyo and the man towards the rich homes of the politicians in the new Toyota comments that "everybody is making things now except us. We Africans only buy expensive things" (p. 140), and the man at work keeps records of slow goods trains shunted into sidings to let the express commuter-consumer trains pass. There is a bitter inverse proportion between the small precious time which the leaders have at their disposal to rush through vast amounts of leisure consumption, and the heavily redundant hours over which the office clerks have to stretch out their tiny amounts of unproductive work. The two categories of experience are mutually determinative. The rich who cram their time with frivolities and novelties are seen to create a vacuum of time for the poor to live and work in, since the government's corrupt neglect of production and services leads to stopped trains, uncollected refuse and bureaucratic boredom in jobs without work. Time "consumed" by big men thus generates a residue of time as "waste" for poor men, time spent inactive in enforced boredom. In the novel of contemporary setting, as in the novel of traditional society, time is marked by what happens in it and has no existence apart from events,[9] but in Armah's railway office nothing is happening. No work or goods are produced: what is produced is time. Redundant time-registers — telephones, morse-telegraphs, overtime slips and clocks — ritually punctuate time, marking moments in a vacuum: there are no events to keep pace with them, nothing to match the clock's motion, and the machines record only the failure and stoppage of motion in the lateness and cancellation of trains (pp. 16, 25). The office is a microcosm of the State, in which repetition is the reality behind an illusion of change. Appropriately, it is staffed by functionaries of time — Time-Keepers, Time-Allocation Clerks, Overtime Clerks. These downtrodden drudges metaphorically produce time which the big men devour and give back to them as waste, processed like food along the ingestion-evacuation circuit which saturates Armah's imagery. The privileged elite's scramble after imported consumer luxuries, ill-balanced by late or cancelled exports (p. 20–21), does not carry the nation forward in any linear progress but traps it in a vicious cycle of borrowing and bankruptcy, paid for by the worker's mirrored monthly loan cycle.

Although their rampant destructiveness is conveyed with the greatest power in its middle section, the novel as a whole testifies to the fatal legacy of Western time values for modern Africa when they become the exclusive possession of a privileged minority and there is no concession to anything happening outside them: "Outside the area of the gleam . . . there was nothing worth pursuing, nothing at all worth spending life's minutes on" (p. 47). Whatever their calendrical variations, traditional African societies adhered to certain commonly-held, minimal time-concepts which governed attitudes towards birth, marriage, work, death and the ancestors. There was a tendency to regard time as the property of the whole community, with the result that the time-ethic was geared to communal values, collective responsibilities and philosophies of leadership. Moreover, the maintenance of the cyclic continuum, in both its agricultural and eschatological forms, was thought to be essential for the continuation of material and social prosperity, so the cyclic conceptualization of time was allied with the ideas of societal well-being and social commitment. But in Armah's contemporary Ghana time has apparently been linearized and appropriated into the elite's general monopoly. The Koomsons "own" time as they own houses and cars: their boat, "The Ahead", is named in their spirit of impatient acquisitive rivalry and early arrival. Koomson, the man of the hour, decrees the time and length of the house visits to discuss the boat purchase and is "unable to take his eyes off his watch" as he concludes, in embarrassed haste, the fraudulent deal, whilst his wife's voice "springs and coils around" like an alarm clock (pp. 138, 37). At each appearance Koomson declares what it is time to do and only at the final crestfallen meeting does the control of time pass from him.

If the traditional society's cyclic conceptualization of time was attuned to the survival and well-being of the whole community, then it is clear that the post-war upheavals and frantic, abortive reform programmes in the new Ghana cause major disturbances in the communal body — note the many links between speed and sickness (pp. 62, 141, 153) — and a splintering of communal bonds. During this period, in which too much happens too quickly and Teacher's memory can barely cope with the "obscure haste", speed not only rots and makes ill; it also divides and disconnects. Traditional ties of kinship and friendship hold no sanction against the sudden loss of the past and break down in an animal competition for survival which enforces the seizure of the present moment (p. 66, 78). The sharp segmentation of chapter 6 into seven phases, one for each year of the manchild and the Independence government which it represents, dramatizes the passage from community to fragmented individualism: the pressure of linearity which it imposes — of time in fractured, finite lengths — carries the diverging voices inexorably from the remembered past into the present's dichotomized order of goal-getting elites and atomized communities. Government by an elite of indigenous aliens is like the handle of the pencil-sharpener in the railway office which "sped round and round with the futile freedom of a thing connected to nothing else" (p. 17): in the new society the disconnected communication lines of telephones reflect the isolative, self-seeking individualism which they serve. Thus the novel's treatment of change devises an alliance between speed, the diachronic sever-ance of the past and human disconnectedness, but this in turn calls into existence an opposing alignment or counter-alliance of slowness or suspension, synchrony and com-munity — a phenomenon most marked in those "ritual moments" in the presence of the sea's continuum when the normal time order and ordinary social identity are suspended.

In the first of these "sea-changes", each of which resembles the experience of liminal "communitas" in a traditional rite of passage, the intuition of a fraternity of fellow-feeling at Teacher's house on the lagoon arises in response to the "slow suspended notes" of a Congolese radio-song about slow arrival (p. 50–52). In the next one, the wee-drug simultaneously erodes psychological and temporal barriers as a condition for the experience of group consciousness and the deeper connectedness of things in nature, thus aligning an almost telepathic togetherness with the ability to "see the whole of your life laid out in front of you" in a synchronic chain and offering its users a brief escape from the one-way destructiveness of historical time (pp. 70–73). Finally, the man enjoys a lyrical immersion of self into the surrounding elements and a remote glimpse of the convivial dockside community when, in a moment of "suspended loneliness", he is "not having to think about time" and the "stillness" and "quiet motion" of the sea give rise to a synchronic apprehension of past, present and future (pp. 112–13). The visions provided in the momentary intensity of these isolated epiphanic episodes are so rare in the prevailing ethos of contemporary Ghana that they appear as survivals from another world, but their synchronic recovery of time as cyclic continuity and sea-process is perceived to be at least temporarily restorative of a sense of community. On the other hand, accelerated change geared to short-term attainable futures and breaking with the past gives rein to a fragmenting individualism which disconnects human lives. Speed divides: its aligned opposites reconnect.

The operation of parallel orders in which time is, respectively, moving at great speed and not moving at all, accounts for the repeated phenomenon of a residual stasis or suspension left in the wake of rapid change: Teacher marvels how something could "turn so completely into this other thing" and, in the next breath, concludes "that nothing in life has changed" (p. 85). Thus the tremendous stasis of the long pivotal sixth chapter serves for a meditation on the mad cycle through which the first indigenous governors rush to their doom, and the man's calmness and gravity impress themselves most strongly in moments of speed and change, as during the urban panic of the coup. This doubleness in the narrative's rendering of time is keenly felt in chapter 8, where the bribe that speeds Amankwa's logs into motion and the workmen's chatter of a small boy's swift rise to ministerial rank and rapid sexual turnover cut across the present-tense narrative's painstakingly evoked monotony of minutes, which the man spends in sleeping, long circular walks and doodling on the morse telegraph. It is equally marked at the beginning of chapter 5, where the man reflects that it is futile to "forever keep up the pretense that the difference between the failures and the hard heroes of the dream is only a matter of time" (p. 46). Ironically, the difference is indeed a matter of time, a question of their existence in different temporal orders, as his continuing reflections show:

> Time in which to leap across yards made up of the mud of days of rain; to jump over wide gutters with only a trickle of drying urine at the bottom and so many clusters of cigarette pieces wet and pinched in where they have left the still unsatisfied lips of the sucker. Time to sail with a beautiful smoothness in the sweet direction of the gleam, carrying with easy strength every one of the loved ones; time to change the silent curses of resentful loved ones . . . time to change all this into the long unforced laughter of tired travellers home at last. But when the approach of the loved ones grows into sound and the pain is thrown outward against the one who causes it, then it is no longer possible to look with any hope at all at time.
> (p. 46)

Koomson's rapid order of success is much in evidence here: the hurried bypassing of natural time processes to arrive at measurable goals, the trampling over symbolic dirt and deprivation, the impatient dissatisfaction of those left behind, the longing for some irreversible change that will turn resentment into its opposite. But the dynamic verbs of motion which characterize the pursuit of the gleam — leaping, jumping, sailing — are here immobilized by the somnambulistic tempo of sentences which are more concerned to register the man's way of experiencing time. The suspension of event in the present tense, the cumbrously adjectival, prepositional and verb-restrictive syntax, and the incantatory Prufrockian repetition of the word "time", which effectively denies time the power of movement, all militate against motion. Time as motion and change is filtered through an almost stationary prose which itself does not change or progress but simply repeats. Those who are resigned to this senseless, un-progressing round because they are unable or unwilling to become like the remote leapers cannot "look with any hope at all at time" as it exists in the alternative mode. For these there will always be their own kind of time, stretching out endlessly in Africa's ongoing continuum.[10]

The recurring pattern of acceleration into inertia, of speed subsumed into stasis, is no mere accident of style, however, but is the keynote of Armah's vision of history, in which the reckless leaping speed of the gleam and its scramble for wealth clog up the historical currents with the resulting refuse of corruption. This unpurged corruption is envisaged as an accumulated, inert mass which, like the decayed consumer junk on the sea shore and the immovable midden around the city bin, fuses with the earth in a permanent stasis (p. 40). The rapid and short-sighted consumption of the rich and powerful, by wearing out and emptying resources, bequeaths a growing detritus and dwindling means to future generations, a process reflected in the novel's entropic imagery. The impetuous haste of government "reform" programmes succeeds only in bringing the State to a standstill and at the end of the regime's term rapid and radical change, improperly distributed, are seen to have had the paradoxical effect of leaving everything unchanged.

A crucial paradox of the novel is that traditionally African attitudes towards historical change emerge from this urban context rather than in opposition to it, a phenomenon principally of the narrative's spatial treatment of time. The failure of meaningful events to mark off one moment from another in lives of clerical drudgery makes it impossible to say exactly when a thing passes into something else and it is discovered that beneath the rapid superficial upheaval of political independence the real change, which has been so slow as to be almost imperceptible, is measured not by motion but by spatial increase. With each new coating of pollution that obscures the flower patterns on the railway building wall, motion petrifies into an accreted stillness and solidity in which the stages of change, as in the case of the banister, are no longer discernible (pp. 11, 12). At some time the colonial administration turned into government by "the sons of the nation", as did the Old into the New Caprice Hotel, but, since these changes were illusory, the time marking their passage seems also to be an illusion: "How completely the new thing took after the old" (p. 10). The presence of more dirt in the environment than can ever be cleaned away — enough to provide the office sweeper with three daily cleaning jobs — is partly explained by the continuities between the consumer habits of Koomson and those of his ancestors. Nothing seems to have changed from "the same people using the same power for chasing after the same enslaving things . . . from the days of chiefs selling their people for the trinkets of Europe" (p. 149). Koomson's hands are "fat, perfumed, soft with the ancestral softness of chiefs who had sold their people and are celestially happy with the fruits of the trade" (p. 131). He is less imaginative than his predecessors but it is clear that little has happened in the time between them apart from their shared corruption, and these snapshot retro-spections to ancestral prototypes of contemporary figures confirm that the past is no place to look for an alternative to the present. The implication is that all the filth of Africa's history is still in existence and the failure to jettison the old has contaminated the new. In an environment polluted by the accumulated unpurged rot of history, things are born dead or rotten, infected by what came before: hence the prostitute's "prematurely tired skin" (p. 35), the putrid polish, the aged new leaders, the rank smell of the new banknote.

In keeping with this immobilization of history in a terminal present, the man's colourful control-graph spatially metamorphoses the stopped time of goods trains into aesthetic patterns that petrify industry into static design and the time hanging heavily over the bored clerks is repeatedly endowed with physical dimensions (pp. 33, 41–42). In the orgies of description lavished upon mere waiting at terminals and routine journeys up a staircase, there is a suppression of event in favour of sheer phenomenology, a hallucinated epic transcription of the world which diverts attention from the object described to the movement of the description around it: the stylistic paralysis turns time itself into an inert weight. There is no denying that such descriptive strategies, as numerous commentators have noticed, are Western in origin,[11] but they are effortlessly and seamlessly absorbed into an indigenous world-view and made to express ideas which are traditionally African, for a massive emphasis of image and reference in the early chapters conveys a single impression of time as a downward spiral: the slow trains circling between Takoradi and Kumasi; the flying ants and clerks going round in their endless pools and aimless routines; the defunct pencil sharpener; the decrepit fan decelerating through its "long, slow waves of time" (p. 33); the dimming orange-yellow light which "came dully, like a ball whose bounce had died completely" (p. 14). The overwhelming impression is of time entropically running down to a point of stoppage. There appears to be a very strong link in Armah's imagination between the endlessly waiting commuters and clerks, eager for the end of the month, and the mood of many traditional West African coastal and river communities, awaiting deliverance at the year's changing. In Robin Horton's words, "the end of the year is a time when everything in the cosmos is run-down and sluggish, overcome by an accumulation of defilement and pollution".[12] As in Awoonor's novel, a number of elements combine to identify the man's role with the traditional rite of the carrier in these village communities; his purification rituals, his pathological compassion even for those who do not seek his sympathy, and a variety of vestigial tribal notions about contagion, taboo, and estrangement surrounding the introjection of communal burdens, each of which will presently be explored in detail. It seems that Armah has chosen to see the last weeks of the accelerated but now torpid cycle of the Nkrumah regime in terms of the traditional year-end, when the old year, run-down and dead, is carried off with its lethal burden of pollutive sins and resulting misfortunes. The important difference is that it is not merely the corruptions of the past year or the Nkrumah period or the whole post-colonial era which are being expelled. Neither is it the century of colonial rule as in *This Earth, My Brother. . .*[13] It is, by massive metaphoric implication, the vast entropized weight of Africa's history which, in the omission of periodic reformation and regeneration, renews only its own decay and bequeaths only its old age to young lives, leaving power in the hands of moribund politicians grown cynical with "the eating of centuries of power" or men like Nkrumah, "a new old lawyer, wanting to be white" (pp. 81, 84). One such politician, Koomson, is misconceived by the man's mother-in-law as one "who can do manly things, and take the burdens of others too" (p. 139). Confusing messiahs and carriers, selfish privilege and sacrifice, family and community, she mistakes his opportunism for the service which the man, at a ritual level, will later undertake: Koomson, one of the novel's false and faulty carriers, in fact bears only the burden of his own acquisitive family and ensures that his token business partners are spared the weight of his affluence.

The intellectual currents feeding Armah's Westernized stylistic experiments are governed by traditional ideas about the running down of time, the piling up of pollutions in African society and its need for regular rejuvenation or annulment. The benumbed society on which the novel opens is the historical culmination of this process, so that the book begins at the end: the regime's careering course has only a few weeks to go, resources are exhausted, the economy defunct. The movement of which time is the measure has ceased and, as we have seen, the early chapters examine what happens to time when nothing is happening in it. In the Ghana of the novel it is in the nature of things to heap up, of speed to ossify into mass, of time to solidify into described objects. The tired standstill of the first part abounds with images of stopped flow: halted trains and uncollected refuse, showers blocked with scum and streams with filth, pockets piled with old tickets and coastal tips with junk. The mountains of consumer waste which stretch back to the days of slave-chiefs become metaphors for the collected past still visible in the present and one such consumer, Amankwa the timber trader, is imaged as a walking antiquity who carries history around with him in his "voice of ages" and "generations of teeth" (pp. 30, 27). Moving through this mounting debris with a quietly insistent pressure is the idea of the backward motion of time to a still visible point of terminal stagnation, a storehouse of heaped-up centuries that have not gone out of existence. The idea of the slow

accumulation of the debris of history into a visible permanence, in which everything which has ever happened
is apprehended simultaneously as if it were all happening
at once and were somehow perpetually present, thus
leads to a "descriptive" or "physical-objective" treatment
of time and pushes Armah's thinking towards traditional
rituals for the disposal of time, conceived in patterns of
cyclical renewal or annulment. Close as it is to traditional
African thought, a concept of time which places ends
and beginnings side by side as in the man's vision of the
sea is necessarily opposed to Western sequential and
evolutionary time concepts and is, in Sunday Anozie's
words, "largely informed by a sense of synchrony, the
static principle of time, and the dynamic permanence of
states".[14] At this point Armah's borrowings from cyclical
theories begin to link up with Mbiti's concept of a large-
scale temporal reverse. The residual permanence which is
entropically shed by speed's dwindling momentum in the
novel is roughly analogous to Mbiti's *zamani* or "macro-
time", with certain differences: in Armah, Mbiti's "grave-
yard" or reservoir of time becomes, characteristically, a
garbage heap stored exclusively with the detritus
of corruption and this visible residue of history
will not pass naturally out of existence with human
oblivion but requires some strenuous act of removal or
reactivation.[15] Moreover, Africa's historical burden of evil,
like Amankwa's corruption, is conceived not only as the
dead weight of the years's detritus, but also as a
still potent living force, a liquid or viscous flux of pollution
still active in the present and recycled in a sea which is
both "thick and viscous, almost solid" (p. 176). The
escape-latrine is home to an antiquity of filth that is still
alive, "as if a multitude of little individual drops had been
drying on the can for ages, but had never quite arrived at a
totally dry crispness", and is still "running with the dark
liquid" of "old mixtures of piss and shit" (pp. 167, 170).

Aged mud holds the shape of rotten cans and ancient rust holds the city bus together. The organic rot of the banister's "diseased skin" is a dynamic force which embraces and consumes, converting all newness to its own "victorious filth" (pp. 11–12): it symbolizes the inherited, compelling force of corruption. Metaphor and narrative flashbacks submerge the historical development of Ghana in what structural anthropologists like Lévi-Strauss would call a "primitivist" perception of time: one which simultaneously disjoins and conjoins ancestors and contemporaries, originators and inheritors, innovators and imitators; one which, with the same stroke, registers the diachronic differentiation of past and present and holds them together in synchronic apposition. Transience is constantly subsumed into permanence. Thus, the nightmare of historical change and its virus of ephemeral gratifications, unleashed at the centre of the novel, disappears into the bored soporific sameness of the residual-contemporary Ghana that surrounds it, and nowhere in the novel is there any simple opposition between a corrupt modern present and an innocent traditional past, to which the man's purely personal code of honour properly belongs: the view of time as historical recurrence or accumulation of evils in a cycle of consumption and disposal is not consistent with the notion that certain qualities were the special preserve of a vanished community.

Armah's monolithic vision in this novel inverts Eliade by turning history into an archetypal repetition of *un*-exemplary events and modes of behaviour, a continuing imitation of worthless models of which white imperialism is only one,[16] and the vision offers no avenue of escape from a bleak determinism of recurring, encycled corruptions. The first novel is concerned with Independent Africa's self-repeating cycle of slavish dependence on the white world and the treadmill-lives of its victims, as the next two novels will concern themselves with the breaking of a "factor-cycle" through which that white world continues to lead a posthumous existence in Africa. The two historical works will chart the quasi-seasonal course of a cycle of colonial sell-outs to "white destroyers" through African history and call for a halt to this process. The major time-scale of *The Beautyful Ones Are Not Yet Born*, anticipating the vast trajectories of the histories, amasses metaphorically whole centuries of corruption to be ritually expelled at the completion of the epic cycle of some Great African Year, the equivalent of that described by Eliade but two thousand seasons long and staggering under the weight of a tremendous store of evil.[17] On the minor time-scale, Africa's colonial-tainted power regimes are pictured as an encycled series of short-lived progeric children or *amomawu* spirit-children born only to die prematurely, doomed to repeat the past until they can confront it and learn from it. Such a death-birth is the anti-Nkrumah coup announced by the Time-Allocations Clerk, the man who knows all about the way time works in contemporary Africa: "Now another group of bellies will be bursting with the country's riches!" "New people, new style, old dance," the man ruefully observes (pp. 157–58). The visionary man with the "keen, uncanny eyes and ears of lunatic seers", "the watching eye and the listening ear" (pp. 12, 153), becomes one of those who, in Eliade's words, must "bear the burden of being contemporary with a disastrous period by becoming conscious of the position it occupies in the descending trajectory of the cosmic cycle".[18] But in Armah's novel there is no guarantee that the "Year" will end, that regeneration will necessarily follow or that the next cycle will be any different. The following exposition of the motif of New Year ritual in the novel will demonstrate, in fact, that Armah's detailed figurative exploration of the carrier's purification not only limits it narrowly to its proper preparatory status, thus denying it any regenerative power of transition, but attaches ironically to it a formalized fear of failure which haunts many communal expulsion rites and which public-ally marks the limited efficacy and relevance to reality of all ritual process. The resulting implications for the novel's moral vision appear to be overwhelmingly negative.

The unnamed man who is continually "pressed down with burdens other than his own" (p. 46) — the anger and anxiety of his family, the insults and unadmitted guilt of the prosperous few and the anguished misfortunes of the many — is the novel's true but unacknowledged carrier and his ritual status is established in the first chapter. Here the prose is saturated by the doom-laden, entropic atmosphere of a community at the traditional year-end, burdened by an accumulation of pollutive decay and awaiting rejuvenation. The monthly cycle of debt and spending is exhausted and already, in imagination, "the fullness of the month touches each old sufferer with a feeling of new power" (p. 2). The feeling of irrecoverable decline and decay is stronger, however, than the sugges-tions of deliverance. Above the "death-rattle" of the rusty old city bus, abuse is screamed at the man, soaked in his own saliva, by a rapacious conductor for whom the new month means only the "marvellous rottenness" of a new cedi note and whose nostrils perversely itch "to refresh themselves with its ancient stale smell" (p. 3). Ghanaian society, represented microcosmically by the bus, has no use for purification because it does not perceive its own decay: the symbolism of water-borne expulsion is thus precluded by streams clogged with "unconquerable filth", blocked drains which create and accumulate the dirt they are supposed to get rid of, and seas almost "solid" with the dumped refuse of ages. Like the hotel-worshippers who lovingly hunger after what should attract their anger, the conductor is so steeped historically in the national infection and so enamoured of his own corruption that he has become immune to its "most unexpected smell", thus anticipating the boatman and watchman who are unable to smell the fallen Koomson because they themselves are of the same tainted order. His initial fears of the entranced man, asleep but with his eyes open and mistaken for a silent watcher, imply that the end of his corrupt personal regime on the bus is near. He imagines the watcher to be "the bringer of his doom" and hears the god-like voice of apocalyptic judgement: "I have seen you. You have been seen. We have seen all" (pp. 5, 4). It seems for a moment that guilt is about to be confronted, confessed and unloaded upon the waiting carrier, the burden of the social organism lightened:

> Only his eyes continued their steady gaze, and the conductor felt excruciatingly tortured as they drilled the message of his guilt into his consciousness. Outrage alternated with a sweaty fear he had never before felt. Something, it seemed to him, was being drained from him, leaving the body feeling like a very dry sponge, very light, completely at the mercy of slight toying gusts of wind. (p. 4)

But then the conductor abruptly changes course and shatters the ritual mystique. He perversely chooses to feed upon the decayed issue instead of expelling it — "The conductor cleared his throat and ate the phlegm" (p. 5) — and compounds his corruption by offering the man a share of his fraudulent takings. Once the mistake is realized and corrected, the imaginatively acknowledged agent of expulsion is himself violently expelled from the miniature society of the bus and, with the aid of the demon-taxi, jerked from the trance-like "long half-sleep" of his ritual condition back to ordinary consciousness. The spray of the spittle which pursues him confers not the sympathetic blessing on the carrier of recognized, admitted guilt but the dissociative curse on the scapegoat which disclaims their common identity.

This scene sets the pattern for the man's treatment in the novel. The characters in turn alienate their various iniquities to the man, vicariously making him guilty of their own sins and then hypocritically defining themselves in oppostion to him. Adopting a facade of moral uprightness, Amankwa affects to judge him as "a very wicked man", and Oyo's viciously acquisitive materialism leaves him with the fear that his own honesty is really a vice. The man's patient accumulation of insults, his martyred interiorization of accusations and general introjection of the world's conception of him, permit the Koomsons' guilty deceit to reduce his idealism to an ashamed folly. Even the conductor evasively shifts to his passenger the embarrassed excremental base of his infatuation with the malodorous money: "Or were you waiting to shit on the bus?" (p. 6).

The traditional carrier's ritual untouchability, following from the fear of recovering ills formerly alienated to a conveyor and forgotten, finds its contemporary equivalent in the man's catalytic honesty, which is dangerous to the corrupt as it steers their forgetful attentions towards what, in this society, are the taboo subjects of legality, probity and justice. Having inherited something of the honest plain speaking that traditionally went with ritual role reversals in New Year ceremonies,[19] the man embarrasses the modern praise-sung chief Koomson with his interjections, and his direct looks and comments frighten the messenger and the "old-new union man" who shifts allegiances during the coup. In addition to serving as the carrier of periodical pollutions, the man is also the metaphoric carrier of the guilt-probing disease of integrity which threatens the Koomsons' security and causes them to regard him not only as the "invisible man of the shadows" whom they are afraid to see (p. 37), but also as untouchable. Estella's handshakes are withdrawn "in an insulting hurry" and "as if contact were a well-known calamity" (pp. 130, 38). People desire to touch the man only when they wish to transfer a shared corruption in which it has become necessary to implicate him, as with the conductor's proffered cigarettes and the timber trader's tainted money, or when, as in the case of the fleeing Koomson, they wish to unload their misfortunes onto him as a prospective saviour: he feels "a certain resentment . . . that in all his prosperous moments it was only now that the Party man should really want to get close to him" (p. 164). But the man's taboo status is double-edged: the Koomsons and their kindred "loved ones" are reciprocally dangerous to the purity of the uncorrupted and particularly to that of the agent of decontagion. Teacher speaks of their blighting touch as "a welcome unto death" and Estella's perfume clings to the man's hand with the same pollutive tenacity as her ruined husband's excremental stench. The man's fanatical bathing rituals before and after contact with the Koomsons indicate the need for constant purification from their polluting presence and the strengthening of his own purity, rendering him least infected and so best fitted for the task of decontaminating his society. At one of these lengthy lustrations Oyo asks him if he has "become a leper" (p. 128), sparking a connection with his boyhood ablutions in streams also used by lepers and adding to his figurative status of social leper an idea of physical contagion consistent with his ritual identity.

The man's parallel, and apparently paranoid, identification with the shadowy, downtrodden figures of the commuter's twilight world are suspect at the level of psychology. His feeling for the young clerk who has yet to learn "that everyone before him had crawled with hope along the same unending path" has the sound of so much patronizing, self-gratulatory wisdom, used to project his own complacent despair, and his sympathy with the night sweeper reads like disguised self-pity: "Christ! Someone actually worse off" (p. 33). His detection of domestic persecution akin to his own in the lot of the night clerk, the coded confessions of the morse-interlocutor, and the shadowed faces of two northerners at the station looks like sheer paranoia. This system of arbitrary identifications and projections most probably has less to do with the man's individual psychology, however, than with his ritual role. Armah's manipulation of his occasionally neurotic mode of perception, identifying with the insulted and oppressed of a community whose filth and waste he obsessively dissociates himself from, turns paranoia into a literary strategy. Paranoid self-projection is perhaps more usefully read as ritual introjection, correspondent to the drawing of society's ills into the carrier's effigy. Even in terms of sheer psychology, Armah seems to have more success with his ritual stranger than Awoonor in *This Earth, My Brother. . .* The man's tortured interiorization of accusations and anxieties is a more intimately anguished and painfully realized process than the detached, merely intellectual assumption of the "burden of terrible truth" by Amamu, who is altogether a more abstract observer and who is more deliberately aware of the ritual aspect of his estrangement than the man:[20] the latter appears to have no inkling of his employment in a carrier-role and his ritual behaviour is made to emerge naturally from what he does in the panic of the crisis, partly because the monolithic, seamless narrative makes no clear distinction between character-impression and authorial comment. On one rare occasion when the man's paranoia is ironically located and judged — the Space Allocations Clerk is not fleeing from loved ones at home but is at the office to collect the early bribe (p. 105) — the misplaced sympathies contrive to telescope the carrier's dual burden of sin and suffering, instanced here by the clerk's corrupt motives and the persecuted sorrows which the man mistakes them for. Thus, ritual ambiguity emerges from psychological confusion. On a note of deeper personal relevance, two of these twilight creatures who are targets for the man's appropriative empathy — the sweeper and the latrine man — are precisely proleptic versions of his own cleansing role and gather in advance the threads of his ritual function.

Both of these figures are caught between the ending and the renewal of cycles, carrying away at each new dawn the dirt which is the end product of society's day. Tired "at the beginning of the night", the sweeper, like the year-carrier, starts at the end (p. 33). Amankwa beholds his sleep-walking delirium "with hostility" and leaves as he enters; as we have seen, the trader is endowed with a legacy of ancient corruption and is later likened to a "forgotten bundle" (p. 107), so that he becomes, by implication, part of the uncollected refuse of ages, about to be swept symbolically away by the giant brush, larger than himself, which the cleaner hauls about in his "strange dance on the lower stair" (p. 33). In the figure of the latrine man the carrier-prototype is revealed with a more detailed precision:

> There is not much light, but not much light is needed to tell one that the man with the shitpan heavy on his head has an unaccustomed look of deep, angry menace on his face, and his eyes are full of drunken fury. Perhaps the smell of akpeteshie would be bathing him if he were not carrying this much stronger stench with him. Surely that is the only way for a man to survive, carrying other people's excrement; the only way must be to kill the self while the unavoidable is being done, and who will wish to wake again? It is not such a usual thing to see the shitman coming at this hour of the morning, a man hidden completely from the sight of all but curious children and men with something heavy on their minds in the darkness of the night. And it is not such

> a usual thing to see a latrine man up close. The last
> shall be the first. Indeed, it is even so. (pp. 103–4)

Many of the classic ingredients of the carrier, as outlined
in Soyinka's portrait of the *Eyo Adimu* for example, have
been graphically transposed to this apocalyptic figure. The
physical weight of the head-borne burden of human
detritus is made to correspond rhetorically with that of the
psychological burden of the troubled souls who share with
him the day's threshold. A drunken delirium must first be
induced for the performance of the carrier's unavoidable
and enervating task: the self-negating, slowly killing
sacrifice from which no permanent reincorporation into
the waking world will be possible. Frazer remarked of the
effigy in the canoe of the original Calabar carrier: "When
the burden is of a baleful character, the bearer of it will be
feared and shunned just as much as if he were himself
instinct with those dangerous properties of which, as it
happens, he is only the vehicle."[21] The carrier in traditional
West African societies does not die the sacrificial "death of
blood" claimed by Amamu in Awoonor's novel, and
Eman's arboreal crucifixion in Soyinka's own play *The
Strong Breed* is an untypical perversion of the rite, but he
does endure a more protracted mode of self-sacrifice and,
as Soyinka points out in his discussion of the Yoruba *Eyo*,
is not expected to survive very long his debilitating ordeal
and the "very lingering illness" which is its legacy: "The
whole demand, the stress, the spiritual tension, as well as
the forces of evil which they trapped into their own person
are such that after a few years they either go insane, or
they catch some mysterious disease, or they simply
atrophy as human beings and die . . . they cease to be
useful members of the community quite early."[22] The
carrier's conveyance of death and dead things has always
made him a darkly taboo figure, instanced in the near-
death of the Onitsha king after his personal assumption of

the exhaustion of the dying year,[23] and in the superstitious convention by which the returning *Tele*, in the Yoruba *Edì* Festival at Ifè, marks out for death within the year the first person he encounters.[24] The latrine man who simulates the carrier's functions in a contemporary context dies a figurative death, having to "kill the self", and the man who carries off the corrupt issue of his guilt-soiled, anxiety-ridden society at the end of the novel is a shunned outcast, a taboo figure secluded from the sight of all except his fellow-carriers along the latrine passages and "curious children", one of whom runs away as the man half-carries the stinking Koomson from the shitman's circuit to the sea (p. 170). In the person of the man the ritualized seclusion and stigmatic estrangement of year-carrier, shit-carrier and sweeper are brought together. Like the sweeper, who is a "lost man from distances far off", the man feels "like a stranger from a country that was very far away" and is imaged repeatedly as a creature of the shadows (pp. 33, 131). Finally, Armah's droll and cryptic Biblical tag energizes a pun which signals the carrier's ambiguous status. "The last" become "the first" has the end-product of the human physiological circuit and social body carried mockingly before, like the symbolic shit truck riding at the head of Nkrumah's motorcade in Awoonor's novel.[25] But coupled with this is the ironic hint and wan hope of some messianic reversal at the expulsion of the old order's dirt. In fact, the coup effects no such change in stations but merely reshuffles power into the hands of men not very different from the ones they supersede.

The man shares with these figures an anonymity which marks their common social invisibility. The novel's carriers are not drawn from a special spiritual elite or the superior aristocracy of suffering which constitutes Soyinka's hereditary "strong breed" and do not have much affinity with the visionary liminars conceived by Priebe after the model of Awoonor's Amamu, whose communion is of a religious rather than of a social nature and is achieved only in death.[26] This does not mean, however, that the man's anonymity and supposed impersonality have anything to do with an everyman typicality or an occupational representativeness as "working man", after the pattern of Western allegory: the man is, in fact, untypical of his class of railway clerks and it is, moreover, necessary that the human being who carries the conscience of a corrupt society be generally untypical of it. His anonymity has less to do with any generic significance than with his society's refusal to grant an identity to one estranged from its values and its incapacity for recognizing value beyond its own narrow definitions. In this Ghana of Westernized go-getters with extraordinary Anglo-African names — Attoh-White, Fentengson, Binful (p. 126) — his traditional ordinariness finds its peculiar expression in anonymity: in a society where naming is itself inauthentic, the man, whose communal representativeness lies in his task and not in his social identity, is marked out as different and exceptional by not being named. Neither should anonymity be automatically equated with impersonality or non-personality. A strong sense of personally alienated individuality emerges from the characters of Teacher and the man which is at variance with the device of the anonym. Significantly, these two are the only coherent subjectivities in the novel whilst the named characters are parabolic constructions who never achieve full psychological autonomy but are used mainly for purposes of satiric representation, being stripped either to the things they pursue or, as in the case of the politician and the timber trader, to their gross physical issue. Amankwa, "a belly swathed in kente cloth", is reduced to the swollen wealth that physically precedes him into the room (p. 27). Koomson, more an impersonation of corruption than a corrupt individual, is "a suit", a shining white shirt and the fiercely glinting cufflinks that turn perception into reception (pp. 37, 38, 131), and, finally, a sack of excrement. His wife is a wig, a gleaming diamond, and a metallic voice, "thin as long wire stabbing into open eyes", which functions with the ferocity of her laser-like dress (p. 36). Nevertheless, the man's anonymity does mechanically identify him with two groups of peripheral characters who are designated only by their occupations: the office's oppressed menials and its corrupt managers and clerks. The connection, in this instance, couples the carrier's interdependent burdens of the community's sorrows and sins: the man's task is to relieve the sufferings and the misfortunes of one group by bearing away the corruption of the other. (In traditional New Year purification ceremonies such as the Yoruba *Edì* and *Bòábù* and their Ibo equivalents, the ritual sweeping or bearing away of the year's misfortunes was at once clearly differentiated from and closely interwoven with the scapegoating of the community's sins by a chosen individual, and in the Ijaw and Onitsha carrier cults the flood tides which awaken disease and suffering also carry the year's accumulated offences away.)[27] Armah's scheme of retribution, making as little allowance for unprovoked misfortunes as the moral order of traditional societies, finally levels the positions of the sinful and the sorrowful. "It is nobody, just the Minister," the man tells the wary boatman during the escape. Fallen from fame, Koomson becomes another "nobody", the term reserved for the man by his mother-in-law, and joins the ranks of the other nameless people on whose behalf the man is seen to act.

In the novel's ritualistic finale the carrier motif, which has moved with a quiet insistence through the novel's metaphoric structure, begins to take control of the action and the correspondences between human and ritual properties become particularly marked. With all the vividly concrete personification of the African oral tradition, the fugitive Koomson is materialized into a bag of decayed body wastes to be evacuated down the national latrine hole. Exuding "flatulent fear", excremental "smell waves" and "the rich stench of rotten menstrual blood" (p. 163), he has become the residual filth of the exhausted, moribund regime toppled at the coup, whilst the debris-heaped shoreline at the end of the latrine circuit surrounds him with an imagery of material deadness which alludes to a much older legacy of corruption. For the second time in the novel, the man enters his own house to encounter Koomson, signifying his estrangement even in his own home, his necessary seclusion and separation from the pollutive object until the start of the ritual passage, and the entirely active nature of his role. From this moment on Koomson assumes the passive, inert status of the object of contamination which must be collected, insulated and manoeuvred into position in ritual preparation for its conveyance. Powerless before the man's invitation to use bath or latrine, the Party man is unable to purge and purify himself but has to have these things done to him: "Koomson walked like a man without a will of his own" and is "like a man completely doomed, unable to help himself" (pp. 166, 175). The meal given him may suggest the fattening of a sacrifice but this does not mean, as Terry Goldie concludes, that "Koomson becomes the scapegoat, the sacrifice".[28] If caught, Koomson would doubtless be made into a scapegoat for the crimes of the regime: as it is, he is, in literal terms, not the scapegoat but the escapee and, in metaphoric terms, does not carry its ills but is himself the ills which are carried. More interested in his object-status as ritual property, Armah reductively depersonalizes Koomson into the symbolic dirt-mound or wooden figurine in the carrier's model canoe: the man leads him across a landscape of "stumps and holes and mounds" and the politician is even described as "walking stiffly", "momentarily rigid", and "like some wooden thing" (pp. 170–71). He is now almost inanimate, a dead weight which is pushed, pulled, held, rammed, gently drawn, steered and dragged by its carrier who, after partly denuding the contamination source during the latrine passage, no longer troubles to avoid contagion by keeping "a fruitless distance between himself and the other" (p. 163). Finally, Koomson is "half-lifted" in the narrow lane behind the latrine in readiness for the carrier's dash to the sea: the "long, circuitous route" by the "little lanes . . . along the latrine man's circuit through life", like the long labyrinthine seaward journey of Awoonor's Amamu through the Nima slums, corresponds precisely to the "narrow lanes" along which the carrier's canoe is rushed to the sea in West African coastal communities.[29] In the manner of his ritual prototype, the man stoops under his burden, "walking painfully in the curve" of the sea-wall to avoid detection. Throughout the passage the man's dealings with his charge are marked by an appropriately impersonal, ritual formality. Up to the moment when he is put to sea Koomson, as taboo-object, is "a dangerous person to be with" and, along with the junked shoreline, the charcoal grit in the boatman's soup which looks "like stranded debris after the tide has gone back in" evokes the ritual anxiety about missing the ebb-tide, with the disastrous consequence that the pollutive ills will not be carried off into the sea's continuum to allow a new cycle to begin but will be swept back to land on the next flow: "There is not much time," warns the man. "There is no time at all, in fact" (pp. 173–74).

Here is the Ijaw carrier in the rite of the *Amagba*, as he appears in Robin Horton's account:

> As the signs of possession appear, a ragged exhortation breaks from the crowd: "Time to go down, it is time to go down!" . . . As the carrier reaches the waterside, helpers take the load from his grasp and set it down in a waiting canoe. No sooner is this done than he becomes himself again: his possessors' work

is finished, and they have gone their way. For a few
seconds he stares dazedly down at the boat, wondering where he is and how he got there. Then he pulls
himself together. Lifting from his neck a length of
palm-frond with a small chick attached to it, he circles
it three times around his head and throws it into the
miniature canoe. By this, he rids himself of any
residue of the destructive forces with which he has
been in such close contact . . . Then one of them
stands up, heaves the miniature canoe and its
figurine into the waters, and mutters for the last time:
"We have taken you down. Do not come again and
worry us. Let evil go out. Let sickness go out!"[30]

The man, as carrier, undergoes a similar derangement and
mystical self-estrangement which leaves him unable to
explain why he is on the boat at all. He hears himself
distantly repeating Koomson's words "as if he were not
himself but someone completely different". The passage
of the exorcism, through delirium and possible madness,
brings the mixed relief of liberation and estrangement:
"The receding town, with its weak lights, now seemed to
be something apart, something entirely separate, from the
existence of the man . . . and the man felt achingly free of
everything in it" (pp. 176–77). But the returning stench of
Koomson and the boatman's warning, with its echo of the
ritual exhortation — "The bay is out there if you want to
go down" — call the man back to himself. "Then the smell
of shit which had never really left him became even
stronger, and when he turned he saw Koomson next to
him. 'You are going back,' the Party man said, against the
engine noise" (p. 177). To return to the community, the
man must rid himself of the smell still clinging to him, or
he must remain with his charge in polluted exile. The
ritual immersion which follows again matches the model
of the coastal carrier, cleansing the man of the destructive
contagion which is felt to physically "get out from him"
when he reaches the shore. In Armah's version the saving

rubber inner tube does the work of the protective palm-fronds, insulating the man from the water's previous pollutions, and, like the fronds, is finally thrown back into the current in the direction of Koomson's tainted boat, carrying with it the last vestiges of pollution. Barely has the man emerged from the ritual process when its tribulations begin to take their physical and psychological toll. In the water he has "the almost exploding inward feeling that he was perhaps no longer alive" and is left with the marooned carrier's peculiar stigma of alienation and exile — the "cold feeling" of "vague freedom" and "untroubled loneliness". As he reaches land he feels the world to be "so very far away from the welcoming sand of the beach beneath him" and he observes the brand-new societal bus and its lubrication by age-old corruption with the spectatorial detachment of one who is now far outside it. Although it is a depressingly complete reincorporation into family and community which is envisaged at the end of the novel, there are lingering intimations of the carrier's return to an impaired existence and slow entropic decline in the man's continuing estrangement and his "never-ending knowledge that this aching emptiness would be all that the remainder of his life could offer him" (p. 183).

Such systematic tracking of behaviour to ritual source gives the impression that the man merely goes through a series of mechanical metaphoric motions in which psychology is overridden by ritual pattern, motivation clouded by motif. For example, the man's presence on the escape boat after aiding the boatman with the starting mechanism makes no sense except in terms of ritual metaphor: the ceremonial pattern demands that the ills of the old year are actually carried a little way out to sea before the carrier endeavours to purify himself of their enervating influence. There is no evidence in the text for Margaret Folarin's idea that the man attempts a half-hearted escape from his domestic commitments and then

apparently changes his mind.[31] The man's apprehension
of the sea as thickly "viscous" prior to his immersion in its
"unbelievably salty water" derives less from his immediate
sense impressions than from the image of an expelled
pollution still sticking to the agent of expulsion, about to
be ritually cleansed. Certainly, motivation is never a
strong feature in the novel and the man is unable to give
a convincing explanation of why he refuses to take bribes
or why he saves Koomson, but in the latter action Armah's
selection and emphasis of motivation tie it to his ritual
motifs with a remarkably logical consistency, so that one
does not detract from but crucially confirms the other. It
has become commonplace in critical commentary on the
novel to assume that the man helps the Party man to
escape because he is already corrupt like him or is at least
tainted by earlier contact with him,[32] or alternatively, if
this is not so, that he becomes corrupt in the process of
saving him,[33] or is moved to help Koomson out of a latent
sympathy with his motives.[34] None of these explanations
are strictly accurate. Firstly, in the matter of the boat deal
the man simply remains aloof from what he cannot
prevent and what little pleasure he takes in the boat is
purely aesthetic, not acquisitive (p. 152). He does not
capitulate but holds out against temptation until his
temporary vindication by the coup, and his pollution
behaviour is consistent with his ability to withstand
pressure: he holds his breath against the fallen politician's
"pollution of the air" as he had earlier held his breath
to keep out the stench of the public lavatory and
the fetid wood of his shower door and as he will do
again in the water when departing from him (pp. 163, 41,
101, 119). Secondly, the man is not necessarily relegated
to Koomson's level merely because he is forced into
Koomson's element — the bribe to the watchman — in
order to save him. Corruption becomes a way of saving
life, not a way of life as it is for Koomson: the man corrupts

to live whilst Koomson lives to corrupt. The man's freedom from moral taint is, moreover, perfectly consistent with the status of his ritual prototype, whose stressful exhaustion has to do entirely with the absorbed entropy of the dying year and is not a moral condition. In the merely cathartic mode of expiation practised in the Ijaw *Amagba*, for example, the year's ills are drawn magically, by shouting and bull-roaring, into the ritual object which the carrying figure simply bears away: there is no bodily casting out and transference of sins by token or violent contact with the agent of expulsion, as in sacrificial modes of expiation.[35] The minimal taint of the carrier, whose own nature is a stranger to what he carries and who does not embody the impurities he conveys, is compatible with the honest individual's inescapable contact with corruption in an excrementalized universe where "all around decaying things push inward and mix all the body's juices with the taste of rot" (p. 40). The man is forced to wade through Koomson's vomit in the latrine and carries his smell home with him: the carrier's inevitable partial infection is instrumental in the restoration of the community's health. But the dissociative phrases and metaphors constantly differentiate between the man and his pollutive burden, maintaining a firm distinction between rescuer and refugee: in the converted lavatory where the boat deal was concluded earlier, the man stands "a little apart from the party man and his boatman" (p. 174).

What precipitates the man into effecting Koomson's escape has passed largely unnoticed, even though Armah hammers it home on every page. Panter-Brick comes closest to recognition with his claim that the man acts "more out of disgust at the change in the Party man's appearance — physical deflation matching at last the inner moral decay — than out of any sense of duty".[36] The immediate impulse to get Koomson away is overwhelmingly physical in its origin: the man simply cannot stand his smell. He can be rid of the unbearable only by bearing it away: "The man himself was filled with only one thought now: to get out of this room . . . he would surely vomit if he did not get out from this foul smell. Hoping to steal a breath of uncorrupted air, he moved toward the window . . . he was about to die of this smell . . . The smell was truly unbearable . . . Even a sigh from him [Koomson] spoiled the air some more. The man tried again, looking for a way out" (pp. 163–64). Faithfully following the pollution behaviour of his ritual model, and with all the exuberance of the oral tradition, Armah has graphically corporealized corruption into a grotesque and obscene physical phenomenon, an all-pervasive rotten-ness whose pollutive presence cannot be endured and so must be expelled. The hyperbole insists on the sheer material urgency of expulsion, to the exclusion of abstract moral significations either of the man's capitulation to corruption or of his upholding of it as a moral and human necessity. There is neither guilty lament over his taint nor moral defence of it, since the ritual meaning effaces the ethical one: his task is simply something that has to be done. Armah is, of course, alert to the complementarity of contraries in ritual forms which invest corruption with positively life-giving elements. Apart from saving Koomson, the daily "kola" of the bribe feeds families, oils Amankwa's logs into motion, and generally keeps energy alive by lubricating the otherwise stagnant commercial life of the nation. But the element of personal humanitarianism and the general respect for human life are subdued, if not suppressed, in the severely formalized rescue of the fugitive politician. Where a saving regard for life should be, there is only physical disgust and moral indifference: "He thought with some surprise of his complete inability to get affected by the feelings and fears of the figure next to him. There was only the awareness of his own acute discomfort" (pp. 163–64). The man's odd quirk of impersonal compassion, on the boat, for "the strange emptiness of two lives spent apart" is for the situation of Koomson and Estella, not the persons themselves. At the rescued man's parting thanks, "the man heard the words, but he felt nothing for Koomson" (p. 177). It is the distanced neutrality of formal ritual, in which the disinterested performer has no personal or even human feelings towards his charge and his task.

Koomson's boat is, like its owner, reduced to a ritual property, resulting in a very precise and physical kind of symbolism. There is in Western anthropology ample comment to the effect that pollutions in cathartic modes of expiation are "understood to be present invisibly in the material and visible vehicle which conveys them away",[37] or that the "primitive mind" is "incapable of drawing sharp distinctions between the symbol and the person or object symbolized"[38] and neither disjoins nor confounds "mystic" and "material" qualities, "nor does it make one the symbol of the other".[39] In fact, these partly denigrating observations testify unintentionally to the power of what, translated into literary terms, is the purest and most highly integrated form of metaphor. The symbol is, eucharistically, what it symbolizes. Like the sin-object of the carrier's model canoe which lies behind it, Koomson's boat is a symbol which is perfectly itself: serving, on the one hand, as manifest evidence of corruption in its fraudulent purchase and provision of tainted food, and, on the other, as the vehicle of its conveyance, escape and expulsion, the boat is intrinsic with or possessed by the spirit of corruption and effectively *is* that thing. The same intimately ritualistic mode of metaphor governs the physical investment of people with the pollutions which their fraud and neglect inflict upon the environment. Taken from the filth and waste of consumer materialism and its corresponding body wastes (faecal, menstrual, perspiratory and expectorative), this imagery invades and possesses its subjects with a thoroughness that turns them into objects. An excremental master-metaphor tirelessly constipates voices, flatulates breath, turns aspiration into urination (the conductor "aiming high" on the city can) and ambition into excretion (the "leapers" and "jumpers" in the office latrine). Koomson finally becomes the collected excrement which is the produce of the gleam's prolific consumption, about to be borne away by the national latrine man and dumped in the sea, itself a pile of pollution at the end of the latrine circuit and the death-cycle of the body. Armah's imagination, in this novel, so obsessively endows voices, figures and movements with consumptive or excremental characteristics that ascribed qualities seem to enter into and become integral with their objects, and it becomes impossible to distinguish the object's intrinsic neutrality from its verbal contamination by the author's attributions. After a hundred pages dense with scatological metaphor, it is quite normal and un-surprising to find a Ghanaian aping English speech described as "a constipated man, straining in his first minute on top of a lavatory seat" or a floor polish as "tired and menstrual" (pp. 125, 118). The drastic fusion of tenor and vehicle in Armah's scatology, in which the "moral" and "physical" partake intimately of one another's nature, is indebted both to the vividly concrete personifications of the oral tradition and to the symbolism of ritual.[40] Moral decay is not merely symbolized by organic decay in the Ghanaian environment but physically produces it: the undisposed-of refuse piled around litter boxes is concrete demonstration of irresponsible consumerism and the accompanying municipal neglect arising from the embezzlement of public funds.

The excrementalizing of almost everything by this impersonal totalitarian rhetoric induces a fatalistic accept-ance of corruption as the total condition of reality, before which individual honesty must wearily capitulate. His resistance worn down by the cumulative force of latrine slogans, the example of fellow-clerks and the general ubiquity of bribery and fraud, the man decides that "there was no more point in his continuing his efforts to keep the rot out of himself" (p. 101). Significantly, after both meetings with Amankwa, he allows his hand to be "clammily caressed by the caked accretions on the banister" and "lets it slide greasily down" (pp. 34, 111). On both occasions there is a formal acceptance of the carrier's token taint by the unavoidable touching of the pollutive substance which, in a world where dirt replaces air, has spread itself throughout the environment. The ritual gesture is made at the moment of submission and the abandonment of struggle; thus, ritual action, by implication a kind of literary last resort, is taken up and marks the moment when real action in the world becomes futile or impossible. Armah negatively equates compromise, resignation or outright capitulation with a ritual tokenism which does nothing physically about evil and it is perhaps instructive to remember at this point the notations of extreme fallibility, of temporary success prior to ultimate failure, which are built into many expulsion rites by the necessity of repeated expiation: the elaborately formalized precautions taken in the Akan *Apo* to prevent the ills of the year from finding their way back;[41] the delay in the Ijaw *Amagba* which risks missing the ebb-tide and having the ills washed back to land;[42] and the merely short-lived rejuvenation of social activities in both of these before new hardships appear with the new year. This awareness of society's failure to reform itself through ritual or quasi-ritual acts informs the mood of grimly guarded hope in the literal and figurative treatment of purification rites in West African writing.

It may also be salutary here, lest my extrapolation of ritual forms from traditional societies to contemporary urban settings, and from one West African nation to another, be thought merely fanciful, and lest the foregoing references to the Apo and to Awoonor's novel have received insufficient emphasis in my own account, to note the following incidental points. Armah is not the only Ghanaian writer to use the motif of the carrier, which has a general currency along the West African coast and hinterland from Ghana to the Calabar river communities of the Niger delta. Awoonor, who hails from the same stretch of coastline as Armah, conceives his city lawyer as "the priest, the carrier, the man who bears his burden of the terrible truth"[43] and "a priest, in the traditional African sense, taking upon himself all the burdens of his people."[44] Of Amamu he writes: "The centuries and the years of pain of which he was the inheritor, and the woes for which he was singled out to be carrier and sacrifice, were being rolled away."[45] Moreover, Awoonor's own variant on the priestly carrier who "runs with a herbal pot on his head, . . . runs himself into a state of trance,"[46] is freely extrapolated from the end-of-year purification ceremonies of the Akan *Apo* and *Afhaye*, and the Ashanti *Odwira*, each of which contain, in the accounts of Rattray and Meyerowitz, elements of the carrier's purification imaged in Armah's novel: the casting of insult and abuse on the year's accumulated ills and broken taboos, embodied in an ox in the *Odwira* and insulated by the customary bundle of palm-stalks in the *Apo*;[47] the carrying of polluted objects, ranging from sacred stools to household furniture, to the river for ritual purification at the time when "the edges of the year have met";[48] the inducement of trances for the rush of carriers to the river and their immersion and ablution at the completion of the rite;[49] the ritual invocation to the year's ills, "Do not come again", and the solemn formalities that perfunctorily fend off returning ills.[50] Thus Armah, like Awoonor in *This Earth, My Brother . . .* and Gabriel Okara in his poetic novel *The Voice*,[51] is merely drawing in his fiction upon a ritual commonplace of the West African shoreline. The results, however, are somewhat different.

In the last third of *The Beautyful Ones Are Not Yet Born* there is a self-conscious shifting of frame from realism to ritual and myth: a complex and largely ironic transposition which half-heartedly disguises escape as expulsion, makes defilement not a sign of defeat but of ritual destiny, and opens up wider speculative fantasies of the panoramic cleansing of history right back to pre-colonial times. Armah uses ritual in ways which explore and expose its limited relevance and turn its inefficacy to ironic effect. Ritual action, nothing more than secondary and substitutive in nature, is never allowed to pass for the main event and in this matter Armah's treatment of the carrier motif is significantly different from that of other West African writers. In this literature the temporary and cyclical nature of a rite that has always to be done again is usually complemented by a more optimistic alertness to the New Year's traditional mood of revaluation and long-term retrospection, which activities may be prologue to some millenial reversal or upheaval quite at odds with the rite's dominant emphasis on the community's failure to effect any lasting regeneration. The ritual expulsion of dying years since the founding of a society or the genesis of a race inevitably implies a repeated return to an initial innocence;[52] consequently, the motif often bears Utopian or millenarian associations, looking either to the recreation of a golden Edenic Africa — "Let us return to the magic hour of our birth for which we mourn" cries Awoonor's carrier-surrogate[53] — or, as in the case of Soyinka's *Bacchae*, to the permanence of an act of political regeneration which frees history from its eternal cycle of repetition. As I have demonstrated elsewhere, Soyinka's carrier-dramas simultaneously suggest a short-sighted repetition and a long-term revaluation of the past.[54] In *The Strong Breed*, for example, the perverted and self-undermining rite is primarily locked into a vicious and futile cycle of repetition, meaninglessly expiating guilt by an act which amasses more. Yet the villagers' final desertion of their leaders intimates that the established order may now have been shaken and the clock wound back on decades of corrupt malpractice, whilst the parallels between Eman's death and Christ's Passion hint at some messianic and ultimate change. The stock-taking spirit of the New Year may result in the reassessment of the value of the rite itself, as in this play, or, as in *The Bacchae*, of the value of the whole civilization and moral order that practises it.[55] Armah, however, appears to be the only West African writer to deny the motif even its customary faint accretions of radical and regenerative change and to restore it to the merely cathartic mode which is its true status. It has been noticed that the novel's treatment of time effectively assigns to its carrier-figure the disposal of the whole of African history: Armah's imagination toys with the historical necessity of a total break with the past, a genuinely new start for Africa's future being dependent upon a sweeping away of ancient corrupt heritages. But the magnitude of such a cleansing is of the impossibly idealistic and mythical order of the novel's many millenarian faiths in messiahs and beautiful saviours, the "future goodness" and "the destroyed people waking up and wanting to make themselves whole again" (pp. 160, 90). The only practical possibility envisaged is a break with the immediate past of the Nkrumah regime, but the inveteracy of corrupt traditions prevents the nation from availing itself even of this limited opportunity. History in Armah's work is an encycled continuity, not a series of Eliadean explosions, apocalyptic annulments or revolutionary restarts.[56]

In this novel the carrier has come full circle to his original position in a preparatory, preliminary rite of discharge and separation. His figurative removal of the

Koomsons and Nkrumahs is one of "the things in the present which would prepare the way" for the "future goodness" like the delta carrier-rite through which pollution is "cleansed from the village, and way made for new life to come in".[57] The rite merely clears the path for the new by evacuating the waste of the old, admitting passage to renewal through negation and entropy. Armah extracts a grim exhilaration from the cathartic release: in the escape-latrine the man imagines "particles of shit doing a wild, mixed dance with drops of stale urine" (p. 166), as if in joyful deliverance from the costive stagnancy of the Nkrumah regime through Koomson's evacuation. But the carrier is only superficially caught up in the fruitful creative-destructive ambivalence, the dynamic complementarity of opposites that hold life together during the marginal period of the year's turning, when everything is of the double-nature of transition.[58] In the narrowly pre-transitional cleansing rites of the Ijaw, Ashanti and Yoruba, the normally multivalent symbolism of blood, palm-fronds and dirt is restricted to singularly negative and cathartic meanings and stripped of regenerative and fertility dimensions, and the dominant mood is of solemn purgative release, scant of rejoicing.[59] For example, although Armah's symbolism clearly makes much of the viscosity of filth, the dirt which, in the rites proper, stands for the waste of the old year owes nothing to the liminal creative power of fertile decomposition, but is dirt pure and simple, an inactive weight of earth restored to its undifferentiated state.[60] Binary ritual models of renewal through transitional indeterminacy and communitas-recharged-structures, such as those posited by Mary Douglas and Victor Turner, are of little relevance to the carrier's very limited liminality.[61]

In Armah's scrupulous choice and deployment of his ritual form, the New Year's fertile binary equivocalities are correspondingly dormant. The renewed bribery by the latest order, following hot upon the escape bribe, indicates that the evacuation of the regime's decay has not restored the social body to a more normal functioning and even the saving implication of excretory release fails to reaffirm the vigour of a healthy organism. The clogged currents of baths, streams and seas marginalize the purificatory and regenerative potential of water: only the "brief gust of wind still lifting off the sea" and "deep breaths of air" fascinate the man with their "freedom from decay" during the ritual sea-passage (p. 171). Neither does Koomson's valedictory stench of "rotten menstrual blood" imply any complementary opposition of fertility and generation. The "tired and menstrual" polish which the man uses on the floor in an earlier episode takes its place in an unproductive "senseless cycle" of futile, ill-paid work which leaves "everything the same", and has "nothing new, nothing encouraging about it" (pp. 118–19). This menstrual metaphor marks simultaneously the ironically named Passion Week (the last week in the month before pay-day, when the worker's cycle of borrowing and debt is most widely stretched) and the coup which ends the short life-cycle of the deep-in-debt Independence govern-ment: hence the coup becomes the ironic pay-day for the Party men who have bankrupted the country. The application of the metaphor to the fugitive Koomson signifies that in the life of the nation, as with the abortive floor cleaning, "nothing really new would happen" (p. 162). The old cycle is complete, nothing has been born, nothing new has even been conceived, and its waste, in the form of Koomson, is about to be expelled so that a new cycle of consumption and waste may begin. In what reveals itself, to discerning sensibilities like the man's, to be not a war but an insidious reciprocity of rots, the new polish is drawn into the crypto-sexual "effortless embrace" of the office banister's ancient wood, like the new elites into the decay of colonialism, leaving only the single monochromatic, unproductive rot (p. 12). Finally, Koomson's excretory "rebirth" through the latrine hole, symbolically naked and pushed "head first" by the man as midwife, is the culminating mock ritual of passage, the irony too deliberately droll for it to be anything but the purest parody. In his last words Koomson ironically echoes the parting formula addressed to the year's ills — "Do not come again and worry us"[62] — and the man repeats them: "We shall meet again" (p. 178). This, and the debris heaped by the returning tide, imply that they will not be washed very far away. In Armah's totalitarian environment, bribery is banished by a bribe: corruption, perpetually self-repeating, must be expelled by more of the same. Like the novel's many personal and communal purifications in private showers and public baths, the cleansing rite creates the dirt it is meant to discharge and there remains only "the doomed attempt to purify the self by adding to the disease outside" (p. 40). Armah's figurative version of the rite, like Soyinka's dramatization of the debased actuality, has the last purgative act of the old order undermining itself by triggering the first guilt of the new one. The natural cycle of guilt, expiation and redemption is not allowed to run its full course but is viciously truncated at its inception, and the purification is powerless to purchase even a makeshift efficacy. Armah's ending does not even permit the customary short-lived rejoicing of the New Year, for the forced celebrations of the coup are tainted by fear and suspicion and the regime is only a few hours old when the bribes begin again.

In the last chapter the unburdened carrier returns from the delirium of his sea-purgation to the unredeemed world which he left and meets Maanan, here an ironic Mammy Water whose power of madness in her sea-element is not the restorative process of the myth but an affliction beyond cure and recovery. In Armah's ironic vision, the carrier's pattern of outward passage preparatory to cyclical regeneration finds its mythological counterpart in the Mammy Water legend, and Maanan moves in and out of her mythological role with the same capricious freedom as the man in his ritual one. Teacher's earlier reminiscences invest Maanan with the symbolic identity of the woman of the sea or sea-goddess with magical revitalizing powers, who allows her faithful lovers to return to the land as visionary healers after seven years in the sea or, alternatively, sends back her betrayers and deserters as madmen.[63] Awoonor's novel combines these into the single consciousness of the visionary madman who carries with him the sea's creative-destructive potential: "And sometimes, after seven years, they come back with a knowledge of life, a complete awareness."[64] Maanan's own doubtful healing magic is the wee-drug which she dispenses to the smokers by the sea shore. The drug's destructive reorientation of consciousness takes its users on a "frightening journey" deep into the individual and group body, linking "everything that was going on inside and outside ourselves", a voyage which both confirms and transcends solitary despair (pp. 72–74). The sea-changed lover's ambiguous status is reflected in the drug's ambivalence — in its dispenser's self-destroying love and ruinous hope, and its users' mixture of elation and despair — and in the alternating perceptions of the sea as terminal dump and as a timeless continuum whose powers of renewal are mythically embodied in Mammy Water's seven-year cycles of regeneration. In Armah's version, however, the "complete awareness" is reduced to a transitory euphoria and an escapist political innocence which can only be destroyed. Maanan's attempt to extend the psychic powers of the drug consciousness beyond their special liminal milieu leads to a dangerous, quasi-religious infatuation with her fantasy-messiah, the *Osagyefo* Nkrumah (p. 87). Betrayed and deserted both by him and by Teacher, she subsequently becomes a collective reincarnation of African womanhood, of "millions and ages of women", and of Mother Africa herself: each assumes the common historical destiny of "a woman being pushed toward destruction" (pp. 72, 79). Mammy Water's mythical cycle of renewal dwindles into the contemporary reality's "senseless cycles" of "little insects caught in endless pools" (p. 2). The strangely isolated girl who, in Teacher's closing reminiscence, waits by the non-functioning telegraph pole "for someone no-one could see" and who looks "like some insect lost in all the vastness of the world" (p. 75) — clearly a figure from the gleam's order of lost connections — is a proleptic image of the wrecked Maanan at the end of the novel, isolated in her madness and waiting on the beach for the sea-lovers who will never return. It is here, in her encounter with the man who has just returned from Mammy Water's element, that the book's ritual and mythological patterns briefly cross.

The book's ritualistic finale holds in apposition the mythical role of Mammy Water, festooned with cyclical images of rebirth and restoration, and the historical identity of Maanan, the real woman terminally ruined by time. The ritual rebirth of the beautiful ones of the wee-group is accomplished in tension with the fact of their irredeemable destruction far back in the past. Thus, the orders of cyclical renewal by sea-change and linear speed and decay are kept simultaneously in view. The "single flower" is born from the egg-like oval painted on the new green bus and the haunting inscription, despite its negative phrasing, stays in the man's mind, its words "flowing up, down, and round again" in a cyclical motion suggesting rebirth (p. 183). Marginally present is the sea's regenerative character: after the mock-birth in the latrine, the two men walk eastwards towards the sea and the rising sun for a more authentic birth-ritual, from which the man returns as if from the dead in a rite of passage (p. 178). But the new social bus belongs to the old order of corrupt speed — the policeman has to be bribed because the passengers are "in a hurry" — and the sounds of the sea are drowned by the harsh noises of speeding military vehicles, specimens of the historical change which has overtaken Koomson. The man's "sea-birth" is out of an old lorry tyre's inner tube, a relic of the world of mechanical speed like the shore's technological junk: all the world's waste and filth, it seems, can be recycled in Mammy Water's element.

The drug administered to the group by Maanan causes a destructive rebirth into reconnectedness which is consistent with Mammy Water's sometimes violent powers of regeneration, and Teacher's sensations of the vital reciprocity between sea and land whilst under the spell of the drug are similarly consistent with the folk-myth's pattern of land lovers being given special powers in return for sea favours. These parallels are carried into the episode of the man's return from the sea and his meeting with Maanan. The man's purifying and liberating immersion in the sea recalls the creative-destructive inward explosion of the wee-smoker, something feared and enjoyed: "He held his breath so long that he began to enjoy the almost exploding inward feeling that he was perhaps no longer alive" (p. 178). From this death, with its resonances of the liminal neophyte, is born the partly changed consciousness of the final chapter. The man returns from the waves to the "welcoming sand" and the diametric opposition of sea and land gives way to a wee-like reciprocity: the new dawn's rainbow of colours on the beach mirrors the sea's "greens and blues, separate", emerging from the water's "indiscriminate dark" (pp. 179–81). But the kaleidoscopic blaze of colour on the sunlit waves is swiftly eclipsed by the shadow of the mad woman. Maanan vainly scrambles to retrieve past moments of time by sifting symbolic grains of sand but, echoing Teacher's speed-confused memories of events, she finds that the "vomiting speed" of the Independence years has "mixed everything", indistinguishably telescoping idealistic hopes and betrayal, early promise and endings (the novel's food–excretion/sex–birth correspondence which images birth as an ending, and the drastic curtailment in private physiology of the route from mouth to bowel, each have the same effect of running together separate stages into a single, abruptly truncated process).

At her last appearance in the novel Maanan parts company with her mythological counterpart. She is now one of the altered, not the alterer of consciousness: it is she, not her faithless lover, who is spurned and punished by madness; the healer, made sick by speed, is herself afflicted by an "urgency in her diseased soul" (p. 180). The pattern of regeneration is replaced by one of irretrievable loss: the seven years of her personal decline poignantly parody Mammy Water's unbroken seven-year cycle of restoration and renewal and more accurately match the senseless life-cycle of the seven-year manchild and the Nkrumah regime which has witnessed her annihilation. After leaving the "reborn" man, Maanan walks away from the risen sun, her shadow in front of her an adumbration of the grave, and the man crosses a desecrated cemetery (p. 181). But before departing from Maanan the man fulfils his role in, and formally completes, the mythological pattern as with the more important ritual one of the carrier. By involuntarily remembering and recognizing features he may never have set eyes upon, he acts as a surrogate lover of this "Woman of the Sea" and symbolically keeps faith with her vicarious memory and inherited hopes. His recovery of her is comparable with Amamu's mythical quest to recover the lost woman of childhood in Awoonor's novel, where the return of the woman rewards a life-long keeping of faith with her memory and spirit, and, as in the folk myth and Awoonor's version of it, his faith is rewarded with a regenerated awakening.

In the more ironic climate of Armah's novel, however, this discovery is not, as in the case of Amamu, a blinding religious illumination which generally corrects rather than confirms his previous experience. The man's somewhat gentler awakening is to a more realistic and discriminating sense of human community and to a penetration of the total complex of corruption, its vitality and stagnation, which has in fact been growing steadily in the course of the novel. As Robert Fraser has remarked, the peripheral references to systems of commerce and economics earlier in the novel make the ethical complexities of Amankwa's bribe endless, ruling out any easy judgements of offerer or refuser: transportation-bribes connive at the moral ruin of the country but also divert a little foreign profit into (albeit corrupt) indigenous hands and keep a flicker of life in the economy.[65] The man's lyrical epiphany by the seashore at the end of chapter 8 takes place in the context and presence of corruption. Amankwa's rotting wood, now bound into a raft ready for loading onto the waiting ship, shifts from its earlier image of an ancient dead weight to a mobile force which depends on corruption to keep work and trade alive. Corruption is what the sea recycles, making any ultimate expulsion impossible: like the ocean's recharged filth and the new life growing from the tree's rotten fruit, the bribe enables life to go on. The man turns away, "almost happy" (p. 113), and the action is duplicated in the final chapter, where the chichidodo's "strangely happy" song over the latrine recalls the seagull crying over Amankwa's sea-bound logs and there emerges, with a much greater strength, the idea of a life-giving and life-saving corruption which is the lubricating energy of a State in exhausted stagnation. Because it is a total condition, through which everything that happens is expressed and through which grows the only life that exists, this corruption can be removed only by recourse to more of itself and attaches even to acts of goodness and love. Though they change their form in the totalitarian order, potentialities for goodness do not disappear entirely. For example, the man understands that the bus driver's closing bribe is not prompted by selfish motives like the conductor's opening fraud but is a gesture of community, performed on behalf of his delayed passengers. The briber is here a victim, not an exploiter, and, having no reason to feel shame, smiles and waves at the silent watcher. Prior to this understanding, the man has in his ritual immersion taken on the character of the sea, which the epithets for the waves — "soft", "gentle" and "noiseless" — have identified with his own nature (p. 171). The indication is that he is now more attuned to cyclical process, to Mammy Water's original spirit, and sees corruption as an inevitable and necessary stage in this process.

At his return to land and meeting with Maanan the man feels "something get out from him, from the endings of the nerves and the fingertips, from every part of his body, sinking into the sand" (p. 181). What finally leaves him, as if of its own accord, is not merely the expelled pollution of Koomson, unloaded by the carrier into the sea. It is also, paradoxically, the illusion that there can be absolute solutions to and permanent expulsions of ills, of the kind which his own ritual task has just simulated. Maanan turns away, "leaving the man wondering why but knowing already that he would find no answers, from her, from Teacher, or from anybody else" (p. 181). The man's awakening is to the reality that there are no millenial deliverances from history; no answers and no saviours (he has just helped one of Maanan's fraudulent messiahs to escape); and no Utopias, prospective or retrospective, to feed glib faiths and fatalisms like those of Teacher.

Absolutist hopes for the community are compromised by the conditions of individual cases and, significantly, there is no mystical transference of the carrier figure's solitary release to the community as in Awoonor's novel. Like the driver, each man must come to terms with corruption as honourably as he can and must learn to live with his "aching emptiness" for a more ideal existence (p. 183). The new perception is a metaphoric growth from the man's psychological affinity with sea-process: his discrimination of individual colours from the sea's "indiscriminate dark" is followed immediately by his discriminating extenuation of the individual case of corruption awaiting his judgement on shore. "Community" is finally enlivened into particularity from its earlier polarized abstractions — gleam and loved ones, leapers and waiters, saviours and saved, Teacher's implied *us* and *them* — and begins to wear a more human and believable face. The siting of psychological discoveries in metaphoric "sea-changes" is not without its problems, however, even in the context of the novel's elastically symbolic realism. The poetics come tentatively to rest in a nature-metaphysic that appears to establish corruption as an absolute and which, as we have seen, is at odds with the narrative's sustained psychological relativism: the man's wandering thoughts are both attracted to and repelled by, but never converted to, the idea of analogizing human behaviour to natural process and his parable of the monstrous fruit seems finally to insist upon the unnaturalness of analogies with the natural.

Kofi Awoonor has said of Mammy Water: "Somewhere she does exist as the final repository of wisdom. She knows the answers. She knows what I must do, what Amamu must do, what we all must do. And I must go with her to acquire this knowledge and survive the truncation of the soul that society imposes."[66] The man elicits no final wisdoms from her human equivalent and his moment of recognition and reaffirmed faith is also the moment of rejection, for he has ceased to search for panaceas: each man must save himself. But his commitment finds support in the cyclical wisdom of the true Mammy Water, and knowledge of her repetitive processes, processes partly energized by corruption, appears to be the only "answer" offered. The explosion of births at the end of Armah's first novel — the flower from the egg, Koomson from the latrine, the man from the sea — does not disguise the fact that there are no beautiful ones waiting to be born at the end of the laborious circuit through which the man has been painfully initiated into this knowledge. The ironic ritual task completed by the man on his return to shore has no pretensions to finality or absoluteness: when the appropriate point in the cycle next comes round, it will have to be done again.

VI

Fragments and the Akan World Order

If Armah's first novel deals with the mechanics of ritual and mock-ritual process, his second novel is more concerned with their religious implications. The first book has "no saviours": this one has two. But there is nothing in *Fragments* to match the consistency of ritual interference with character and incident which peaks at the climax of *The Beautyful Ones Are Not Yet Born*.[1] Here the motifs have to be coaxed out of the naturalistic action and move in and out of a complexly interwoven and uninsistent myth-fabric which has a structural rather than a narrative presence in the novel. This seamless tapestry of myth and ritual is crossed by a number of spectral passengers: carrier, cargo-ghost, reincarnated ancestor, the mermaid's singer-lover, the sacrificial offering, and, not least, the dying year in whose regenerative transition the dying come closest to those about to be born. The recurring pattern in these concurrently advancing motifs is that of a going to come again: this consists of an outward passage, an actual or figurative death and rebirth into an altered state, and a beneficial return, bearing what may be doubtful blessings. Sentences like the following, from Naana's dream — "But Baako walked among them neither touched nor seen, like a ghost in an overturned world in which all human flesh was white" (p. 15) — conflate allusions to cargo-ghosts, the ancestral dead turned white in the spirit world, the lonely African in American exile, and the ritually invisible and untouchable carrier walking unheeded among contemporary Ghanaians. In the fictive space occupied by the dual consciousness of Baako and Juana, the combined artist-psychiatrist, converge the common traits of the carrier and the lover of Mammy Water: a visionary estrangement, a power of healing, and the assumption by an "expanded consciousness" of a maddening burden of knowledge or, in Baako's words, "all there is to know about loneliness, about love, about power" (pp. 171–72).

Fragments is divided by its thirteen Akan-titled chapters into the thirteen lunar months of the traditional Akan year, at the end of which Baako, the persecuted artist transfigured into an unmistakably sacrificial carrier, is hounded by his family into the mental exile of madness. "A been-to, returned only a year ago," comments one of his captors (p. 248). After running his pursuers into exhaustion Baako walks "deliberately down the remembered path of his first day back home", as if his run has magically exorcized the torments of "the blighted year behind" (pp. 235, 187). In a series of quasi-ritualistic scenes culminating in the chase across Accra, Baako symbolically takes over the burden of communal frustrations, anxieties and neuroses of which he has become the target. His natural partner in this process is the Puerto Rican Juana: the psychiatrist as sin-carrier, a common figure in world literature. But, as in Awoonor's novel, the recovery or rebirth prepared for by the healing derangement seems to be eschatological rather than social. In the last chapter, which brings the novel's year full circle, Naana dies from a world of impenitent materialism and, in her own mind at least, is reborn into the world of the ancestors. Meanwhile, in the here and now, there appears to be little prospect of new beginnings, most particularly in the light of Baako's painfully slow emergence from his entombment in the asylum, but also in respect of the weight brought to bear upon Naana's cyclical vision of eternal renewal and conservation by the terminality of her impending death. Naana stands as the sole survivor of a lost past, so that her beliefs die with her and her release into the spirit community betokens the continuing captivity and incorrigibility of the living one. The flashback of the chapter "Efua" offers a cautious glimpse of possible redemption. In this moving episode Efua takes Baako to the ruined foundations of her unbuilt mansion, where she formally lifts her curse on the son previously convicted of the "refusal of ritual joy" at his homecoming and confessionally off-loads onto him, as priest-carrier, the accumulated burden of false hopes, material cravings and "strange feelings" which he has inspired in her. Yet the purity of Efua's "soul cleaning" is suspect because her relief at being lightened of the weight of her dreams is still mixed with regret that they could not be fulfilled. The grudging withdrawal of her accusations and formal abandonment of hope in her son leaves Baako with a load of guilt which becomes the crucial factor in his drift towards madness. Juana optimistically prepares an "unused room" in her house in readiness for Baako's release, as a realistic alternative to Efua's unbuilt dream-house, and her final rescue of him from the clutches of his family brings the novel to rest on a note of muted hope, but this exists entirely on the personal level. Her urgent concern is with salvation — or, more precisely, salvage — not with social regeneration or redemption.

From the opening libation to the resurrection hymn that swells from the cathedral opposite the asylum in anticipation of Naana's death, the metaphor of salvation, and the idea of saviours come to rescue imperilled minds and souls from a diseased and paralysed Ghanaian body, blaze a luridly suggestive trail through this novel. Juana makes "small saving attempts" against the prolific human damage wreaked by the city and thinks of the child's escape from death under the wheels of the tanker as "the lucky moment of salvation" (pp. 33–34). Baako, who is himself regarded as a saviour from "some disease that has descended upon us" by the old woman in the airport taxi, talks to Juana as if he were himself "a doctor probing into a diseased body" and locates the sickness in the ruling elite's opinion of themselves as "the happy plucked ones, saved . . . a brand plucked from the burning" (pp. 85, 145, 210). The "damned" of the countryside deludedly "look to the grinding town as if some salvation could be found there" (p. 22). The titles of the novel's pivotal central chapters turn upon the stem of the Akan verb *gye*, to receive or inwardly accept (in this case, salvation): *Osagyefo*, the Saviour (here, Juana, though with ironic references to the Head of State, whose cultural propaganda machine is seen at work in the chapter); *Gyefo*, the Redeemer (coupling Juana with the fisherboy who for Baako signifies the redemptive power of art); and *Igya*, the hopefully redemptive blood-sacrifice (here, Skido). The essentially private nature of the Protestant salvationist ethic is, in theory, alien to traditional ideas of an interdependent community of spirit-ancestors, living and unborn in Akan theology,[2] as, in practice, its ascetic, individualized spirituality is unknown to the materialistically-minded Christians of Akan stock who flock to beach messiahs in the novel. But what emerges from the mesh of mixed loyalties and apostasies is the broad truth that Armah's Fante-Akan have lost touch with their ancient faith without wholly adapting to their new one and it is a fitting incongruity in such a community that the mantles of traditional ritual and mythology — the healing carrier and sea-goddess — should fall upon the shoulders of the expatriated outsider and the foreigner. In their transposition of African priestly functions to the roles of contemporary psychiatrist and artist, the "Catholic pagans" Juana and Baako reject the quasi-Protestant option of the Western artist's solitary vocation held out to them by Ocran. For Juana, the "salutary cynicism of Protestants, their ability to kill all empathy, to pull in all wandering bits of self into the one self, trying for an isolated heaven in the shrinking flight inward", is not enough. To it must be added the outward passage into a community of souls, the assumption of the social burden, the cleansing communal empathy which are the carrier's stock-in-trade: "Too much of her lay outside of herself, that was the trouble. Like some forest woman whose gods were in all the trees and hills and people around her, the meaning of her life remained in her defeated attempts to purify her environment, right down to the final, futile decision to try to salvage discrete individuals in the general carnage" (p. 177). The community's suffering is, familiarly, introjected until the purifying protagonist has made it his or her own, but with an anguish, both personal and professional, which goes beyond the man's in the first novel: "Juana not only saw the pain, but felt it in herself and was holding down something straining to scream out from within her own body" (p. 191). This process is paralleled, at the family level, by Baako's interiorization of his mother's and sister's anxieties and disappointments, in the course of which he sets up their values in his own mind to pass judgement on himself, and by his frustrated attempts in his screenplays to share his vision, "to say things in my mind, to let other people see". "That sounds like a priest," Naana responds (p. 220). Paradoxically, it is modern Africa's rejection of Baako's traditional priest-like approach to his art that drives him reluctantly inward into the position of the Western artist-recluse. Juana, as healing saviour, sees that this "high flight of the individual alone, escaping the touch of life around him", is as dangerous for Baako's temperament as a wholly conformist, annihilating identification of the self with the cargo-minded society (p. 271). As she tells Ocran, "Salvation is such an empty thing when you're alone" (p. 276).

In *Fragments* the carrier's functions are divided between

Juana and Baako, whose peripheral empathizings from positions of professional detachment and artistic isolation are acted out against a ritual backcloth of healing and salvation. Taking up where the the man left off, the long-expatriated Baako is addressed by almost everyone in the novel as "stranger" and is first seen indulging a misplaced compassion for a fellow exile who purchases a picture-postcard to send home in Orly airport. Juana, who as an expatriate professional undergoes an "unavoidable estrangement" (p. 18), is a more likely saviour than Baako insofar as she is directly involved in the daily salvaging of human wreckage, and during the drive to the old slave castle at Christiansborg her emotions lead her to a wider racial identification with a defeated people whose heritage she shares. Juana and Baako are more humanly, less ritually conceived than the man of the first novel. They lack the necessary ritual purity, the sterile immunity to the disease they probe: they hunger for contact with, for a "human touching" of, the tainted body. But for both figures contact contaminates and corrupts, remains both desirable and dangerous. The colour and nature symbolism which surrounds them habitually equates touch with pain and the only exception to this torturous algebra is the bond of physical intimacy through which they find comfort and release in each other — an intimacy emphasized by the sexual explicitness of the love scenes. Both characters, like their counterparts in Soyinka's play and Awoonor's novel, are reluctant to embrace their destined missions and attempt evasions that bring them circularly back to a fulfilment of them. Baako senses "that everything he had done in about the last half year had been intended as a postponement, a pushing away of things to which he felt necessarily called" (p. 74). Preferring the carrier-archetype's secondary resonances of millenial reversals to its primary pattern of doleful periodicity, of repetition and return, Juana infuses into her struggle-seeking pilgrimage to Ghana "the hope of constant regeneration, the daring to reach out toward a new world . . . the brilliance of an always imminent apocalypse . . . the making of another world" (p. 45). But the outward passage returns her to "another defeated and defeating place" where she is confronted again by " the living defeat of whole peoples — the familiar fabric of her life", and old sorrows "burrow inward, travel along everywhere with the carrying mind, and mix their old traces with the sights and sounds of every new place the traveler came to" (pp. 17, 45, 42). Those individuals who are marked out to bear the burdens of the many cannot escape what, in its essential nature, is not a revolutionary transformation but a saving mission — a series of periodically repeated relief-actions which, to Juana's despair, "save people who had found the mess insupportable and had somehow flipped out of it after too much pain long endured", only to give them back "the outer toughening they would need so they could be flipped back to get messed up some more" (p. 21). Her makeshift solution is to see less, adopting "a narrower vision every time the full vision threatens danger to the visionary self" (p. 46). The necessity of fragmented perception and a limited wholeness is restated in the example of Naana's blindness as a refuge from insanity, "which would surely have come with seeing so much that was not to be understood" (p. 14).

It is, however, the painfully "expanded consciousness" of Baako (he has seven chapters to Juana's four) that occupies the larger space in the novel. The American who sells Baako his guitar warns him that "he had begun to run from human beings" (p. 93), and in the narrative of Baako's return he is an eternally running figure who spends much of his time in flight. Following the sudden headlong flight from Paris, he is next seen running to give birth to his sister's child, the parturient blood smears on his hand investing him — as if a stigma in this sterile land — with a peculiar taboo which provokes horrified looks and hasty retreats from the taxi drivers he tries to flag down. Baako's provision of passage for a new life is elaborated afterwards in conversation with the new mother, who insists that he has given the child to her along with the blood taken from him for her transfusion:

> "Truly, what I meant was this: if you had not come back yourself, I would have lost this baby also . . . Do you know how many times I tried for this child and failed?"
>
> "Only husbands know, no?"
>
> "I'm going to tell you anyway. Five times." She counted fingers and thumb. "Five good times. It was when you were writing those letters which made us doubt so much whether you would come. And then you got ill."
>
> "Yes."
>
> "I would carry him for months, and then just as I was getting happy thinking of myself as a mother, everything would pass away in such a river of bad blood I could have died. Now see, it is such a good thing, your coming. Already you have brought me this, the baby. Other blessings will follow, that I know."
>
> "I don't know."
>
> "You won't ever go anywhere away from us again, Baako. Stay, and the baby will stay too. Baako, he is yours. He will be named after you." (pp. 121–22)

Araba's faltering fertility and short-lived maternity are seen to grow, by a mysterious analogical process, out of Baako's mental breakdown during his stay abroad and his eventual departure from America. The significance of the Akan blood-bond between child and maternal uncle will be discussed presently but it should be noticed here that not only does Baako, in a semi-sacrificial way, literally give his blood to usher in the new life, but his temporary derangement and debilitated return, in a carrier-like capacity, also figure in a healing, creative process which enables new life in society to get born. The ritualistic implications reinforce a simple moral point: in a pleasure-seeking world too paralysed by illusion to produce anything of its own, Baako represents a hard, painful road to truth, and the self-sacrifice necessary for creation. But the intuition quickly evaporates. A flick of Araba's wordly imagination whisks him out of his sacrificial role and into that of a modern cargo-bringer, a bearer of "other", material blessings. The quick, instinctive life of the child for which he gives his blood is, by a logic both moral and material, an extension of his own creative energy which his family is unable to make use of and which therefore values as nothing. Neither Baako nor the child stays: one is rejected unto madness, the other neglected unto death.

Baako's final fugitive run across the city takes him back into familiar archetypal territory. In the faces of his ensnarers he senses "an assumption of some terrible knowledge shared" and immediately prior to the ritual chase he makes a symbolic effort to vomit forth from himself the spiritual sickness of his family which it is his task to take into his charge: at one of the visible symptoms of this sickness (Efua makes the banal insinuation that his artistic self-communings are signs of madness) "the huge vomiting fever came draining out of him, tearing itself out of a body too weak to help or resist it" (pp. 231, 227). Following the classic course of neurotic behaviour, the sick ones stay well by making the well ones sick: the family passes its own madness onto its son who expresses its illness for it. The carrier's own illness is a necessary part of the cure that makes others well: "I've been very sick before," Juana tells Baako. "Coming here was part of the cure" (p. 168). The frenzied pursuit carries him out into the wilderness of the city's waste ground and through the familiar labyrinthine maze leading down to the sea, and throughout he retains the untouchability of the ritually dangerous, the transmitter of received pollutions. "Stay far from him. His bite will make you also maaaad! . . . The same thing happens if he should scratch you," cry his demented pursuers, and Baako later tells Juana and Ocran, "You shouldn't be coming too close to me" (pp. 243, 272). Like the carrier in Soyinka's play, he is stoned when he tries to return home and carry the "evil" of his imaginary madness back into the house. After running into exhaustion the pursuers whose real madness he has led to the city gates and figuratively abandoned there — a madness given full rein in their panic phobias and superstitions — Baako experiences a "lightness" and "happy feeling" which recall the man's feeling of "vague freedom" and relief upon taking leave of Koomson and returning to shore. But there has been no corresponding purgative release in those around him: the accusers and persecutors are waiting for him when he returns as surely as the uncleansed society awaits the man's return from the sea.

The chase sequence uses the metaphors of ritual transference to precise moral effect. As in *The Strong Breed*, the mechanics and symbolism of the carrier are parodically drawn upon in the depiction of what is really the coercion of a scapegoat. Baako's "madness" does the work of the ritual effigy: it is a manufactured, invented thing in which are projected and embodied the collective neuroses that, in the Onipa family and the wider society, issue from a narrowly acquisitive and philistine materialism. His persecution, like the murder of the dog by the sexually disabled and the novel's pivotal infanticide, is an attempt to exorcize a general impotence. The implication is that this community is jealously resentful of any creative energy or quickness, and either destroys what it cannot itself create or tries to make those who possess this gift responsible for its own frustrating sterility, perversely demanding that they also be made like its own barren self. In accordance with scapegoat-psychology the family, like the general public in the first novel, dissociatively alienates its sickness to Baako, who makes it his own. After the apparently demented yet, in fact, sanely visionary inspiration of the cargo-conceit which marks the acme of his insight, Baako then really goes mad, his infection by the collective insanity demonstrated by his insistence on the correctness of the cargo mentality in the asylum. The family's guilt is transmitted to Baako, as victim-vehicle, in the twisted form of shame at disappointing their expectations and is expressed, finally, as clinical insanity.

The inefficacy of this ritualized behaviour is directly proportionate to the impurity of its motivational origins, a point made clear by the proleptic dog-slaying outside the Kalifonia Moonbeam Cafe. The destruction of the dog, like the locking away of the alleged lunatic, is ostensibly a public service undertaken for the safety of the community. But in the Ghana of this novel communal feeling is a negative thing which has degenerated into isolated outbursts of violent destruction just like this one. Juana sees instantly that the killer is "a man who needed something like the first killing of the dog for reasons that lay within and were far more powerful than the mere outside glory open to the hunter with his kill" (p. 27). The dog's madness becomes an occasion and excuse for the fulfilment of private needs driven by an inner corruption, and the same is true of Baako's "madness" and incarceration: after failing to bring back the expected wealth from overseas and then resigning his lucrative sinecure at Ghanavision, Baako is simply written off as a bad investment, a useless person and a drain on the family's resources. As in Soyinka's play, ritual behaviour demonstrates the sicknesses it is designed to expel, so no purgation ensues. The sacrifice of the dog fails to renew the masculinity or the potency of its killer: the killing is a cowardly act and the pent-up, festering sickness craving release still clings to him in his orgasmic shudder at the moment of impact and the pseudo-sexual ejaculation of poisonous matter from his diseased scrotum. Similarly, the unexorcized spiritual sickness of the Onipa family is given quintessential expression in its hounding of its sick son.

The ritual pattern of the first novel is a monotonously cathartic one, suffused by the symbolism of purgative, excretory release: the February coup which carries out the Nkrumah era is linked with calendrical rituals of discharge and relief which clear the way for the new to be born. But in the second novel the more openly aggressive and destructive pressures to conform demand a more challenging response than the man's passive endurance and solitary relief. Juana cannot be content with a periodic patching up of broken souls that will always have to be repeated since it merely sends "the once destroyed back to knock again against the very things that had destroyed their peace" (p. 34), and a desire for "real change" energizes the protest-art which Baako defiantly pumps into the Ghanavision propaganda machine. Moreover, whatever traditional gods or moral orders these modern pressures offend demand heavier sacrifices and repayments than are obtainable by mere relief-actions. The intolerances of Ghana in this novel, and white America in the next, demand offerings for the altars of their materialism and purblind racism and, since their sins against humanity are deadlier and less forgivable than the corruption in the first novel, a correspondingly higher price must be paid for their purgation. The man in the first novel is a carrier; Baako and Modin are, more immediately, sacrifices. One is a vehicle, the others are victims. In the asylum Juana reports to Baako Naana's words: "I didn't understand her, but I think she said they tried to kill you" (p. 270). Only Naana is able to understand the sacrificial ritual dimensions of the attempted "killing" of Baako. In the cases of both Baako and Skido, the merely symbolic death of the outward passage is unsatisfactory because Skido brings back unwanted, unvalued cargo and Baako, materially, brings nothing at all. In the case of the child, the electric fan that kills it also scatters the collection-money, the cargo which it brings into the world. As a result of their failings all three are pushed towards a real death and a literalization of their metaphorical ghostliness: contemporary reality has been ritualized, in part, by the excesses of the new cargo-cultism which has bitten so deeply into the Ghanaian mentality. But, beyond this, the characters are destined to die as scapegoats, to release the community from the burden of false hope and subsequent shame which it has heaped upon their several heads, and, hopefully, through the pain of loss and remorse at their deaths, to restore to that community the traditional wisdoms which were missing from its management of their lives.

The sacrificial perspective called into play in *Fragments* skirts the more violent territory of transition. Baako's peculiar mode of transitionality is, however, a purely ritual phenomenon, not the usual historical one. He is not the conventional been-to figure, the transitional African whose Western education leaves him ill-equipped to deal with African society — as Obi in Achebe's *No Longer At Ease*, for example. Baako is not caught between Africa and the West or even between a modern and a traditional Africa, but between the West and a vulgarly Westernized Africa: he is a reverse been-to who reviles the place he returns to only insofar as it imitates the one he has fled from. His "liminal" experience and personality consign him to a state of transition that really exists betwixt and between states in a number of contexts: his family and the needs of the larger community, his own and others' view of himself, Ocran's option of the isolated artist and his own "priestly" concept of his vocation. By the light of Juana's intuition, Baako's personal psychological "cataract" is his deluded desire to banish conflict and come to rest in one of these spurious polarities. His belief that he can be completely at one both with himself and with his society drives him between the rival insanities of total conformity and solipsism, in neither of which he belongs and can remain for long. Carried by conflicting currents "all at once in too many undecided directions", Baako is, like the hovering child he has a duty to protect, one of the "sudden" or "uncertain ones", a traveller between worlds: a status consistent with the "posthumous" ritualization of the been-to into a kind of cargo-spirit (pp. 138, 183). Only when finally persuaded that he can neither wholly compromise nor island himself is Baako allowed to take up residence in the asylum's auspiciously-designated "transitional ward". There is, however, no clear evidence that his private zone of transition is a source of regeneration for family or community; it remains uncertain whether any painful knowledge or moral growth has emerged from his sacrifice. In the ironic vision of the early novels, ritual hope exists in tension with brute fact: Baako's mental disintegration, Modin's futile death in the next book. But a shift away from the entirely negative rituality of the first novel is apparent in the reluctance to believe in total loss and waste which is given its purest expression in the unifying perspective of Naana's energy-conserving cycle.

Naana, in whose traditional system of belief all things are connected, can make no sense of the new Ghana. No longer able to penetrate to "the particular meaning of the particular moment hidden some depth beneath the surface" and unresigned to the mindless reception of the modern world's confusing material impressions, she seeks sanctuary in blindness and "rest in despair, not trying again to regain the larger meaning and the peace that can come from the greater understanding" (p. 281). *Fragments* has more than enough fragmentation to justify its title. In a Westernized Africa besotted by commodity and status, the uncritical "beholding eye" is overwhelmed by the dazzling fragmented beauty of externals: the airport's gaudy technology; Brempong's lighter "sculpted entirely out of light"; office doors luminous with pompous titles which, Juana observes, Ghanaians invest with a "deadly seriousness"; the glittering confusion of Brempong's welcome and the Onipa outdooring. As in "An African Fable" and the gleam-worship of the first book, the "unconnected eye" which is mesmerized by this superficial beauty perceives only unconnectedness. The failure to see beyond an impressive outward show to an inner paucity, thus mistaking the visible form of the thing for the thing itself, fragments form from meaning, perception from understanding, and results in non-functioning literary quarterlies like *Kyerema* (in Akan, "show" or "exhibition") and empty ceremonies which are evasions rather than expressions of reality. In Armah's portrayal of modern Ghanaians this notion of partial perception, uninformed by a guiding moral or intellectual vision, is reinforced by a style which physically fragments them into partial people who sometimes appear to be little more than a collection of disjointed limbs operating independently of any organizing consciousness. Brempong's sister is a whirling mass of kente, teeth and buttocks, and his wife "the generous mass of a wig protruding above the seat . . . Beside the wig a hand suddenly shot upwards and sideways, its blackness cut off from the blackness of its coat sleeve by a lucent white cuff, and a single finger summoned an advancing stewardess . . . Out in front a dark head crowned with the mass of a wig stood suddenly upright" (pp. 60, 69). Hands and fingers dismember themselves at will: it is the head and the wig, not the woman, that jerk to attention. The droll satire toys with the pretence that there is no thinking human presence animating these spare components from the human limb factory and, connected up, the parts would not add up to a complete human being. As the rhetoric of the first novel graphically endows characters with excremental characteristics that take on a quasi-literal status, that of the second novel affects to disintegrate them, rendering them as fragmented and humanly incomplete as their perception of the world.

The general pattern of fragmentation is also reflected in the divisive effects of the much-abused extended family system. This system, once the linchpin of the traditional community which acted as a bulwark against social strife by ensuring some share of prosperity for all, now undermines it by turning against it the self-serving interests of a few powerful careerists and their families, into whose hands wealth and influence have been concentrated. Both family and state have ceased to be a solidarity of reciprocal interests and have become channels for one-way manipulation: the striking syncretic image of the white fish's cannibalized body in the first novel gathers together in a logical chain the ruling elite scrambling after white power from the corpse of colonialism, the cannibalized communal body fed off by a few families, and the family members themselves feeding parasitically upon the single providing "big man".[3] The system of false sharing in Ghanaian socialism by mutually corrupt, cut-taking partners, instanced in the confederacy of fraud offered to the man by the venal conductor of the first book, is thus a refinement of the perverted family system, in which the public body is made to bear the weight of private welfare: "WHO BORN FOOL/SOCIALISM CHOP MAKE I CHOP/CONTREY BROKE", runs the cynical latrine graffiti.[4] Brothers in corruption only, people are united by what most divides them, together in the rivalry to "get ahead" which keeps them apart, and, in Armah's sociology of the oppressed, violence in the vanishing communal body is never directed outwards against oppressors but always inward, as in Kofi Billy's suicide and Bukari's breakdown, against the oppressed self.

In senses other than the thematic, however — namely, at the structural and imagistic levels — *Fragments* is the least fragmented of Armah's novels. Juana and Baako do not meet until the fifth chapter but their parallel third person narratives have a tonal uniformity and imaginative rapport: fine psychic vibrations, touching upon race-consciousness and the nation's criminal legacy, pass between their contemporaneous second and third chapters, to be taken up later by Naana's closing retrospections to slave-chiefs. The circular phrasing of Naana's opening monologue percolates ironically into Juana's observations of the repeated breaking of the circle of slayers in the pseudo-sacrifice of the dog (pp. 14, 16, 28–29) and, reciprocally, Juana's rejection of the idea of solitary salvation in her last words to Ocran reverberates through Naana's final speculations on her release into a community of spirits (pp. 276, 286). Baako, who has an unspoken sympathy with his grandmother, thinks habitually in terms of circles and cycles, thus allowing Naana's thought patterns to infiltrate the mainstream of the narrative so that the intermittently interlocking viewpoints effectively form a single diffused consciousness.

At the imagistic level the novel is bound by a sometimes over-suggestive network of foreshadowings and echoes which, when too artful and heavy-handed, make it read like a tone-poem in which a limping narrative and dialogue are carried along on the rhythm of recurrent leit-motifs: the Parisian and Ghanaian madmen who try to walk and look through barriers of brick and water to other worlds, reflecting Baako's transitional passage; the spectre of the murdered dog that prowls the pages of the succeeding chapters, spreading a general aura of persecuted pain and resurfacing metaphorically in the hounding of Baako across the city. More subtle and significant is the occult orchestration of coincidences that allows the paths of Juana and Baako to cross many times before they meet. Towards the end of her first narrative Juana meets Efua, as religious cultist, on the beach where she and Baako will later make love and the chapter ends, perhaps over-neatly, with the two women searching the sky for the aeroplane which we see Baako boarding at the start of the next chapter. At the Cafe of the Silver Shooting Star Baako, in the company of his brother-in-law, unwittingly encounters Juana's laboratory assistant, Bukari, also afflicted by a cargo-clamouring mother and now grief-stricken at her dying before he could fulfil her expectations. The characters themselves remain peculiarly unaware of their common ground and the plot takes little cognizance of it: although Juana mentions a visit to the Onipa house during Baako's breakdown, no reference is made to any earlier acquaintance with his mother, which appears to exist at a numinous level of association and has no life in the action of the novel. One possible inference is that Armah's employment of coincidence and prefigurative devices is designed to reassemble the random "momentary happenings" of which Naana speaks and recover the "larger meaning" formerly given them by a unified whole before it shattered into a thousand useless pieces (p. 280). The aim is to put the pieces back together in the only kind of order and wholeness — an artistic one — that is now available to them. The novel's handling of the pivotal episode of the child's death implies, however, that Armah's occult restructuring of consciousness purposes something deeper than the token resistance of material fragmentation by a fragile aesthetic unity.

The fourth chapter "Awo", which is set about a month after Baako's return to Ghana and covers the week of the child's life, halts abruptly on the Sunday morning of the premature outdooring in which the infant is fatally exposed to the electric fan. The chapter closes with a grim presentiment of the child's death by Naana, almost "inarticulate" with a "huge terror" of the doom which Efua's and Araba's abuses of custom are tempting: "He must be protected. Or he will run screaming back, fleeing the horrors prepared for him up here" (p. 139). The abridged narrative of the central chapters then moves forward over the events of the next year, during which no reference is made to the child's death, an event which is finally narrated in flashback in the eleventh chapter from the viewpoint of Baako's incarceration and subsequent madness. Thus the reader is placed in the odd situation of waiting over seven chapters for something which has already happened. When the revelation finally comes, the clairvoyant Naana is discovered using the past tense for what, in the present of the flashback, is still a future event. "You should have saved the child," she admonishes Baako, as if the child is already dead. "My mind can see him, lying in state now . . . They've got him shrouded in rich clothes and now they turn this wind on him" (pp. 262, 266). The event has been awarded the certainty of what has already happened: firstly, because Naana's sombre prophecy invests it with an inevitability comparable with the assured consequences of violating a ritual taboo; secondly, because it has indeed already occurred within the book's temporal structure, on that unfinished Sunday in an earlier chapter; thirdly, because it is implicit in almost everything which *is* narrated both before and during the waiting period. The deferred death has a protracted imminence in the mind of the novel. Armah's liberties with the restriction and release of information take tremendous risks with psychological realism and the delayed flashback of "Iwu" raises doubts about the twin narrative's linear progress between Naana's two monologues since no thought of the child's death crosses the mind of either narrator during the following year. But the artistic reward reaped from these risks is another grand crystallizing, culminating image, in this case for the premature truncation of life which pervades the novel. The failure of the Onipa family to keep its offspring alive because of its greed for riches has a broad mythopoetic inherence in many local details: the aborted public utilities of schools and roads, quickly abandoned by self-aggrandizing governments; the shut-down distilleries and disused industrial rail tracks; the architectural miscarriage of Efua's house which is the sequel to the actual miscarriages of her daughter. Omnipresent in the novel is the impotent destruction of whatever fails to provide instant fulfilment by those who cannot themselves create.[5] Significantly, the slaying of the dog is presented as a series of aborted, deathly births performed by men with huge bellies that "pushed into the open world" and monstrously swollen syphilitic scrotal sacs that emit poisonous afterbirths of yellow pus and clotted blood (pp. 26, 29). In the fishermen's episode, Juana's imagination transforms the "beating flesh of still-living fish" in the "bag net, vaginal and black", into sperm thrashing in the vaginal passage and prevented from fertilizing: in the next instant the fish are neither nourishment nor sexual potentialities, but dead commodities for sale at market, trampled in the stampede for money (p.184).

Northrop Frye has described ritual as "a temporal sequence of acts in which the conscious meaning or significance is latent; it can be seen by an observer but is largely concealed from the participators themselves".[6] The child's foreseen and awaited death occupies little space in the plot and the complementary narrative consciousnesses: it has a more elusive existence in the implied collective psyche or "ritual consciousness" at the invisible core of the novel. In *Fragments* the single saturative consciousness which dominates the first novel has been broken down into three partial and often mutually uncomprehending viewpoints. Naana is unable to make Baako understand traditional wisdom and Juana fails to interpret the ritual implications of Naana's words on the "killing" of Baako. Baako explains the Mammy Water myth to Juana without registering its relevance to his own situation: by the logic of the fable, madness will follow upon Juana's absence and his desertion of her values for the materialistic ones of his family, and the harsh lesson learned by the sea-goddess's abandoned lover predicts the pain that Baako must learn to live with, the "pure, impossible longing" and "impending disappointment understood" in the final scene in the asylum (p. 275). The visionary consciousness at the heart of the book is never wholly possessed by any of them and, in the last analysis, has its unity only in the mind of the author, yet each of the narrators participates in and contributes some important mythological fragment to it: Baako, more intellectually self-conscious than the man and able to theorize about his ritualized functions, tentatively grafts a cargo-mythology of the ritual dead onto imperfectly understood beliefs about ancestors gathered by the novel from Naana's prologue; Juana, meanwhile, sits for Baako's portrait of Mammy Water and supplies the idea of the "carrying mind". But the viewpoint which comes closest to complete identification with the book's ritual psyche is that of Naana, whose oracular utterances about the "human mother" who "dreams against the coming of her own flesh" preface the main narrative (p. 3). Naana is the novel's "ritual observer", in Frye's term and in the dual sense of "keeper" and "perceiver". As one who foresees and reviews and who subsumes the deteriorative motion of her family's history and the minimal progress of the nation into the flow of a great cycle of being, she acquires considerable authority as the novel's time consciousness. Naana's cyclical vision encircles a discontinuous linear narrative, thus carrying the novel finally back upon itself like the poetic interludes in Awoonor's novel and giving an impression of events as

statically enclosed within an effective timelessness or
time-suspension — a pattern of non-progression enhanced
by the apparent simultaneity of Baako's and Juana's
fugitive flights in the second and third chapters and the
mesmerized slow-motion rendering of event into descriptive tableau in these parallel narratives. Her present-tense
incantatory prologue holds the whole of history together
in a synchronic continuum — "The great friend throws
all things apart and brings all things together again" (p. 1)
— and, as in the first novel's "ritual moments", aligns a
cyclic conceptualization of time with intuitions of an
interconnected traditional community and, additionally in
this novel, an interdependent community of humans and
ancestors. Furthermore, as a fount of traditional wisdom
and spirituality, Naana has an important, if problematic,
practical role as a moral and theological touchstone. Not
only do her monologues and reported conversations insist
upon the superiority of a lost order of value and the
ancient Akan faith in which it had its roots but, more
specifically, her poetic reveries give some guiding indication of the seriousness with which implied continuities
between beliefs about ancestors and a contemporary cargo
mentality are to be taken.

Armah's Ghana appears to be afflicted by many of the
requisite standard conditions for a modern cargo-faith and
the been-to fits with deceptive ease into the prototype of
the cargo-prophet as a well-travelled man trained in
alternative cultural assumptions.[7] But it is a commonplace
of studies of millenarian activities that such faiths must be
cast in traditional moulds if they are to take root
in indigenous cultures and this important condition is
missing from the novel.[8] Baako's inspired exposition
stumbles upon and surprises into expression a set of
bizarre correspondences between the warped mentality
of contemporary cargoism, vaguely grounded in increasingly remote beliefs about ancestor-intermediaries, and

the logic of Melanesian cargo cults. His parallel is an ingenious conceit, not a literal reality, and the divisions of intermediary and dependent, inventor and copier, white and black, are not seen to inhere in traditional mythology, as is often the case in the cargo cult proper, but derive from an inferiorizing and humiliating historical inheritance: "Not a maker, but an intermediary . . . To think of being a maker oneself could be sheer unforgiveable sin . . . The most impressive thing in the system is the wall-like acceptance of the division. Not inherent in the scheme, this acceptance. Inherent mainly in the INTERPRETATION people give the system. Saves thought, I suppose" (pp. 224–25). Caught up in a dependency complex inherited from colonialism, Armah's Ghanaians readily alienate to the white world god-like powers of invention and innovation which they are unwilling to develop themselves. The apathetic Public Works engineer at the ferry — "I was patient, and waited, that's why I have my present post" (p. 200) — represents a whole nation which waits for things to be done for it whilst mindlessly taking over colonial routines which leave it incapable of independent enterprise. Baako's emphatic capitals caution the reader that the cargoist twist and the unthinking acceptance of a slave mentality are matters of modern interpretation, not things inherent in traditional assumptions, and this perception is reinforced by Naana's perspective.

Naana is, of course, herself to blame for implying many beguiling and disquieting resemblances between traditional Akan beliefs about the spirit world and cargoist credulities concerning returning ancestors:

> I saw Baako roaming in unknown forbidden places, just born there again after a departure and a death somewhere . . . All the people were white people all knowing only how to speak the white people's languages. Always, after saying anything, however

small or large, they shook their white heads solemnly, as if they were the ones gone before. Some touched hands, slowly. But Baako walked among them neither touched nor seen, like a ghost in an overturned world in which all human flesh was white. And some of these people bore in their arms things of beauty so great that I thought then in my soul this was the way the spirit land must be. (p. 15)

Naana's dream analogizes America to the "other world" of the Akan *samando* and the stock cargo motif of black men departing to be reborn as white ghosts carrying "things of beauty" is not inconsistent with the Akan belief that the ghosts of the recently departed are, when visible, dressed in white and act as intermediaries between the living and the ancestors.[9] As Baako is about to be "swallowed", cargo-fashion, like a "gentle ghost" by the aeroplane, her imagination transfigures the airport lounge into the Akan royal palaces and her spirit-analogies even slip into cargoist phraseology, the "overturned world" echoing the prophet's announcement that at the millenium "the world would be turned upside down".[10] Naana admits that she herself has not been immune to the "things of heavy earth" and, preparing at the end to cross to the spirit world, asks forgiveness for the "thousand things I had gathered round my body to give it comfort" (pp. 4, 286). Nevertheless, the reader would be ill-advised to embark upon a search for the roots of cargoism in Akan religion. In most West African beliefs the intermediary role of the "living dead" who have recently joined the ancestors entails the conveyance of prayers, not the things prayed for: the spirits are a transmission line for requests and responses, not for the goods themselves.[11] Supplications to the newly departed in Akan dirges and laments are often materialistic ones but they are usually accompanied by a sceptical irony and realistic misgivings about the spirits' power to confer bequests, expressed in the attendant refrain: "If the Departed could send gifts / They would surely send something to their children."[12] Secondly, Naana's conflation of the human and divine worlds, and material and spiritual journeys, is perfectly in accord with the traditional Akan world-view and has little to do with the idolatrous materialism of cargo-faiths: in the seamless fabric of this universe, where one world is always immanent in and contiguous with another, the equality of humans and spirits and the interrelatedness of all experiences within the cycle are a matter of course.[13] Naana's direct communications with the "Great Friend" and *Nananom*, the community of ancestors, penetrate the ritual veils which divide worlds in traditional belief: since, in van Gennep's phrase, "seeing is itself a form of contact", her blindness in the visible world distances her from it and carries her closer to the unseen one.[14] Thus it is natural and proper for Naana to give to Baako's journey between earthly locations at least an analogical continuity, if not a common identity, with the spirit's passage between lives for the reason that "spirituality" is a dimension of all travel since departed spirits are thought to watch over the passage of travellers both into and within this world and to intercede with the ancestors for their safety. Every voyage is a rebirth into a new reality and returns the voyager wiser than when he went: "But what is a traveller just returned from far journeys started years ago if not a new one all over again?" (p. 4). Thirdly, Naana's supposed materialism. The interdependency of spiritual and material in traditional African thought, which has led some Western commentators to deny asceticism to African spirituality, tends towards a corporeal conception of spirits.[15] The Akan live very close to their dead, who are a constant and contactable presence. Indeed, the dead are kept posthumously and materially alive by nourishing food offerings and libations (*Nananom* puns on the plural for "ancestor" and "the ancestor drinks") and are in turn accosted by the living with requests for material returns. Naana sees nothing fundamentally wrong with Foli's mundane exhortation to the spirits for such "blessings and their fruits" at the departure libation (p. 8). But in Akan religious practice the apparently cynical exploitation of spiritual channels for material gain is counterbalanced by the reciprocating spirituality of much apparent materialism. The model for Naana's reverie — its journey motif, compressed allusiveness and incantatory repetition and assonance — is the Akan dirge, and J.H. Nketia's researches into this genre demonstrate that gifts requested of ancestors are motivated less by material greed than by the need for expressions of an ongoing fellowship and solidarity between, on the one hand, the "ones gone before" and, on the other, the living who acknowledge their continuing existence and protection through libations and other acts of communion: a reciprocity instanced in the dirge refrain, "Send me something when someone is coming / Father, you and I exchange gifts."[16] Moreover, the funeral address to ancestors looks for corporate rather than personal gain, and materialism diffused into a communal property ceases to be materialism in its most crude and naked form.[17]

The real change in modern practice, Baako discerns, is not from the spiritual to the material but from the dispersive communalizing of materialism to its intensifying privatization by the Western nuclear family. Additionally, the emphasis in the dirge falls not upon the motif of the returning ancestor, as in the cargo-laden resurrections of millenarian faiths, but on the reverse passage of the spirit's circular return from this world to the next, the "going" here which, Naana insists, will be a "coming" there.[18] A striking and significant similarity between the dirge and Naana's reverie is the play of a material-based imagination around tenuous hopes, vague yearnings and wishful projections. The cargo mentality concretely vulgarizes these into specific expectations and requests, perverting the uncertain and gestural into the explicit and material, as cargo cults proper visibly vulgarize the unseen ancestor into flesh and twist a spiritualized into a spiritless materialism. Drawing naturally upon the devices of analogy and parable from Akan fable, Naana's materializing imagination plays around Baako's American exile as a figure for the spirit's sojourn in the *samando*. The "strange lands" crossed in her mind are no doubt partly prompted by the increasingly foreign Ghana in which she herself has "become a stranger" (p. 14), but essentially Naana thinks — and dreams — in metaphor and, as in many dirges, the similes and conditional expressions confirm the figurative status of the envisaged reality: the white people in the vision shake "their white heads, *as if* they were the ones gone before", Baako is "*like* a ghost in an overturned world", and Naana speculates that "this was *the way* the spirit land must be" (my emphases). Her final proviso about the soul-killing material beauty which Baako needs "protection" from — "Only it was a beauty that frightened also" (p. 15) — undermines the analogy of the two worlds almost as soon as it is made. In her closing monologue Naana admits to the roaming poetic licence which fosters subjective correspondences between the spirit-journeys of Baako and herself, "the habit those about to travel have of seeing a like readiness to go in all else around themselves", but the passage of her human essence into the spirit world and Baako's spiritual crises during and after his American sojourn have already been carefully differentiated as logically distinct experiences which involve quite different readings of "spirituality" (p. 283).

Naana's traditional religious values are not drawn into the cargoist ethos except as sacrificial victims to the new god of materialism, on whose altar Baako's remaining writings, in parodic cargo-fashion, are also offered up. Contrary to Ron Rassner's claim, there is nothing millenarian about Naana's patient faith in Baako's return.[19]

Such faith is intrinsic to a properly ritualized system of behaviour which, measuring out gifts and rewards, duties and dues, governs the cycle of departure and return in traditional belief and selflessly places the individual at a mere stage in a vast cycle traversed by a community of souls. Her moral horror at her family's avarice is in no way diminished by the occasional failure of her own immunity to material temptation, and her vision constitutes an exemplary model of African ascetic spirituality which links moral self-denial and unwordliness with the recycled incarnations of the *okra*, the encapsulated spirit or ongoing human essence. Naana's final anticipation of her rewards from the spirit-community she is about to enter — returns worked, not waited for — could not be further removed from the slavish dependency and fatalistic apathy of the cargo mentality, given its most extreme form in the providentialist faith of the "nexologist" and roundly condemned by an Akan culture which prizes thrift and personal independence. "I am in need, please do this for me," runs one Akan proverb. "That is how some men become slaves."[20] Naana's tracing of both slavery and modern consumerism to the psychology of dependency follows traditional lines of thought: "The origins of slavery were traced by the Akans to the loss of independence by shiftless persons who depended on others for their livelihood and security."[21]

When her grandson and companion-spirit, exhilarated by his own ingenuity, further explores the correspondences of Naana's dream in the more discursive form of the cargo conceit, it is with an awareness that the connections are preciously poetic, not solidly historical ones, and that African religious faiths have no more nor less cargoist potential than any others. But the closeness of the poetic analogies indicates how less discerning sensibilities than those of Naana and Baako might be deceived into discovering unholy continuities between the two. In a faithless age the search of the surviving religious emotions of awe and wonder for a correlative object in the external world drives them to modern technology's glittering profane paradise of material objects. The novel's "unconnected eyes", unable to see beyond surfaces, crudely materialize the narrators' metaphors by treating returnees as reborn cargo-spirits. "Oh, they have made you a white man," cries Sissie Brempong. "The big man has come again . . . The air where he has been is pure, not like ours" (pp. 81, 85). Efua beholds her newly-arrived son as a semi-supernatural being, enquiring after his car "in a near-whisper filled with wonder and gladness" (p. 101). The demented fantasy of Bukari's mother, who cannot wait for her son to "come again" with his "many things", is seen to transplant the Western world of commodities visited by the been-to into the spirit-world: by the pseudo-logic of the new magical materialism, her unseasonable death is a sign of her impatience to get into these regions of purer air (p. 132). Both Efua and the old woman at the airport act out the pathetic faith of Baako's surreal nexologist, respectively squandering savings on house foundations to get back the return of the whole edifice and spending a "last cedi . . . to come and welcome someone's swollen peacock" (p. 85). "Kill the pigs, burn the crop and wait with faith," comments Baako. "Throw the last coins, brokeman" (p. 229). These welcomers follow "no mere laid-down ceremonies", however, but ones of their own devising, prompted by private greed. In Armah's fictional polemic cargoism is not an emanation from traditional faith but is tied up with colonial legacies — is, in fact, another gratefully received product of the ex-colonial West. Its samples (Mercedes cars, neon advertising, wigs and skin-lightening creams) are aimed by Euro-American powers at the markets of underdeveloped countries with a view to keeping these imitative of and magically dependent upon themselves by creating demands for products which the buyers can ill-afford and which deepen their degradation. In Naana's mind, cargoist dependency is an inverted continuation of slavery, with white salesmen and black buyers replacing black salesmen and white buyers: it is rooted in "the same long destruction of our people when the elders first . . . split their own seed and raised half against half, part selling part to hard-eyed buyers from beyond the horizon, breaking, buying, selling, gaining, spending till the last of our men sells the last woman to any passing white buyer and himself waits to be destroyed by this great haste to consume things we have taken no care nor trouble to produce" (p. 284).

Such is the transforming energy of corruption brought by a strenuous modern ingenuity to bear upon traditional forms that it is easy to overlook the fact that the novel's myths and rituals are as innocent of corrupt intention as are traditional beliefs about ancestors of any lurking latent cargoism. Far from having any inherent potential for the insidious ends they are made to serve in the modern world, traditional practices serve as the source of an alternative and corrective moral vision. In *The Beautyful Ones Are Not Yet Born* ancient customs appear to be still moribundly alive and potent with their own corruption, like the still viscous, aged filth in the latrine tunnel. In *Fragments*, however, the commanding impression is that they have died and been cynically resurrected in altered forms which have no kinship with their original spirit and, as if having ghostly lives of their own that refuse to be denied, are set to revenge themselves upon their violators. In 1965 S.G. Williamson wrote of the contemporary Akan that, although competitors for "an untraditional economic and social opportunity express themselves in traditional attitudes . . . financial considerations appear to have taken precedence over correct behaviour towards the spirit ancestors" and ancient customs are "valued because they are traditional rather than as expressions of a live belief".[22]

Correspondingly, in the Ghanaian 'sixties of the novel, the traditional order appears to be fighting a hopeless rear-guard action from underneath a deadening weight of dislocating subterfuges and obfuscations. Asante-Smith camouflages his sycophantic opportunism as traditional respect for elders — "Yes, Mr Onipa, we'll be taking pictures of your elders who freed this nation" (p. 214). Praise-songs pass to toadying television producers, folk-myths into neo-colonial propaganda. "The myths here are good," Baako tells Juana. "Only their use . . ." (p. 172). Rituals like the outdooring ceremony resurrected by the Onipas are no longer "expressions of a live belief". Nevertheless, the sudden death of the past and its baleful residual effects notwithstanding, the traditional order is given a more positive and dynamic continuity with the present through its living representative and spokes-woman, Naana, and its dead order of value insinuates itself as a living presence in the novel. This presence is felt in the opening libation which transports Naana "away into a past" where everything is "full of understanding . . . as if all this crowded present had never come at all, and days and years already gone had come again to live with us" (p. 6). Foli's ritual utterance momentarily conjures into being the hallowed interdependent community of humans and spirits bound together by the libation in traditional belief — "You are a piece of us / of those gone before / and who will come again" (p. 5) — and, in Naana's surrounding reverie, this stands in sharp moral contrast to the fake contemporary community and false sharing of this world, in which the family exhorts the traveller to deny his own interests only in order to further its own: "Do not be persuaded you will fill your stomachs faster / if you do not have others' to fill. / There are no humans who walk this earth alone" (p. 6). Prior to the outdooring's misplaced emphasis on the exhibition of private wealth and prestige, Naana issues proper reminders both of the original communal importance of the rite of incorporation which carries the child from one corporate existence, among the spirits, to another, in the living society, and of the subsequently precarious status of the child, "only a traveler" between the worlds of spirit and flesh.

The novel's metaphorical complex of birth and impotence also touches upon important links with the past. Mbiti writes that an African woman's "failure to bear children is worse than committing genocide; she has become the dead end of human life, not only for the genealogical line but also for herself".[23] In Akan myth this dramatic association — the pseudo-murder of not procreating — takes the form of the barren and destructive Earth-goddess whose namesake in the novel, Efua, is suspected by Naana of "looking hard for ways to push me into the earth deeper than where my navel is buried" (p. 278). Efua tells Juana that children are the most important things in life, "giving the statement the quiet finality of truths held to be self-evident", and a few moments later tears the green stem from "a yellowish leaf, freshly fallen" (pp. 50, 52). The deathly symbolism with which Armah surrounds birth and growth draws powerfully and graphically upon traditional fears in its ritual equation of infertility and infanticide. Those murder who do not create, those who cannot make destroy: the syphilitic dog-slayer; the impecunious nexologist who impotently destroys what little he has left; the contemporary cargo-devotees; the television technicians wrecking the last disputed set which, as short-lived as Araba's child, has only "a brief moment in which to reflect the sunlight" in its "pearly smoothness"; Araba herself, effectively sterile in the miscarriages which leave her childless. Juana discovers that only "abortions of contact" are possible in the "aborted town" of Accra, where green is the colour not of freshness and growth but of sickness, premature decay and death: the "green filmy luster" on the Principal Secretary's teeth, the green-gauzed windows of maternity wards which turn away expectant mothers, and the green fruit which, in Naana's analogy with Baako, is plucked and devoured "too unwisely soon", causing sickness and disease (p. 282).

"The barren have no face in the Other World," runs one Akan proverb, expressing the customary fear of the long-term consequences of childlessness.[24] Naana's reference to an old woman as "the pregnancy that will make another ghost", telescoping the stations of the circuit of birth and death, is an instance of the extreme humanism which conceptualizes the ancestors as dependent children who have to be fed and cared for by living adults (p. 10).[25] "Be kind to me: a new child coming back to you," is Naana's final prayer (p. 286). A death here is a birth elsewhere and the destinies of the newly born are bound up with devotion to the ancestors who watch over them and with care of the elders who are closest to the ghost world from which the new shades or *sunsum* are sent. Foli's scanted libation simultaneously cheats "those who have gone before and even those coming after us", and Efua's more serious omission at the outdooring draws Naana's parallel comment: "They do not look to those gone before, and they do not see the child" (pp. 9, 263). But what is most pertinent to Araba's childlessness is the belief that new pregnancies perpetuate the memories of future ghosts. The begetting of children to secure one's "personal immortality" is traditionally a prime reason for marriage. The dead have their lives prolonged in the remembrances of their progeny, who give them a continuing earthly "face" or identity during their stay in the ghost world, and are apt to bring down illness and misfortune upon living relatives who deny them personal immortality by forgetting them.[26] "Did no one also teach you the power of the anger of the departed?" Naana rebukes Foli, claiming that the neglected spirits would have turned their anger against Baako (p. 12). In the perfect circle of Naana's belief a similar fate attends the early forgetting of those who, either in the physiological or ritual sense, are not yet "dead". Such hasty oblivion is certain to take its toll on the careers of those literally not yet born — the child fails to come five times and then comes prematurely — and of those who have left the womb but have yet to complete all the ritual phases of birth. In Akan belief, to have forgetful children is as bad as to have none, and the childlessness visited upon Araba is a traditional form of poetic justice: those who quickly forget the old ones are allowed no progeny so that they themselves will be quickly forgotten at their deaths. Neglected ancestors and elders alike withdraw their protection from the newborn, and there is more than a hint in Naana's thought that the rapid succession of Araba's five miscarriages betokens a punitive spirit-child's whirling circle of untimely deaths and re-births: "one of the uncertain ones" who has "refused the world several times", the child may be "only a disturbed spirit come to take a brief look and go back home" (p. 138).

In the actual circumstances of the Onipa outdooring, the allusions to the undermined order of value become more specific and damning. In one traditional version of the ceremony, the *kpodziemo* of the Ga people of Accra, "the child is blessed by an old person of the father's lineage, chosen for his (or her, if the child is a girl) admirable character, which is supposed to be impressed on the child." Wine is drunk only "after the ancestors have received their share" and the ceremony always takes place on the eighth day after the birth: "After birth the child is kept indoors for seven days; it is then held to have survived seven dangers and is worthy to be called a person."[27] This traditional yardstick makes glaringly conspicuous the Onipa family's general remissness, in the matter of the fifth day staging, and its particular omissions, namely the libation and the grandparent's formal contact with the new arrival to keep the birth-death cycle intact.[28] Naana's warning that the child is still "in the keeping of the spirits", expressing the traditional fear of supernatural trouble during the first week of a baby's life,[29] goes unheeded, and the family's impetuous refusal to observe the proper timing and sequence of events causes them to lose and change their places in the natural cycle. Thus, the newcomer is sent back into the spirit world ahead of its great-grandmother and the career of a potentially normal child is accelerated into that of the ghost-child whose feared presence is traditionally a threat at the Fante outdooring ceremony: "For the first eight days after birth, the child is regarded as a 'ghost child' who may return to the land of spirits; it is therefore treated rather negligently; it lies on an old rag or mat . . . it is not really encouraged to feed at its mother's breast . . . On the eighth day, the *Ntetea* rite is held: the father brings gifts to the mother and child."[30] The grotesque exaggeration of selected negative elements of the tradition in the novel is tantamount to its total denial. The ritual pattern of systematically restrained negligence is made to license a maternal apathy — "It's so tiring, having to deal with the children" (p. 123) — which is crucial in the fatal neglect of the child. Similarly, by reducing the offering to a few dregs and finally to nothing, Foli crudifies the half-welcoming, half-discouraging ambivalence of the libation, which traditionally offered the ancestors morsels to prevent them from joining the feast.[31] For the Akan reader there is an additional sinister resonance in the father's gift, which in this case is an untraditional one but which is nevertheless full of dark associations from traditional folk-lore. The outdooring present draws upon the ancient Akan song "Owuo Papa", the Death Fan whose winds blow the "uncertain ones" back into the other world of the *samando*, which traditionally "a place of shades and cold" in Akan belief and is, in some African beliefs, the generator of whirlwinds inhabited by hostile spirits.[32] A line from the song which remarks upon the fan's weak current stresses the fragility of the *sunsum* or unformed personal ego: "With no more force than the wind stirred by a fan, Death can at any time blow the *sunsum* into the other world."[33] With a chilling obviousness, Kwesi brings the gift of death to his son. His eager fifth day present transforms the palm-leaf fan of the song into the monstrous modern form of an electric fan, capable of generating a blast which is more than enough to return the infant to the shadow world. Naana, at the end of her life, is so close to this other world that she no longer feels the cold when she sits outside in the evening — "I'm a person no more" — and figuratively conceives it as a place "filled with many winds" (pp. 2, 15). In a sense, the death-winds from the *samando* are blowing towards the sons of the Onipas throughout the novel. They rustle through the conversation at the meeting of Efua and Juana and when the former speaks of the importance of children and is asked about her love for her son, the wind ominously carries her words away unheard (pp. 50, 52). The clairvoyant, ghostly Naana is especially sensitive to the "new confusing turbulence of wind" in the household and her instincts tell her that her own destination and that of the child, "shrouded" funereally in rich clothes, are one and the same: "What do they want with this wind machine? . . . Everything is wrong now" (p. 284, 266–67).

From the moment of Araba's return home with the child, an occult congregation of random instances in the chapter "Awo" implies the gathering forces of an offended moral order and envelops the coming ceremony in an aura of unnaturalness and mounting danger. In the course of the chapter the signals are posted at increasingly short intervals: Baako's horror at the urgency of the desire to make money out of the child; Araba's unnaturalness as a mother, demonstrated by "the plain fear she had of being left alone with the child"; Araba's sexual blackmail of Kwesi, using her "secret weapon" to subvert the sexual reciprocity of husband and wife in a way that puts Baako in mind of the deathly copulation of insects (pp. 123, 128). In the latter business the moral logic is transparent: the withdrawal of the procreative act engineers the event which destroys the fruits of that act, since it is Araba's threat which causes Kwesi fatally to advance the outdooring. The vignette in the Cafe of the Silver Shooting Star furthers the impression of approaching danger. The example of Bukari's mother warns against disrupting the natural cycle of events by precipitate action, and the ominous background song is about a "stranger" (echoing the "little stranger", Araba's child), who will be "away tomorrow / giving life to worms" (p. 134). Baako, in unwitting rapport with Naana's thinking, warns Kwesi that "special care" must be taken over the premature child. More portents of the monstrous and unnatural enter with the drunken sacrifice of the ram by the hunchback Korankye, who drinks most of the libation himself and, the botched ritual over, desecrates the family's solitary stunted mango tree by wiping his blood-stained knife on its leaves. Naana's warning, at the end of the chapter, of the dire consequences of the early outdooring comes as the natural culmination of these forebodings chiefly because of the trouble Armah has taken to orchestrate events in ways which invite the reader to view them from Naana's moral and teleological perspective.

Underlying the whole presentation of the child's birth and death is a layer of references to Akan mythology which reinforces Naana's world-view. Araba's child is born in the last week of September and dies after the early outdooring ceremony five days later, on the second day of October. Its short life straddles the week between the autumnal equinox and the New Yam Festival which marks the turning of the traditional agricultural year in southern

Akan states.[34] The changeover period between years in traditional cultures, when the end is very close to the start and the dying closest to those being born, is also a time of cross-over when, in van Gennep's words, "the dead leave their abodes and come to have a taste of earthly life", and this mythology of the periodically returning dead informs a number of the novel's features: cargoism, the "reincarnation" of elders' characteristics in their grand-children which links Naana with Baako, and, most important in the context of the outdooring, the idea of earth-spirits standing guard over the newborn child during its first week of life.[35] It is significant that New Year purification festivals like the *Odwira* were also first fruits festivals which involved regenerative blood-sacrifices to the goddess of the Earth — *Asase Efua* in her fertile, procreative mood, *Asase Ya* in her barren persona.[36] In Armah's Fante-speaking part of the Akan world, however, the earth is known only as *Asase Efua* and in her vindictive, destructive moods carries the tag of "the killer Mother" and "the Mother of the dead".[37] "Awo", the title of the chapter which covers the child's week of life, means "birth" in Akan, but *Awo* was also the word cried aloud at the *Odwira* before the offering of human sacrifices to the Earth goddess: according to legend, *Awo* was the first human being offered to *Asase Efua* to make the earth fruitful, with the result that the name became synonymous in Akan lore with human sacrifice.[38]

Armah has woven into one of his fragments a deft web of traditional ritual and myth. The mother, Efua, is repeatedly linked with the earth: not in its fruitful character, however, but in its negative associations of worldliness, materiality, infatuation with the things of earth. Her dreams for Baako are, in Naana's words, "woven of such heavy earth that they will load his spirit down and . . . it will never fly again", and the walls of her dream-house get no higher than the earth, her own desire to fly frustrated by earth-bound lusts. The newly born in Akan belief come up from the underworld of spirits and the eight day period between their departure from *Asase Efua's* element and their public outdooring coincides, in the case of this birth, with the interval between the harvesting of her fruits and its ceremonial observance at the First Fruits Festival. The money-making outdooring ceremony which thus substitutes for the harvest festivities, giving artificial pay-cycles priority over the seasonal cycles of nature, is turned by Armah's web of allusions into a sombre Earth-ceremony, a grim inverted fertility-rite presided over by Efua in the role of the "Killer Mother" who murders the grandchildren arriving with the harvest. "A human mother should not have such dreams against the coming of her own flesh," says Naana in her opening indictment of Efua's unnatural behaviour. "Even cats have learned to turn the hunger for the newly born against their own entrails" (p. 3). In the death-scene it is Efua herself who switches on the fan, "turning the air current directly against the cradle" (p. 265).

The offended Akan Earth takes a double revenge upon its misrepresenting mother. Firstly, the ancestor-spirits whose sacred day (Sunday, the day of the *Adae's* commemoration of ancestors) is appropriated for the outdooring and to whom no libation is offered, take back into the underworld the child still in their keeping. Secondly, the earth-spirits reject Korankye's bungled sacrifice and are made by the poetic logic of events to demand the greater sacrifice of the child itself: a fitting punishment for those who abuse the earth's fertility at the time of year when it is ritually renewed. The idea of "natural justice" executed by an angry earth is repeated one year later in the death of Skido in the chapter "Igya" (sacrifice). Skido brings the harvest to market but his lorry is held up at the ferry for three days by those who, like Efua, value things (in this case, steel) above human lives and who spurn the nourishing fruits of the earth on which life depends. Consequently, in the panic rush to board the ferry, Skido dies a recognizably sacrificial death, an offering to the river with his skull crushed like that of the dog.

Armah's recourse to Akan religious mythology and, specifically, to sacrificial ritual practice is not merely gratuitous or ingenious but has a twofold purpose. Firstly, it demonstrates how far modern Ghanaians have strayed from the beliefs of their ancestors and how the most vital human values enshrined by those beliefs — the sacredness of human life, the gradualness of growth by natural time-processes — have been abandoned for the worship of the trinkets of Western technology. Against a framework of ancient faiths, the latter idolatries acquire the force of a monstrous blasphemy against life. Secondly, the patterns of sacrifice focus the sombre insight that it is only the trauma of death, whether from maternal neglect or bureaucratic incompetence, which has the power to shock contemporary Ghanaians back into a sense of real value. The sense of human dignity reawakened by Skido's death prompts the ferry people to what is only the second spontaneous act of community in the novel. This is the nocturnal recovery of Skido's mangled body by men and women working quietly and impersonally together in the dark in a collective disgust with, and defiance of, bureaucratic indifference. Only the crises of birth and death bring out what is still good in Armah's Ghanaians — "Brother, it's only the blood of a new human being," declares the kind taxi-driver who rushes Araba to the hospital — and only in these sudden moments of fraternity can Baako find any faith in his people. At the ferry he helps to haul in the ropes with the others, recalling the fishermen pulling in the nets to the boy's song in the other "communal" act of the previous chapter. Here is a different Ghana, an inverted night-image of the day's anger, danger and death, the calm after the sacrifice, but the peace and dignity are heavily purchased at the price of Skido's death. One of the many possible reasons for Armah's deferment until the eleventh chapter of the revelation of the child's death is the suggestive juxtaposition of the chapters "Iwu" (Death) and "Obra" (Life) before Naana's epilogue. The placing of these chapters invites the reading that something of value emerges as the fruit of sacrifice: most particularly, there is the inference that Baako's recovery from madness somehow grows out of the death of the child with whom he is constantly identified, thus reversing the earlier metaphor which made the child's coming analogically dependent on Baako's re-emergence from his American breakdown. The word "Obra", which emphasizes the ethical life, infuses a hopeful hint of moral enlightenment and the getting of a bitter wisdom from error into the scene of Baako's final disintegration.

The connection between Baako and his infant namesake and the traditional avuncular responsibilities urged upon him by Naana at the outdooring draw upon arcane areas of knowledge but the import of the allusions is revealing, both of the extent to which Baako falls short of the traditional order of value and of this residual code's limited applicability to contemporary life. "Why did you not stop your sister and your mother also from this foolishness?" Naana demands of him. "Kwesi is the father. I have heard you. But the child is yours to look after . . . The blood that flows in Araba is yours, Baako, and the child is yours also if it is hers. So what has he done, that you will fold your arms and let them destroy him?" (pp. 139–40). In Akan belief the blood-bond between child and maternal uncle is a strong and fundamental one. But it is a bond which exists by way of or through, rather than with, the sister: significantly, before offering his own health-giving blood to save Araba

and the child, Baako dissociatively washes away the taint
of her blood, the "rivers of bad blood" mentioned in her
talk of miscarriages. Furthermore, since the maternal
blood, or *mogya*, in Akan spirit-physiology is the substance
from which is formed the ghostly *saman*, the spirit or
shade of the person at death, whilst the paternal *ntoro*
does not go on to the spirit world, the bond is not the
crude physiological nexus proposed in Robert Fraser's
account but, on the contrary, is of a ghostly, ethereal
nature.[39] Both travellers who hover between worlds,
Baako and his infant charge are bound by their common
transitionality. The child, "uncertain" like his temporary
earthly custodian and still under the guard of his spiritual
ones, is yet part ghost and is soon to be made one again by
the family which also tries to make a ghost of his uncle:
firstly, a symbolic cargo-ghost in the funereal departure
libation, and finally a real ghost in the murderous chase
across the city. That Baako's "invisibility" is not merely
that of the cargo-ghost, whom Efua looks through and
beyond at what he is meant to provide, is indicated by
the fact that he becomes "invisible" to his mother at
the precise moment when he is prompted by Naana's
exhortations into a feeble gesture of protest and protection
regarding the child (p. 141). Because of the blood-bond
which, in the most literal sense, he shares with his sister to
help bring the child from its ghost-existence in the other
world and which will be the substance of the child's
eventual life as a spirit, Baako has most influence over the
child in what pertains to its spirit-being: it is his task to
take the child into his moral custody and watch over its
welfare during the crucial "ghost-phase" of its transitional
passage between worlds. At the end of this period its
ghost-status is terminated and it is formally received into
the community in a rite of incorporation in which the
blood-bond of the child and the communally-minded
uncle again figures. In the matrilinear society of the Akan,

social obligations and communal status derive from the blood-group. The maternal *mogya* provides for a solidarity with the extended family (and, through this, with the wider community), beside which the personal and clan ties of the paternal *ntoro* are of secondary importance.[40] Thus Baako's failure to stop the debased ritual marks the capitulation of corporate values, vested in the blood-nexus of the matrikin, to the new exhibitionist individualism, as represented by the wealth-displaying patriarchs at the ceremony and the selfish behaviour of the father.

As so often in the novel, the progress of events colours the narrative with Naana's world-view. Baako, in his disinterested concern for the child's welfare, is a better father than Kwesi, whose sexual anxieties allow him to be pressured into endangering its life. But there are limits to his upholding of the past. In Fante custom the authority vested in the *wofa* or maternal uncle, an authority which is residual in Foli's baleful influence over the family, gave him the power to remove his nephew from the father's care in the event of poverty or negligence.[41] Baako acts spontaneously to bring his spiritual ward into the world, but he has no power or will to stop Kwesi's and Araba's abuse of the ceremony. His saving act is too sudden and too late and, since he has no conscious knowledge of them, he is, in any case, unable to recognize and honour the special obligations enjoined by obsolescent customs. "The world has changed," he answers Naana from the standpoint of the Western nuclear family. "I'm only a relative. I cannot stop them from doing what they want with their own child" (p. 140). Moreover, no one looks for moral guidance to Baako, an immature fledgling maternal uncle: they seek only the prestige which his educated presence lends to the proceedings. Although he is intuitively alert to the wisdom of traditional ethical imperatives, Baako's own moral malaise shows that they no longer have any currency in the contemporary world or claim upon the new generation of Ghanaians.

As much of this chapter has been given over to speculations about the peripheral role of the traditional order in the novel, it would perhaps be wise to close with some assessment of its real value, measured against its effect on the action. In this respect, the dormant Akan ethos of *Fragments* behaves very much like the purification rite in the first novel. The order it draws upon is one of positive value but it is a dead order, artificially resuscitated by the author to infuse some moral energy and vision into a spiritual wilderness, and systematically declaring its absence from and failing relevance to modern life. The centrality which it assumes in the novel's composite psyche is disproportionate to its minimal influence on individual behaviour. Once again, Armah has gone to great lengths to draw up a detailed backcloth of non-functioning values from his knowledge of traditional ritual practice and belief. This ambivalence, generally present in the workings of Naana's framing narrative, is most poignant in her epilogue's mixture of reaffirmation and despair. The novel's finale holds in apposition contrary ideas of cyclicality and terminality, process and endings, after the fashion of the Mammy Water/Maanan apposition at the end of the first novel. Naana's death, in her own view, is subsumed into a cycle of renewal and restoration, and the historical decline of which it is part is only another development in the unceasing progress of the spirit. But from the more material viewpoint of her age, the deteriorative historical process has already subverted this circular motion. As it closes the cycle of the novel's year, Naana's death leaves hanging over the end of the book the impression of having also brought to completion the age of cyclical belief. "Naana" is the singular form of *Nananom*, figuratively rendering the grandmother as the last fragment of a community of elders and ancestors: indeed, she sees herself as "the remnant of something that passed by and was immediately forgotten" (p. 278). In the final and most realistic analysis, the Akan world-view which permeates the novel's ritual psyche and colours its value-structures exists only in the consciousnesses of its sole surviving elder and its author. Naana effectively sings her own funeral dirge since no one in the family will sing it for her and, accustomed now to its scanting of ritual dues, foresees that "in the end there will not be too many left to close with dust of gold" the body's apertures to ease the spirit's passage to the next world after Akan custom (p. 279).[42] Moreover, there is a sense in which the death of Naana's beliefs precedes her own death. Not only is the perfect circle irreparably broken and its sequence unnaturally disturbed — "The little one is gone; soon he will be the elder of his great-grandmother there" (p. 284) — but the family's shameful neglect of her last days makes Naana herself a reluctant accomplice to this dislocation by provoking her into an equally unnatural welcoming of death, a trespass beyond the proper fearful resignation of custom which she is fully aware of: "Such inward readiness to go does not come if this world here has room and use for us" (p. 278).[43] The prologue's confident affirmation that "nothing in the end is lost" is answered by the epilogue's painful realization that nothing of the end of her life is worth conserving since it has not "brought with it peace and the good stillness which understanding brings" (p. 279). In the closing reverie the characteristic circularity of Naana's thought is accompanied by other and quite foreign concepts of death as the linear arrival of the individual soul at some final rest or relief, as a permanent state rather than a phase in an ongoing sequence through which the spirit moves in an endless round. The eternally reincarnating *okra* or impersonal human essence has now become "my soul looking to find its home . . . where there is understanding to give a tired spirit rest" and arriving at "the last of my veils" (pp. 282–83, 287). Naana speaks of the segmentation of experience into broken pieces by the veils of this world, "veils that rise in front of us, cutting into easy pieces eternity and the circle of the world" (p. 286). In effect, the disruption of the ritual passage has turned the afterlife into another fragment, broken off from the other phases of the circle. Naana's valediction, with its circular refrain of "going" to "come" at an "end" which is also a "beginning", owes more to the Akan dirge and ceremonial hymn than to the Book of Revelation, but it is prefaced, significantly, by a Christian resurrection hymn.[44] The linearization of Akan eschatology into Christian salvationist and apocalyptic terms, vulgarized in the religious slogans on buses and mammy-wagons, and the growing emphasis on the personalized soul in her meditations suggest that Naana has not escaped complicity with the decline and demise of her traditional African beliefs. Their infiltration by notions of terminality signals their own impending termination.

There is no other force in the novel which is capable of halting this decline. Naana's spiritual successors, the indigenous and foreign outsiders Baako and Juana, are both too far removed from knowledge of the ancient traditions which she cherishes to purge them of modern infections and restore value to them. Uncomprehending of and unresponsive to her overtures, Baako is culturally and temporally remote from the traditional community which is the source of Naana's wisdom. "But these days the community has disappeared from the story," he theorizes to Juana: it has been replaced by the family which is "supposed to get rich, mainly at the expense of the community" (pp. 146–47). "The community" retains its currency as an idea in Baako's head but it has, in practical terms, disappeared from the second novel as from the first. Baako, who has visited his ancestral village only once and long ago, expresses a "desire to find out more about the illiterate people's images and myths for use in his work", whilst conceiving of the people themselves chiefly at the level of myth and allowing them only the shadowy and remote coherence of screen images (p. 218). When he confronts them in the flesh, in the fishermen-scene, Juana surmises that "he was seeing all this for the first time in his life" (p. 182). The boy's gift to the fishermen of "something they didn't have" makes his song a communal service, a vehicle of a collective vision, since they take it over and briefly make it their own, and Baako struggles to find something of relevance to himself in this sample of the traditional artist's role. But his own "songs" — his abstract screenplays and cargo-theories — are not expressed in the impersonal, self-effacing, communal medium of traditional African art and, appropriately, it is the boy-singer who is allowed to walk off with Mammy Water's trophy, in the form of Juana's washed-up bra, whilst Baako flounders in self-consciousness. Juana's parallel and more practical quest after social solidarity leads to the first novel's familiar anti-community of locked-in lives: only here the more violent tensions and repressions demand an equally violent release — "something that had stayed locked up and poisoned the masculinity of his days" is discharged from the dog-killer (p. 29) — or an emotional outlet like the frenzy and hysteria generated by the fraudulent fraternity of the revivalist beach-prophet. The only "authentic" community which the meditating minds of the novel have to offer is not an earthly one: it exists in Naana's prayers, in the form of *Nananom*, the community of ancestors.

Given the naturalistic mode of Armah's fiction, a reversion from Baako's modern cargo-intermediary of flesh and blood to the original "unelaborated system" of a spirit community answering calls of human distress — a world "where the been-to has yet to make his appearance" and the departed "intercede on behalf of those not yet dead" (p. 224) — is never a real option for modern

Ghanaians. The cyclic passages and transactions between the seen and unseen worlds which haunt Awoonor's novel have no significance beyond the metaphorical for Baako who, unlike his grandmother and Amamu, is not ready to trade a physical for a spiritual existence. Naana's monologues offer an abstract, other-worldly alternative, not a practical corrective. The strong intimations that her traditional view of the universe is better than what has replaced it, or what it has been corrupted into, are balanced by the realistic admission that there is no longer any way to draw upon the old in order to improve or temper the new. *Fragments* does not fatuously urge a return to values rooted in a way of life that has vanished: Naana's is a lost and failed order that cannot be restored. The problematic positioning of her circumscriptive narrative at the outer ring of the novel, implying at once an absolute overview and her peripheral remoteness, her distance from the centre of things, leaves uncertain the final value which is to be attached to her religious vision. Juana's sections, placed at both the centre and the edges of the book, provide a more balanced and accurate focus on the contemporary setting than Naana's shadowy metaphysical presence. It is perhaps significant within the novel's fine mesh of correspondences that when Baako addresses the dead Skido, as Naana does the ancestors, he is insane, and when he picks up her musings on encycled ghosts he is at the verge of mental collapse. Naana's spiritual meditations, like Baako's artistic ones, are, it seems, tokens of madness in a materialistic age. The hedonistic ethic of the Ramblers' song overheard by Juana fragments time into a succession of discrete, intense moments — "Happy are those whose life is today and only today" (p. 47) — and Juana's itinerant thoughts linearize life into "a long stretch of danger with both ends unknown" (p. 33). The timeless perspective of the Akan world-view which frames and contains the novel's interior linearities is also undermined and exploded by them. Naana's is not the least word in the novel, but neither is it, except in the most literal sense, the last one.

VII

Colonialism as Erotic Ritual: The American World of *Why Are We So Blest?*

Following the tremendous formal accomplishments of the first two books, Armah's next three novels show serious failings on formal grounds. More particularly, the African presence in these novels, an increasingly polemical and ideological one, is disappointingly thin after the richly textured early work and, since it is not the kind of presence that I have been concerned to investigate in this study, I shall deal with the latter half of Armah's career in more summary fashion.

In *Why Are We So Blest?* Africa has only a mute, peripheral presence, consistent with its focus on Africans spirited away from native cultures by Western education. The lonely pondering minds of its anglophone and lusophone narrators record no family ties and few memories of home, and only three of the novel's journal entries have sub-Saharan settings. Even then, "setting" is a misleading word because, except in the vivid rendering of a war-dilapidated Algeria under the thin guise of "Afrasia" at the beginning and the desert atmosphere of the close, Armah takes little trouble in this work over the sensuous evocation of authentic fictional locales. Places are no more than their names: Harvard, Washington D.C.,

Lisbon, Laccreyville. The book, like Modin's journal, is "more like concatenations of ideas" than a novel.[1] In the static 170-page expanse of diary entries between Solo's first two narratives, in which the appointment with Jorge Manuel is made, and his last two narratives, in which the appointment is kept and comes to nothing, most of Modin's output and all of Solo's are given over to pure exposition. During these "exchanges" — a rapport which is not the interaction of living people but the posthumous dialogue of ghosts — there is minimal or zero narrative development and a rarefied thinness of texture which is unparalleled in Armah's writing. It is as if the discursive sixth chapter of the first novel, or the screenplays and cargo-expositions of the second, had suddenly expanded into the narrative and assumed command of the entire fictional structure.

"The beauty comes from the patterns," says the Moroccan engineer who tempts Solo with a simplifying panoramic view of Laccreyville from an overlooking hill, and the novel's partly self-undermining aesthetic is one which shows more interest in patterns and processes than in the individual complexities of people. In terms of Modin's abstract model of high and low, according to which there is "high information in the centre, low information on the peripheries" and "overall clarity is potentially possible only from the central heights", the novel's own viewpoint is the safe, lonely eminence to which Western education has removed the alternately assimilated and alienated African intellectual (p. 33). It is the view from Olympus, comprehensive but simplified by its remoteness: a vantage point variously manifested as the hilltop retreat where the failed revolutionary Solo privately cultivates his agonies of shame; the lofty peaks of the Ivy League paradise where the African student is guiltily drawn into the ranks of the American "blest"; and the plush upstairs U.P.C. offices and managerial mansions to which the executives and diplomats of the revolution have been carried by the struggles of sacrificed militants. If the blest in the novel are thinly-drawn caricatures who reveal little of their inner lives, the damned, from the prospect of their distant heights, are also faceless abstractions, comprising one crippled *moudjahid* and an anonymous army of orphaned beggars. The exclusive focus on the personal careers of the half-blest, half-cursed who wander between them has the disadvantage that it tends to make the guilt-traumas of the *évolué*-conscience seem more interesting and important than the mass deprivation it agonizes about. Moreover, it fails to give concrete embodiment to the politico-economic processes by which educational selection-procedures and Western monopoly-capitalism collaborate to retard the client state's growth, and the subsequent over-emphasis on the personal wickedness of Western educators takes the novel into the magical realm of conspiracy theory and the metaphysical one of inherent racial diabolism. "You interest yourself in abstractions. There are concrete problems," Ngulo tells Solo, and the novels stands accused of the same charge.

The three-storey universe of *Why Are We So Blest?* is an ideographic construct with the dramatic evidence and character histories left out and the enemy easily identified: it is "The West" and, beyond that, the whole white race, fired by a pathological lust for destruction and materially powerful enough to replenish its spiritual void by draining the superior vitality of its victims. In the first two novels the West is not wholly diabolical: it is at least the source of Ghana's post-war prosperity and the writers' workshops of its universities nurture Baako's creative gifts as well as generating the hostility to Western materialism that drives them. In these works the main enemy is not the white world but the Ghanaians who, mindlessly or cynically, adopt its worst elements, and the many vignettes of taxi drivers and street sellers leave no doubt about the Ghanaian people's collaborative infatuation with the alien values that are destroying their culture. The third novel crudely polarizes this more densely textured world into a Western "centre" and "peripheral" masses awaiting Promethean deliverance from its "manipulation, mystification, planned ignorance" (p. 33). Armah has not entirely lost sight of the Koomsons and Brempongs who enslave their people from within but now even the betrayers are recast as victims. The Jorge Manuels are themselves manipulated and, albeit willingly, programmed into positions of privilege and prosperity by Western educational schemes which isolate them from the people whose revolutions they profess to lead.

In *Why Are We So Blest?* the intricate metaphoric labyrinths of the first two novels have given way to a bold diagrammatic design, the richly complex symbolism to a single-minded telegraphese. Into a single archetype are subsumed the "thick walls" that protected the original slave-factor, the "thick-walled dishonesty" behind which America trains his modern counterparts, and the steel walls of the colonial mansions of the Maghrib, penetrated but not demolished by revolutionary bullets and now insulating the revolutionary elites: their manifest differences are carelessly dispersed, the fine distinctions diffused. The colonial regime in Kansa sees Africans "the way a hunter sees a snake" and, to Modin, the departing French soldiers have "the look of beasts of prey cheated of their prey but still eyeing him" (pp. 40, 275). Between them come the Afrasian managerial cadres who absorb agronomy from colonial textbooks, spend their nights hunting hyenas and live in ex-colonial fortresses decorated by paintings of hunting beasts. This facile, uninvestigative kind of symbolism — really a kind of mechanical insignia, spotlighting only superficial similarities — gives a spurious inevitability to the conclusion that the French-educated Tahar is, in some vaguely associated and unspecified way, a new variation on the old theme of colonial predation. It overlooks the complexities of the case at hand: in this instance, the question of how a war-impoverished nation, damaged at birth, can be expected to survive except through its existing resources and inherited expertise. Sometimes the paradigms are too blatantly signposted and clumsily stage-managed, as with Modin's remembering a childhood visit to the old slave-castle during his flight to America and the awakening of an atavistic lust to re-undertake the middle passage. With a too artful precision, the remembered pains in his back and neck look backwards to the tortures inflicted by American slavers of the past and forwards to identical wounds inflicted upon himself by one of their contemporary academic equivalents. The flight into the future returns him to the past: "Factors then, factors now," runs the underlying message.

The race–sex archetypes picked out by Solo's doubtful x-ray vision regress in the course of his narrative from slaves and mistresses to imperial plunderers and prey. Following his opening match-flare impression of Modin as proudly displayed showpiece-Negro in tow to a fake white radical, Solo observes: "He just sat silent, looking at the girl. There was so much pain expressed in his long look . . . For a moment I saw something elemental in that look, something so old. The face itself was young, but the expression on it could have come from the depths of ages and ages of sadness" (p. 59). Modin's premature ageing at the hands of his American persecutors is a thin covering for a mythical substratum which fixes him in the ancestral attitudes and postures of the "niggerized" African, obediently suppressing his initiative in attendance upon the white girl whose pack he carries. Modin's quiet feline movements are ill at ease beside her "long, loping strides" and "awkward angularity", so their identical outdoor dress suggests that all the integrative accommodation has been on his side. Seldom allowing the symbolism to speak for itself, Solo concludes that they are "two people so different, yet so willfully assimilated", and his ensuing rhetoric of "wide, endless expanses, dotted with lifeless things, hard and unbreakable" as the "perfect environment" for Aimée's "destructive wildness", telegraphs the novel's ending (pp. 56, 62). Aimée is a barbaric being who belongs in the wilderness but, more specifically, she is a creature of that figurative desert which, in this novel and the next, symbolizes a ubiquitous and desiccated white culture whose vampiric existence is maintained by draining the non-white world of its vital resources. "There is nothing here, not even sand," runs Modin's last entry. "Everything is hard, stony" (p. 278). This "nothing" is Aimée's natural element: in its endless, undifferentiated expanse the universal monolith of white civilization is able to reveal its true nature. Here, all modes of whiteness — terrorists and liberals, racists and revolutionaries, Europeans and Americans, all apparently alike in their attitudes to blacks — need no longer feign enmity but can combine their destructive passions. "You're just like him, you know," Modin tells Aimée when she fails to understand that the O.A.S. driver stops for her and pretends not to see him. Incredibly, with Modin bound in the back of the O.A.S. jeep about to be sadistically murdered and the driver already speaking of him "as if he were dead", Aimée blithely muses: "The desert was open. A lot of space. I forgot the situation I was in. There was freedom out there. It made me happy to be here. The driver turned into a sandy area . . . The dunes were identical in some places. When he stopped he said with a loud, free laugh: 'Eh bien, nous sommes arrivés'" (p. 284). They arrive in a nowhere which is everywhere, a white landscape in which everything, like themselves, is the same. The setting is a mere prop for poetic concepts, a backdrop for symbols:

the novel has taken flight into a region of pure metaphor. *Why Are We So Blest?* is an over-insistent, self-conscious piece of myth-making with hard symbolic outlines and low specificity. As such, it is the least "African" of Armah's works, and Solo's vague allusions to the "African soul", or Modin's speculations about a new *maji* to combat Europe's status-seeking individualism, do little to disguise this fact. The novel opposes to its stereotypical idea of the West an equally stereotyped, stage-set Africa, shorn of its multiple complexities and contradictions, and the higher visibility and sparser texture are especially noticeable in the areas of ritual and mythology. One of the secret strengths of the early novels is the subtle subtextual pattern of ritual process which runs beneath and often counter to the narrative. The ambivalent mood of apocalypse and regeneration which envelops the purification motif in *The Beautyful Ones Are Not Yet Born* invests the coup with the momentousness of a potential turning point in Ghanaian history: the opportunities for fundamental change and new beginnings are there, even if the collective will proves too weak to make use of them. Similarly, in *Fragments*, the Onipa family has the theoretical option of embracing the artistic gifts that Baako, like the singer in the Mammy Water myth, brings back from across the sea, though in practice they see him only as a transmission line for material cargo. These ritual options in the fictive subconscious are absences which have the power of presences, negatives which function, albeit with guarded promise, as positives. In the third novel, however, these quiet potencies have been dissolved along one of two courses: either modes of behaviour are stripped of their familiar ritualistic dimensions or the latter are emptied of their suggestiveness by being made explicit and overt. Among the first kind, the revolutionary carriers in the paradigm offered by Solo to the crippled *moudjahid* are not even mock-sacrificial figures who gesture towards revolutionary awakenings but cynically duped pawns, their lives wasted to fuel a war which installs a new French-supported hierarchy in a "colony only freshly disguised as a nation". Solo's introjection of the real or imagined accusations of practically everyone he encounters — the engineer, the *mutilé de guerre*, Ngulo, the beggars — is pure paranoia, an entirely personal guilt-neurosis. Both narrators employ ritualistic terminology for the figurative burden of their complicity with a hostile white culture. "The initiation was a quick death of the hopeful spirit," writes Solo of his discovery that the inequalities of white institutional structures have infiltrated black revolutionary leadership. But the burden borne by these spiritually ailing figures is an individualized one of guilt-ridden privilege which separates its carriers from the African community, not a common burden of shared suffering which links them with it. Aware that they are unable to remove any of Africa's suffering, Modin and Solo wallow in a private remorse that daily distances them from it.

Under the second category, the unapparent is made too apparent, the subconscious becomes self-conscious. This is due to a change in the nature of the novels' rituality, from a covert subtext, charged with independent potentialities and determinisms drawn from an outgoing African tradition, to an overtly extraneous, self-advertising presence peculiar to an incoming American one. This is the "alien communal ritual", the grotesquely artificial arrangement of the American educational process to which the African is humiliatingly subjected. No beneficial enlightenment awaits the neophyte at the end of this passage, which inculcates not intelligent apprehension but mindless obedience to the dogma of Western superiority. Modin's intelligence penetrates the "rites of secrecy" to discover that the priests of the American Olympus educate the crossovers from the Tartarus of the

Third World only because these have certain roles to play and needs to fill within the imperial system: firstly, to foster Western values and protect Western interests in their own nations and, generally, to govern them by proxy for Western overlords; secondly, to serve as the object of America's philanthropic charity and proof of its munificence and thus to demonstrate to the world the fundamental rightness of an unequal system which allows the high to help the low without any real danger of dissolving the divisions; thirdly, to provide America obligingly with an opposing fantasy-image of "primitive inferiority" to complement and consolidate its own complacent self-image of "civilized superiority". In this latter role, the modern "factor", the scholarship holder, is paid on the condition that he will dutifully decry his race when prompted and confirm that his exceptional intelligence proves the general rule of African stupidity. Armah's white Americans have no interest in the African's mind or, indeed, in any aspect of his individual human reality, but only in "mythical qualities" concocted by the fantasy life of the Western sexual imagination, such as a special animal vitality and extraordinary sexual prowess, and the compliant humouring of these fantasies entails the numbing of the spirit and the voluntary death of the intelligence. By day the obedient puppet of his neo-colonial academic masters, Modin is by night the exotic rarity needed to titillate the jaded appetites of their wives and daughters: "I was another rare creature, an African vehicle to help them to reach the strange destinations of their souls" (p. 167). After Europe's economic plunder of the continent comes America's psycho-sexual consumption: either way, the West uses Africa in the pursuit of its own ends. The whole process of this "elitist ritual for selecting slave-traders" enjoys, on both the political and sexual levels, a kind of doomed pre-ordination which makes white values and neuroses the black man's fate and the African's life a creation of whites. "Our disease is ordained," Solo concludes. "What is ordained for us I have not escaped — the fate of the *évolué* . . . the assimilated African" (pp.222, 84). In a world where white-imitative aspirations permeate even anti-white revolution, it is no surprise to find the novel's sole traditional African image — the mask of Ananse — in the custody of a black American academic integrant. Neither is it odd to find the complementarity that marks much African ritual process viciously appropriated in the defence of universal inequalities by that most pernicious product of the American academy, Mike the Fascist: "Matter of fact, blessedness as a state can't exist without its opposite . . . Paradise has two poles now . . . It's got heavens — and hells, as you say — built into it . . . There's Olympus. Below that there are the plains of mediocrity. Then Tartarus. You must agree that's a much superior arrangement" (p. 100). This Western-controlled, fabricated form of rituality is given its most deliberately theatrical expression at the "sacrificial" climax, where the French terrorists swoop in, fate-like, from the desert to crucify and castrate Modin on the back of an O.A.S. jeep whilst Aimée, as malevolent American priestess, erotically prepares the passive victim and then catches his blood.

The new ambience of self-conscious pseudo-ritual allows Solo to toy, in bitter self-mockery, with the notion of his present stagnation as the liminal phase of a purification rite, as the fertile dung from which a new cleansing energy will issue: "I should help myself survive here by pretending my bathing in this present filth is a preparation, a sacred apprenticeship, a getting ready for some larger purifying vocation, but I cannot . . . This filth is no mere station. It is my terminus" (p. 84). The ritual symbolism no longer undermines but is itself undermined: it does not control the protagonists but is now controlled by them. The character-narrator Solo, as chief editorial agency, has moved into the place of the author.

Robert Scholes has written about myth: "Once so much is known *about* myths and archetypes, they can no longer be used innocently. Even their connection to the unconscious finally becomes attenuated as the mythic materials are used more consciously. All symbols become allegorical to the extent that we understand them."[2] If *Fragments* corresponds to Frye's account of ritual form as a sequence in which "the conscious meaning or significance is latent" and is "largely concealed from the participators themselves",[3] then the over-sophisticated analytic style of *Why Are We So Blest?*, which contrives to bring myths and archetypes into the full glare of consciousness, is closer to Scholes' model. One of these, the myth of Prometheus, is given a powerful thrust in the novel's metaphoric structure by the pervasive allusions to fire, entrails, livers and predators, but, at the same time, the very contrived explicitness of the allusions insinuates a self-critical element which bodes ill for Prometheus' credibility as a figurehead for African liberation. Modin is, of course, an ironic Promethean whose attempt to shed privilege and place his gift of education at the disposal of oppressed humanity dooms him to a useless and unenlightening death. His is the fate of that most pathetic product of a Western liberal education, the academic revolutionary who, without the practical skills necessary for participation in a proletarian struggle and already half-poisoned by the values of the oppressor, actually hampers the revolutionary process. Moreover, long before the final fatal fellation which is a gruesome variant on Prometheus' punishment, the harpy-ridden hero is weakened from within, torn by the torturer he carries on his own back: the predatory Aimée, an American version of the Promethean eagle fastening onto what Solo calls "black carrion". His every move monitored by an Olympian, Modin is effectively a counter-revolutionary force and he is not alone in his predicament. At the headquarters of the Congherian

revolution in Laccreyville (Lackeyville?) he is surrounded
by parody-Prometheans like Jorge Manuel, their entrails
hardened to nothing except their own hypocrisies and
their revolutionary ardour burnt out by the destructive
white fire they bring back from the West in the form of
European and American mistresses: a fire designed to
burn its bearer, not illumine his followers. Addicted to a
folkloric faith in revolutions as dangerous and exciting,
Aimée goes to Kansa because "if there is fire left anywhere
that should be the place" (p. 143). But no fire, political or
sexual, emanates from the white-washed Kansan ministerial elites Aimée sleeps her way through — "The fire
doesn't exist anywhere. I'll always be bored" (p. 145) — or
from Congheria's revolutionary exiles. Beyond these basic
ironies, however, the novel's polemical scrutiny of its own
metaphors raises doubts about the value that the Promethean legend, or any item taken from the mythological
store of the oppressor, can have either as a blueprint for
revolution or as a model for progress in Africa. America,
in the novel, assumes that it has a monopoly on everything that is desirable (including white women) and, like
colonialism in Fanon's dictum, wants everything to come
from itself, even models for revolution. But, since it is
Olympian fire that is stolen in the fable, the Promethean
model is necessarily tied to an irrelevant Western myth of
progress along divisive Olympian lines which are either
inadequate to Africa's very different needs or downright
destructive of her potential. In the last analysis, Prometheus is another Western undesirable whose fire, a
Western-originated gift contaminated at source, is not
worth the stealing. Far from serving as a source of
regeneration and illumination for Africa, Armah's
America is a leech-like creature which revives its exhausted sensibility by siphoning off the emotional and
sexual energy of its African visitors. Instead of absorbing
life-enhancing knowledge, Modin squanders himself on

the sexual rehabilitation of what kills him. America offers the black Prometheus no knowledge that is worthy of the name — its "advanced study" constitutes the stale racist propaganda that Africa had no history before the white man came — and the only reliable knowledge he acquires is not from the system but of the system: a paralysing knowledge, since it does not tell him how to change it.

In the Promethean image of the third novel the lone champion-hero and burden-carrier reaches his simultaneous apotheosis and exorcism in Armah's work. The Promethean Superman becomes the supreme expression of a European heritage of elitist individualism, deeply opposed to the communalist solidarities of the African tradition, and is viewed as a built-in component of self-glorifying Graeco-Roman cultural myths which America, as Mike reminds Modin, has proudly made her own: "The crossovers, the heroes, were proof of Olympian justice . . . because of them everyone could see the deserving among men rising to Olympus" (p. 102). The system of "Promethean" reverse-crossings devised by American educational programmes co-opts into power a minority from the underprivileged to help it keep the many out and, in Armah's cross-cultural conspiracy-cartoon, ensures that the cause of black revolution is perpetually self-defeating by maintaining a subversive input of Western-educated intellectuals into the leadership. America expends a few philanthropic flames to dampen the revolutionary blaze and the small loan of fire by their Promethean bearer is returned with interest to stoke the Olympian furnace. The prototype for the real revolutionaries — the slain or mutilated militants — is not Prometheus' free enlightened descent but Sisyphus' blind uphill struggle, futile because its repeated failure is ordained within the Olympian system. Fleeing the bad faith of the U.P.C. office, Solo feels something of this toiling futility: "All the way up I must struggle against a force that seems many times stronger than the one that pushed me down" (p. 15). Modin's overriding preoccupation with the creation of new value systems and ideologies out of the African sensibility, to replace those taken from her and as an alternative to borrowing from the alien, effectively rules out both the Promethean and Sisyphean options as foreign models, prejudicial to Africa's progress upon independently and authentically African lines. At the same time, one of the weaknesses of *Why Are We So Blest?* as political polemic is its failure to define the course such progress would follow under a new *maji*. The silent presence of alternatives is sensed during Modin's heated exchange with Mike in the dining hall:

> "Even staying in your mythology, you shut out the Promethean factor."
> "I guess that's a reverse crossover. No. I didn't want to shut it out. But it's unique. Besides, who has the idiotic ambition to go through the crossing twice: first a heroic, then a Promethean crossing? That's insane."
> "Only according to your mythology. There are other myths, you know." (pp. 101–02)

Of course, the mythologies of Modin's West African coast are abundant in gift-bringing reverse-crossings: Ogun's recrossing of the transitional gulf to unite gods and men, a recurring motif in Soyinka's work; the visionary return of the singer from the sea in the Mammy Water myth; the manifold circular returns of neophytes to structures in African rites of passage. But the novel's internationalized voices say nothing of these "other myths" and contrive to give the impression that, on a Europeanized earth where Africa is a mere prop to Western supremacy, African myths are either extinct or have lost their authenticity; that there are no remaining intellectual or spiritual properties which are not white-originated. The novel's symbolism of the Quest for the Centre — with its Sacred Mountain, its zone of Absolute Reality and ritual desacralization on the initiate's return to the profane world — is, in fact, common to most world mythologies.[4] But Armah's separatist vision in this book makes it the exclusive property and ploy of the alien, a Western (and so anti-African) weapon which can be allowed no African parentage. For the first time in his work, the "other myths" are completely silent.

This despair of a positive political mythology is reflected in Solo's anxiety over appropriate artistic form and his awareness of his complicity with the Promethean pattern. When the black race has to borrow the style and narrative techniques of the destroyer to bewail its own destruction, writing itself becomes an act of betrayal. The novel's aesthetic form reflexively declares its achievement to be worthless, signalling its author's arrival at a terminus and the imminence of some radical formal innovation: "There is no creative art outside the destruction of the destroyers. In my people's world, revolution would be the only art, revolutionaries the only creators . . . I search these notebooks . . . speculating, arranging and rearranging these notes to catch all possible meaning. Is this creation?" (p. 231). It is not, Solo argues, because, informed by no coherent and constructive ideology, his rearrangement is no more than an aesthetic refuge from chaos, a spurious unity patterned from fragments. The dislocated time schemes and multiple consciousnesses express only the splintered life of the Europeanized évolué and, more seriously, the fragmented art — what Solo calls the "discrete beauty" — of a despised European modernism. Solo's seduction by Western aestheticism parallels the political and sexual entrancements of Manuel and Modin: his art bears the Olympian seal of approval and is essentially designed for Olympian/American, not African, consumption. Employed at the *Jeune Nation* office alongside Frenchified Arabs still obeisant to European culture, Solo lives the vicarious life of the Western translator, "consuming quietly other people's works of art" and producing imitative works which, like the reverse-crossover of the educational model, are diversionary and gestural, not revolutionary. He makes interesting art out of defeated revolution, aesthetic success from political failure. *Why Are We So Blest?* is Armah's *Prometheus Bound*: it turns thwarted rebellion and its punishment into high tragedy for the purification of an Olympian conscience which perversely craves remorseful, exorcizing insights into its own iniquity. Its editor is an artistic middle-man or factor: "To be an African now, and a mere artist: to choose to be a parasite feeding on spilt entrails" (p. 232). Of no practical help to Modin's Prometheus, Solo becomes another of his parasites and voyeurs, using his diaries to realize his artistic purpose as Aimée uses their author to realize her perverted sexuality. By his own account, he is not a creator but a "bloat-eyed watcher sitting over other people's pain, using it, surviving on account of it" (p. 149).

The novel is a milestone along Armah's chosen route out of the circle of the African "blest". More particularly, it signals a way out of the dilemma of the African "factor-writer" who is invited to enrich himself by writing about black oppression for a primarily white audience: this literary capitalization on distress is, of course, one of the channels through which revolutionary energy is disarmed and harmlessly absorbed from circle to square, periphery to centre, plains to sacred mountain. Armah's dissatisfaction with inherited artistic forms was already discernible in *Fragments*, although it had not at that stage come to include the narrative itself. Ocran's reclusive, self-enclosed art creates rings of sculpted heads which progressively refine "inward torture" and "extreme agony" into "sweet repose", and the female chorus of Afro-American singers at the airport gives the lone male voice something "to catch his pain and make it into something almost sweet".[5] Mammy Water's lover makes his richest music from pain and loss at her departure and at the end of Baako's country tour the villages full of "maimed people and sickness . . . remained beautiful in his mind" (p. 190). Even the fisherboy's song, though dynamically involved in the work-process and able to lift the men temporarily above the materiality of their work, is, in the end, discarded and forgotten in the stampede for fish: even this vestige of the African singer's traditional art is finally functional, sublimatory and merely self-rewarding. At Orly Airport Baako looks up from where an old man skates endlessly round in a circle to read an inscription: "TOUT HOMME CRÉE SANS LE SAVOIR / COMME IL RESPIRE / MAIS L'ARTISTE SE SENT CRÉER / SON ACTE ENGAGE TOUT SON ÊTRE / SA PEINE BIEN AIMÉE LE FORTIFIE" (p. 74). Armah seems to have in mind here the stereotype of the Western Romantic artist who wrestles with his own unique individual destiny and narcissistically cultivates his private agonies without making any attempt to break out of the circle of the self. This sublimation of suffering and beautification of pain for the purpose of private purification, effectively justifying it in the name of "tragedy" or "necessity", is regarded by Solo, and by the oracular narrator of the next novel, as a deadly perversion.

The radical shift of focus goes hand in hand with a "deritualization" of the fiction which enables it to break free from the fatalism implied by ritualistic and cyclical structures. No doubt, this was partly prompted by the fear that carrier and scapegoat archetypes enshrine the cult of the special, outstanding individual and uphold a subjectivism which Armah has been keen to avoid in his later work. There was also, perhaps, a growing distrust of ritual process as a diversionary substitute for real change: a kind of opiate which distractingly subsumes social and political action into metaphysical idealism, leaving obscure the exact form that change would take and the ways in which it would differ from the present dictatorships of elites. But most important for the artist, the process of ritual introjection from the collectivity to the individual and the merely intellectual absorption of ills were suspiciously close to the Western artist's aesthetic sublimation of the general woe into some "inner space", the private consumption of public suffering alluded to by the airport skater and inscription. When the carrier figure was himself miscast as an artist, the similarity was doubly apparent: for "ritual form" could be substituted "aesthetic form". The more reflexive form of *Why Are We So Blest?* clears away much of this earlier confusion. Unfortunately, however, its explosion of obsolete ritual structures is succeeded by the manufacture of some specious new ones, which are most conspicuous in the novel's minefield of sexual metaphors and myths.

In this book metaphor does not merely encroach upon reality but infiltrates it entirely, turning itself into it, and the main responsibility for this lies with the author's determination to see interracial sexual relationships as a microcosm of Africa's historical encounter with the West. Aimée's frigidity creates for her a compensatory need to sexualize everything in the world, and to hunt down in public reality what has been denied her in private: African politicians are simply there for her to sleep with, political history lectures exist to feed sex fantasies, and orgasms are sought in Psycho Labs. This makes her a ready tool in a politico-sexual allegory which telescopes one thing so obsessively into another thing that it effectively becomes that thing, turning association into identification, correspondence into confusion. The tenor of a metaphor is frequently submerged in and swallowed up by its vehicle, so that Armah, perhaps, imagines he is telling us about political processes — principally Africa's deadly molestation by the West — when he is, more probably, speaking of sexual ones and, even then, with such scant objectivity and slavish recourse to stereotypes that one thing is seldom made to stand convincingly for another. Jorge Manuel sums up the novel's thesis: "Look, an African in love with a European is a pure slave. Not a man accidentally enslaved. A pure slave, with the heart of a slave, with the spirit of a slave" (p. 255). The irony of Manuel himself dancing attendance on a ghastly, nigger-hating white hag makes his scornful indictment self-inclusive and, tacitly, all-inclusive. Still clutching at a decaying liberalism, Solo speaks in his opening narrative of the "mysterious thing of love . . . the attraction of one person to his opposite, the power that brings the white to the black and leads them all to open to each other areas of themselves which they have long kept hidden from everybody else" (p. 12). His subsequent disillusionment frames the perception that, far from changing the collective situation, attempts at private remedies by individual blacks and whites only re-enact racially predetermined roles. The refuge from history which Tahar hypothesizes for Modin and Aimée — "a place where people can love and not be disturbed" (p. 243) — does not exist, and it is Solo, trained in the more intolerant Portuguese assimilation programme which demanded the cultural self-extinction of its évolués, who is made to see what the more liberally anglicized Ghanaian cannot: that the lethal aspects of Western imperialism extended beyond the political and military arena even into the most private corners of individual relationships. By the racist tenets of the novel, black expectations of white friendship, under the misguided impression that certain basic human values transcend racial divisions, are universally suicidal. In this book, any American who is led to suspect the presence of an African culture which is opposed to white domination and which refuses to glorify its supposed benefactor is immediately and involuntarily seized by the killer-instinct:

witness the sudden hysterias of Oppenhardt, Jefferson
and Aimée. The moment its mystifications are challenged,
as by Modin, America's grinning condescension cracks
into psychopathic rage.

Armah does not merely suggest that black–white relationships which are destroyed by inherited cultural
stereotypes are common and therefore typical. His argument seems to be that the colonial model of exploitation
and servitude provides the definitive pattern for and is the
key to *all* such relationships. From here it is a rapid
rhetorical stride to the inference that colonialism and its
modern variants are in fact most supremely themselves,
and find their quintessential expression, in the terms of an
interracial erotic ritual. The result is that each of the
novel's sexual relationships is passed through a political
"blender", in which personal and political fates — the
private disposition of black to white and Africa's relationship with the West — are so mixed as to become virtually
indistinguishable. The acquisition of white mistresses is
not merely incidental but is integral to Ndugu Pakansa's
refusal to join the independence struggle and Manuel's
introduction of a class hierarchy into his government-in-
exile. The colonial-sexual paradigm postulates a quasi-
organic, causative connection between the events, which
are physically present in one another. Under its govern-
ance, the proximity of the white woman universally spells
the magical debilitation and emasculative decline of the
black man, and the sexual attraction of blacks to whites is
uniformly characterized as a "sickness" or "disease". One
of the many bizarre metaphorical transpositions is of the
West's consumption of African economic resources to a
correspondent draining of sexual energy: "What kind of
love fires the white-haired American, sucking life that
cannot fertilize her dryness, from sources already several
times desiccated?" asks Solo. "What is her species of love
but the same ancient white hatred of Africa, taking rotten

form in her dry, decayed body? What is she doing if not taking care to kill the possibility itself of anything good being born in Africa?" (pp. 208, 229). Armah is careful to leave Solo's mysterious "failure of nerve" as an activist both undescribed and unexplained, and the methodical elimination of alternatives inevitably thrusts personal responsibility for the undermining of his political aspirations and his present defeatism onto the frail figure of the Portuguese girl Sylvia and a single rejected marriage proposal. The corollary is that avoidance of close contact with whites and, most especially, resistance to white sexual charms are promoted into articles of the new revolutionary faith. Unfortunately, this habitual identification of white seduction with political infiltration, fusing political tenor with sexual vehicle, leads to some absurdly false and unreal oppositions, such as the American stud service as the been-to's natural alternative to renewed contact with his people's deprivation (p. 208), and to some oversimplified and misleading parallels, notably that of Sylvia's browbeaten submission to her society's petty racism and Aimée's vicious psychopathy (pp. 139, 149–50). Only an allegory of black–white relations, presented in remorselessly destructive sexual terms, could overlook such gross inconsistencies: redeeming white virtues are outside the scope of Armah's racial polemic, as the white depravity manifested in genocide and slavery are outside the scope of Mike's crass Thanksgiving editorial.

The novel's sexual allegorization of 1960s American politics produces a gallery of flimsy white stereotypes and repetitive relationships in which revolutionary energy, black and male, is sapped by the powers of reaction, white and female. Paternalist conservatism, preaching a politics of deference which urges the black man to "prove himself" to the white man whilst infantilizing him into something between a child and a pet, is represented by the Jeffersons. Sandra stands for liberal reform and a civil rights-

based integrationism which balks at intermarriage, and
Aimée typifies a bogus, thrill-seeking Marxism which
attaches itself to the causes of underdeveloped, and
especially black, minorities. Finally, there is the black
American Naita, the tender and expert lover who warns
Modin off white women and in the next instance shares
with him the complete and fulfilling orgasm which he will
not encounter on any of his crossracial sexual forays. Thus
is black separatism swiftly indexed, in the allegorical
scheme, to a monoracial sexual harmony and equality, as
is integration to sexual discord and exploitation. Each of
these vignettes is successful within the paradigmatic
limits: the model begins to wear thin only when the
pressure of a fully developed character — Modin, Aimée
— is brought to bear upon it.

The Radcliffe girl bored with the brilliance which gets
her "the inevitable A" every term, Aimée is meant to
represent, along with her myopic professors, the shabby
best of American academe. The jaded scholarly appetites
of the Harvard dilettantes — "They looked tired, like
people who were looking for something new to do"
(p. 121) — are clearly intended to be seen as the academic
equivalents of Aimée's sexual ones. Moreover, these
American historians fashion Africa and Africans after their
own stale and ignorant images, as Aimée does after hers,
and Armah hammers home the sex-scholarship connection by giving the settler-uncle of her rapacious
colonial fantasy the name of Jahnheinz Reitsch and having
her fantasize orgasms to the statistics of massacred Maji-
Maji rebels in history lectures. Black American apologetics
furnish ample evidence of America's hobbled white
intelligence which, brilliant in other respects, mysteriously fails when it has to deal with black people. Afflicted
by this syndrome, Aimée can admit the sharpness of
Modin's mind only after reducing him imaginatively to a
serving-boy. But even outside of the race-context, Aimée's

embarrassing juvenile gaucheries and abusive slogan-eering rhetoric — "He was bourgeois . . . He was slow to embrace revolutionary experiences" (p. 138) — are not the marks of an arguing intelligence. Alternatively, her Faustian flaunting of rebellion before a failed rebel, fantastically promoting Solo into "an indispensable part of the machinery of bourgeois reaction" (p. 140), shows the academic facility for abstracting ideological models and types from human complexities to be advanced almost to the point of insanity. At the realistic level, the characteriz-ation of Aimée outrages the reader's desire for objectivity and fair play as well as his common sense, and it seems more plausible to regard her, as does Robert Fraser, "not as an individual person, but as a matrix for all those vices which Modin comes to see as most characteristic of white America".[6] It is as a generic concept, an artificial construct harbouring the collected vices and racial neuroses of her country, that the character coheres, and its origins are neither literary nor African but are to be found in black American polemics of the 1960s. "Unless we call one white man, by name, a 'devil', we are not speaking of any *individual* white man," wrote Malcolm X. "We are speak-ing of the *collective* white man's historical record, the *collective* white man's cruelties, evils and greeds, that have seen him *act* like a devil toward the non-white man."[7] Black separatisms founded on the principle that there is nothing of value in white civilization were the logical rejoinder to integrationist concepts founded on the princi-ple that there is nothing of value in black civilization, concepts now dismissed by Black Power as "a subterfuge for the maintenance of white supremacy".[8] Out of this polemical crucible came the unanimous attitudes towards whites in the book and the character of Aimée.

Aimée is an almost allegorical personality, seen as an agent of destruction — a "devouring spirit", "an instru-ment of death" — rather than a human individual. Armah suppresses whatever complexity she might have and gives her virtually no traits other than the frigidity which represents white America's arid sensibility and, contradictorily, the depraved sexual hungers which symbolize the West's plundering of the manpower and material wealth of a subsequently impotent Africa. Aimée's rapacious sexuality is principally a political metaphor, significant for its exploitative and reactionary nature. In Africa she sleeps with the bourgeois elites and identifies with dead *colons* in bullet-holed bedrooms which revive her fantasy of Modin as Mwangi, a colonial serving-boy. Her lecture-theatre fantasies, in a bullet-like splatter of semen and blood which anticipates the last bloody fellation in the desert, release libido not for the promotion of revolutionary violence but for its violent suppression (p. 185). In the light of the novel's overtly politicized sexuality, the improbable finale is perhaps best read on a purely abstract level: for example, the terrorists' use of Aimée to arouse Modin so as to moisten her, in turn, for their own use, can be taken to signify the white world's tantalizing temptation of the African with privileges which he desires but is not allowed to enjoy, whilst perversely siphoning off Africa's energies for its own profit. The politico-sexual allegory also makes some damaging intrusions into the characterization of Modin since it requires him, in his representative role of Africa, to be an innocent sacrificial victim and infatuated slave to Aimée, in her role as imperial America, even though it must be obvious to his intelligence that her sick fantasies repeat to the last detail the Jeffersons' earlier scenario of white impotence, nymphomania and revenge which almost killed him. Modin is both theoretical analyst and participant in the process he analyses, and his stupidity in the latter role is irreconcilable with his personal astuteness in the former. The overworked symbolic shorthand which transforms Modin from articulate African separatist to look-alike white, resulting in the absorption of Dofu ("the one who loves") into Aimée ("the loved one"), is of the same order as the bleaching of the uniforms of the Congherian rebels as they change from a Citizens' Revolutionary Army into a white-imitative hierarchic institution, and makes the same point: in a white-owned world, whiteness always wins.

Africa is still Armah's subject in *Why Are We So Blest?* but the informing background to this book appears to be predominantly American and to relate to a particular period of black American politics. The novel has its setting and genesis in Armah's first American visit and education at Harvard, from 1959 to 1963, but it was completed after his second visit, from 1968 to 1970, and its provocative racial polemics and sexual myths represent a stage of black revolutionary thought much later than that of the period in which the book is set. In the intervening years black American consciousness had come of age and, following the failure of the civil rights movement to achieve any concrete changes in black living conditions, integrationism had given way to a militant separatism. The sources of racism were variously located and different remedies sought in social reform, Marxism and Islam, but usually with the tacit agreement that racism now had a life independent of its origins, that it had become an all-pervasive phenomenon ingrained in the national sub-conscious and, whatever its causes, would not disappear with their removal.[9] Accordingly, black people were now to be regarded as a wholly separate group, identifiable solely by race, transcending frontiers of class, religion and nation, and not affiliated to any liberal or radical white body. The new polemics, not content with the rejection of selected racist elements of white civilization, branded whites as, unexceptionally, "the enemy" and dissociated themselves from the whole white edifice, including white revolution. The Black Muslim hymn which furnished Armah's novel with the metaphors for its secularized political theology proclaimed that "The White Man's Heaven is the Black Man's Hell" and it seemed safer to assume that white blessings were automatic portents of black damnation than to view them as interests which black people could identify with.[10] Clearly, the new separatisms coloured Armah's thinking in his third novel and prepared the way for the amputation of black values from white cultures in the novels which came after. In his American-published essay on Fanon at the end of the decade, he scorns all alliances with white radicals and, in the novel, Earl Lynch's secret Marxism is derided as another racist "white philosophy" which seeks only to overturn white social classes. More particularly, Black Power apologetics provided Armah with his prototype for Aimée, the sensation-seeking, fake white radical for whom revolution, like crossing the Sahara, is merely one more touristic coup: "All too frequently, many young, middle-class white Americans, like some sort of Pepsi generation, have wanted to 'come alive' through the black community and black groups. They have wanted to be where the action is — and the action has been in those places."[11] In the lurid terms of the Fanon essay, white liberals, left-wingers and hippies have a common need for "the exciting experience of black suffering" and a "splashing in someone else's blood so they can feel alive", and identify with blacks because blacks are "in their minds the same as poverty, dirt and the smell of syphilitic goats".[12] "Do all Americans think revolution is the same as filth?" Solo enquires of Aimée (p. 261). The Black Muslim preachers supplied the novel with its rhetoric of "white devilry". "There would be no reason to talk to a European as to a human being," Mzee Nyambura tells Aimée, who is habitually imaged as an engine of destruction or demonic contraption, an "object" or "thing" mistaken by Modin for a human being: "Why could he not see his companion? This was an object, destructive, powerfully hurled against him from the barrel of a powerful, destructive culture" (pp. 37, 115). The opposite of human, Aimée and Manuel's satanic white mistresses are "mere bodies" or "dead tissue" from which the spirit has fled and which have been inhabited by a succubus-like sexuality that "sucks life" from black prey (pp. 159, 95, 200). They are last seen in the conspiratorial performance of some kind of diabolical "white" mass in the café, in celebration of Aimée's ghoulish triumph in the desert.

The novel's racial polemics are best seen against the backcloth of a 1960's black radicalism which interpreted American race-oppression as a species of internal colonization and, specifically, against Black Power's systematic comparison of American integration schemes with French and Portuguese colonial assimilation programmes: an exercise which revealed the operation of a colonial-style practice of co-optation markedly similar to the isolation of elitist African "factors" outlined by Modin, and an ethnocentric racism tied to the white supremacist concepts of the *évolué* and the *assimilado*.[13] Conversely, as the African experience, according to Black Power, became the American one, so the American experience, for the visiting been-to, became the African one. Solo is finally spat upon and called "nigger" by Aimée, Modin is addressed as "boy" by American academics. The agonized face of Lynch's Ananse mask presents an African image of its owner's compromised life, marginalized and disembodied almost to invisibility, but its overall implication is that the elitist been-to entangled in the web of Western education and the black American academic, "caught in the white net of minds", are alike in their predicaments (pp. 32, 163). For both, Ananse the Spider's conventionally misguided wisdom has not furthered his usual exuberant freedom of invention but has opted instead for a meanly self-preserving, self-denying entrapment. Ironically, the mask mirrors the very condition which prevents its ignorant owner and, to a lesser extent, its African admirer from properly understanding it. The drift of Armah's meaning is that some Africans are as deeply compromised by Western culture and as radically severed from their own as American blacks, so that the American "Negro" is no longer a unique hybrid but occupies an extreme position along a line being rapidly travelled by each newly-uprooted member of the black race: the common fate is "the utter alienation of himself from his people and his past". Subsequently, the traditional black invisibility which runs through American writing from Melville's *Benito Cereno* to Ellison's *Invisible Man* becomes, in *Why Are We So Blest?*, the lot of the African, whose education is "designed to reduce us to invisibility while magnifying whiteness" (p. 31). Sylvia reacts to Solo's proposal "as if she had suddenly been asked to search for something invisible" and the novel's white women automatically walk past and talk over black men as if they did not exist (pp. 63–64, 39). As with Indians, so with blacks, Modin informs his Harvard colleagues: "Your forefathers wiped them out physically. Every year you wipe them out symbolically. And your intellectuals wipe them out mentally" (p. 99). An American-style racism, with its fine shades and gradations, has even eaten its way into the fabric of African revolution. The Americanized race-hierarchy within the leadership pyramid of the U.P.C. makes Jorge Manuel, an educated mulatto of mixed African and Portuguese parentage, an "honorary white", superior in his first-floor luxury to the pure Negro Estaban Ngulo, "the dark, silent African" who did not get beyond elementary school and who must make do with his ground-floor austerity. The African and Afro-American experiences have become interchangeable.

America's race-myths are also the principal source of the novel's sexual mythology. Armah approaches one of these through the figure of Sandra and her wedding-night confession to having had a black lover (Modin), a confession which toys with the stereotypical myth-complex of white virgin purity assaulted by the fiery dragon of primitive black sensuality. In its revised version, however, the white damsel's desire to have her virile black dragon-lover as well as her chaste white knight-husband destroys both of them and proclaims herself the only winner (p. 157). By this point in the novel the conventional white stereotype which opposes a black sensuality to a higher white spirituality has, in any case, been overturned, since it is the white women who have given themselves over to a crude and unfeeling sexuality, divorced from any higher emotion, and who now feed upon the more wholesome and integrated sexual energies of black lovers: "They have accepted themselves as mere bodies, killed the spirit in them, or put it at the service of insatiable bodies" (p. 159). Remarking upon the failed instinctual lives of white Americans and their "inability to renew themselves at the fountain of their own lives", James Baldwin stressed the need "to respect and rejoice in the force of life, of life itself, and to be *present* in all that one does, from the effort of loving to the breaking of bread".[14] Armah postulates a similarly disunified, unintegrated white sensibility, in which the mind has no physical apprehension of what it perceives and is not immediately present in sexual communion — an aberration given its most extreme form in Aimée, whose weird fantasy life has gone off into an independent orbit, hysterically divorced from feeling. The sublimatory flight of sex-instinct to the head has brought a general banishment of the instinctual life which can be revoked only by the most extreme physical sensation. In the fantasy world of images and myths that is the novel's sexual landscape, no one makes love to the one they are with. Mrs Jefferson has to pretend that her husband is Modin before she can be aroused, Aimée that Modin is her fantasy-creature Mwangi. The revenge-fantasies of the integrant Lynch and the compensatory sexual ones of the inept Kansan politician Longai indicate that white-committed blacks have not escaped infection by these sexual disorders and respond with their own variations (pp. 31, 144, 163).

Armah's essay on African socialism argued that white sexuality has been brought to this sorry plight by Western civilization's constructive use of sexual repression, siphoning off libidinal energy for use in industry and empire-building "in a process that takes the potency out of persons and invests it in powerful technological artifacts".[15] The Marcusian notion of the West as technologically brilliant but emotionally and sexually backwards was one which black apologetics of the 1960s were quick to capitalize on,[16] and its outcome in the novel is Aimée's frigidity and a collective impotence of academic males, from which the subsequent nymphomania of wives seeks refuge in some mythical black prowess. Even if one allows for novels like Ngugi's *Weep Not, Child* and for the peripheral sexual elements with which francophone authors like Beti and Oyono endow colonial psychopathy, it is still clear that the book's racial typology of sexual jealousy and revenge, rape and castration (not to mention a Negro called Lynch), owes more to black America than to colonial Africa, and that it is black American polemics that supply the scenario for its sexual psychology. "The American Negro," wrote James Baldwin in 1961, "is penalized for the guilty imagination of the white people who invest him with their hates and longings, and is the principal target of their sexual paranoia."[17] According to one popular paradigm, recorded in the pages of Malcolm X, race-guilt over the rape of black womanhood, dread of revenge and fear of his own sexual inadequacy conspire to create in the mind of the white man a paranoia about black men and, concomitantly, a perverse desire to see his deepest sexual fears enacted.[18] White male impotence and female frustration combine to project imaginatively upon "the Negro" or "the African" the sexual vigour that is respectively lacked and craved. The woman's desire is not only spiced by the lure of the forbidden but is enhanced, masochistically, by the threat of detection and punishment and, sadistically, by the prospect of violent revenge on her imagined violator for his unnigger-like presumption. Armah adheres closely to this model of deeply secret white longings and phobias: "What they craved was the nearness of danger, and that a human being, an African, a stranger here, his presence loaded with the heaviest fears known to white men's minds, was bound to bring in time . . . These women I have known have had deep needs to wound their men. I have been an instrument in their hands" (pp. 162, 167). The sexual set-up devised subconsciously by the Jeffersons follows the pattern of the erotic ritual with all too few original additions. Mrs Jefferson uses Modin, in imagination, to arouse herself for her sexually dormant husband as the French terrorists, apparently fearful for their own potency, use him in actuality to arouse Aimée. In so doing, she betrays him and then, the next evening, dutifully fills the air with her orgasmic moans to guide the enraged husband to the spot so that he may, in prurient self-torture, briefly relish his wife's forbidden pleasures before assaulting their supplier. The O.A.S. terrorist who offers Aimée the fatal lift is afflicted by the same neurotic ambiguity. He looks "like a man cheated, a creature deprived of something that should have been his birthright" (p. 280) — namely the white girl, whose preference of the black to himself both fascinates and appals him and who, in the climactic scene, is as profoundly excited by the white men's restraint upon her as by the black man's desire. Armah transposes this essentially American model to a colonial context. The mentally overdeveloped nations in receipt of African sexual aid appear to need, to revive their exhausted sensibilities, fantasy re-enactments of the original colonial violence which deadened them. In their sexual recolonization of Africans the two white women orchestrate their respective orgasms to the phallic stab of a knife-blade and the explosion from a gun barrel aimed at the head of a steward-boy seducer: during the real-life enactment of the Mwangi fantasy by the O.A.S. thugs, Aimée reaches the peak of her sexual excitement at the moment of Modin's lethal castration.

Robert Fraser has noted that, although half of the novel's plot unfolds in Saharan Africa, "the ethical judgements brought to bear on it derive from America in the years of racial confrontation".[19] At the abstract level of Armah's polemic, the alienated, Westernized African and the entirely uprooted, American-formed Afro-American are given a spurious fraternity under the umbrella of "the black race", and America is pressed into service as an unlikely and unreliable microcosm of global race relations. Apart from the contrived death scene and the Sylvia vignette, the dramatized "proof" of Africa's victim-status in Modin's theory is drawn entirely, and tendentiously, from his treatment by whites in the American scenes. Paradoxically, the "Negro experience" in America is called upon to justify not only Africa's disengagement from the West which is Armah's prime concern but, by implication, the separation of the black from the white race: an option which, geographically and culturally, is in fact least available to the American black himself, bound as he is in a deadly symbiotic intimacy with the white society that created him and irrevocably unmoored from his African past. But the major weakness of *Why Are We So Blest?* is that, instead of establishing countertruths, the novel is itself steeped in stale sensationalist myths, often white-originated, about race and sex: it is a racist fiction about racist fictions. By the canons of Armah's race-mystique, white racism is inexplicable and incurable. It is not to be located in the historical determinants of class, creed and nation, but seems rather to be of the fundamental nature of a biological or inheritable genetic disorder. It is merely in the inhuman nature of whites to fear and despise blacks, the result of some mysterious inherent diabolism which places them beyond ordinary understanding. As such, racism in the novel assumes almost metaphysical proportions — the "disease is ordained" — and the polemic is pushed dangerously close to the specious determinisms of sects like the Black Muslims. On the sexual front, the promotion of sexual myths by fantasy is itself seen as an organic malfunction peculiar to the white race. White sex, apparently unable to exist outside of a theatrical dream-world context, is universally manipulatory, "clitoral" and fantasy-ridden, whilst black sex (Modin and Naita) is reciprocal, "vaginal" and wholly directed towards the present partner.[20] The collective pursuit of Modin by white womanhood amounts to an endemic sexual illness. To give Modin his due on the individual level, he does insist that Aimée's trouble is purely psychological: he is no special sexual performer but simply completes her fantasy of primitive black sexuality. But at the mytho-symbolic level on which this novel has most of its life, this mythical property is pursued with such unanimous ardour that we wonder at times if the author believes in it too and if his symbolism does not merely assent to those white-promulgated myths which flatter the black's self-image whilst decrying those which degrade it. White sexual deficiency, though an innate racial disability, can, it seems, be remedied by the black super-stud who has resisted assimilation, and blacks are themselves susceptible to it only when they come under the baleful influence of white culture. Longai's ineptitude, Pakansa's impotence and Lynch's moral emasculation are all signs of the instinctual sacrifices which are the price of their absorption into a white world. Powerful in its symbolism, this motif is weak in its logic. Once it is allowed of white civilization, as of colonialism in Fanon's maxim, that "everything comes from itself", then it is possible, with a fatal facility, to blame all the troubles of contemporary Africa upon it. The remarkable change of moral focus in Armah's third novel does exactly that.

VIII

Griots and Guerrillas: *Two Thousand Seasons*

In *Why Are We So Blest?* Armah's suspicion of inherited Western aesthetic forms, noticeable earlier in his treatment of artist-figures in *Fragments*, engulfs the novel's own narrative mode, which reflexively pronounces its ultimate valuelessness. The African artist seduced by European aestheticism into borrowing its techniques to lament the betrayal of his own race himself becomes a parasite and betrayer. "There is no creative art outside the destruction of the destroyers," Solo declares. "In my people's world revolution would be the only art, revolutionaries the only creators."[1] Once these warning signals have been registered, the next book will not be the total shock to the sensibility which appears to have been its actual and intended effect upon Western readers, and the radical discontinuity of Armah's literary career may, in retrospect, seem less real than apparent. Following logically upon the third book's despair of appropriate artistic form, the fourth, written during a six-year stay in Tanzania, marks its author's search for a narrative mode which would approximate to more genuinely African forms and provide a focus both more explicitly African and more revolutionary than that offered by his previous novels. Nevertheless, after the psychological intricacies and historical particularities of the early books, the fourth one, with its panoramic sweep across time, its Manichean reduction of humanity to primal racial forces, and the relentless polemical harangue of its collective narrator, comes as an alarming corrective.

Two Thousand Seasons uses as a microcosm for the historical experience of the whole African people the troubled migrations of the Akan nation (here called "the people of Anoa") from its supposed Sudanic sources, through slavery, exile, Arab and European imperialisms, guerrilla resistance and decolonization to its settlement in modern Ghana and its future task of reconstruction.[2] As such, it is only in part recorded history and the narrative draws not upon specific local tribal memories but upon the hypothetical race-consciousness of a fictitious pan-African brotherhood of undifferentiated ethnicity, whose names are taken from all parts of the continent. In this book Armah surprisingly bursts the bounds of historical realism, period-setting and naturalistic narrative and moves into the terrain of myth, legend and racial memory. The group experience is now paramount, so characterization is minimal and concerned with the representation of collective states and feelings and, most particularly, of collective heroism, rather than the fine delineation of individual personalities and deeds. The reader is addressed by a pluralized narrative voice, an anonymous and timeless "We" which represents the whole social body throughout its wanderings across history.

Two Thousand Seasons does not purport to be a "novel" in any sense of the word and to approach Armah's daring experimentation with the techniques of indigenous African narrative forms with the critical assumptions governing discussion of European fiction is to mistake both the formal design and the spirit of his book. It seems rather that a strange and arresting new literary form has been evolved out of his refashioning of the devices of an African tradition which has, in fact, an ancient pedigree: the tradition of the griot, story-teller or oral historian who speaks with the voice of the whole community and whose legends, folk-tales and proverbs are stored in the communal memory. Few novels create deliberately unmemorable characters who are merely functions of a collective will or ramble episodically over vast spans of time in pursuit of racial destinies. Even fewer novels start from the premise that certain racial groups and their imperial underlings have engrossed most of the human vices and are wholly predictable because helpless before the evil of their own natures, whilst others have acquired a monopoly on the virtues. Although Armah's narrative makes no simple distinction between foreign vice and indigenous virtue, the pre-colonial disruptions of the community from within are chiefly of interest for their anticipation of white colonial values and the black idiot-kings and askari-zombis who are targeted for abuse are entirely the creation of the whites whose work of destruction they do. Abandoning critical investigation for partisan invective, Armah makes no claim to criticize his "destroyers" and "predators" and their African quislings but simply hurls abuse at them, more after the fashion of the Ewe *halo* than that of Western satire. These features are, more often, the stock-in-trade of epic, saga and chronicle, both in the African oral tradition of the griot and in its written equivalents: namely, those Homeric and Norse marathons which have also had occasion to trace the migrations of whole peoples and celebrate the founding of nations. Doubtless, some Western scholars would claim, however, that the latter use stock epithets with more ironic discrimination and with a more novel-like, fair-minded openness to the variety of human experience than those that are to be found in *Two Thousand Seasons*.

Armah's self-consciously staged griot-like discourse is concerned to contest and correct the method of narrating African history as well as the history itself. There are, therefore, some significant departures from otherwise valued story-telling traditions. As Isidore Okpewho has observed, the collective narrator's avowedly anti-elitist standpoint shuns the griot's customary glorification of the matchless deeds of past heroes since the destiny of a whole people is too important to be entrusted to individual heroism.[3] The supernatural is rejected along with the superhuman and, contrary to traditional practice, the narrator's single creative personality is denied any domineering proprietorship over the events narrated. Armah's discourse, essentially secular and humanist in its worldview, makes communal and egalitarian ideals not only potentially realizable in the contemporary world but so certain to be achieved that the goals can be described as having already been won. His narrative strategy emphasizes accordingly the griot's self-effacing assumption of a common identity with both the specific audience which his tale is designed to educate and the characters of the tale itself. Thus *Two Thousand Seasons* is not only *about* reciprocity: its technique *enacts* reciprocity between the story-teller, his tale and his listeners.

The plural voice of Armah's newly-Africanized narrative form formally announces its agnostic viewpoint in the opening chapter:

> We have not found that lying trick to our taste, the trick of making up sure knowledge of things possible to think of, things possible to wonder about but impossible to know in any such ultimate way. We are not stunted in spirit, we are not Europeans . . . What we do not know we do not claim to know. (p. 3)

In his first two novels Armah's scepticism about the differences between the present and an ultimately irretrievable past contributed to their ironic and pessimistic vision. In *Two Thousand Seasons*, however, he capitalizes upon the uncertainty of the past and turns it to positive ends. The narrator does not proceed to a cynical negation of all retrieved "authenticities", ironically thin though the line may be between the supposed rational ideology of "the Way" and its rivals, those sentimental mystifications and nostalgic hankerings after unreal pasts which are presented as betrayals of the Way's essential aims. His didactic purpose is to cure an errant Africa of its diseased distrust in its own indigenous forms and values, not to reproduce the exact historical origins and developments of those forms and values. It is accompanied by an awareness that the communal memory drawn upon by the "remembrances" of oral narrative is no more unreliable than recorded history, especially when the written record is a European one coloured by colonial prejudices, and that a starkly monochromatic portrait of white devilry and black victimization is at least compatible with Africa's narrow experience of the white man as slaver and colonizer, as material and spiritual destroyer. The dogma of the Way works from the premise that one made-up ethno-centred history, serving one set of ideological needs, is as good as or better than another one which serves different and alien needs. *Two Thousand Seasons*, as Soyinka has observed, stands in the same relation to the work of black ethnologists and historians such as Cheikh Anta Diop and Chancellor Williams as Rider Haggard and Conrad do to the Eurocentric ethnology of Western scholarship.[4] The Prologue's rhetoric of fragmentation and dismemberment issues a reminder that it is the fragmented part of Africa's history — the colonial period which cut the continent off from its past — that, until recently, has alone constituted "African history" in Western study. Of course, the past is not a total void into which any fiction may be projected. There is a bedrock of verifiable fact to provide yardsticks for authenticity and even Armah's highly postulative, theoretical history, though less concerned with the past than with promise for the future, retains a strong attachment to historical, time-bound reality: witness the Arab invasions, the slave-trade, the many historical personages. The griot's didactic purposes may, however, license imaginative additions and historical inaccuracies: for example, the notions, in *Two Thousand Seasons*, that kings, social classes, private property and even adult genesis-fables were all foreign importations (pp. 61, 64, 82, 95, 96), and African hunting skills merely defensive (p. 14). The poet-historian of the African oral tradition is, if only by way of compensation, as entitled to his vagaries of chronology and causation as the Western historian is to his. Armah's story-teller, for example, mixes anticipation and retrospection so freely as to leave less than clear the accounts of those indigenous disruptions of "reciprocity" which appear to predate the Arab invasions and of the odd infiltration into the fleeing community of the twisted values of its tormentors.

Armah's innovative, pseudo-oral narrative is, of course, a simulated exercise, a literary affectation. It is rendered in English, not in Akan or Kiswahili, and, since communal readings of novels written in English are rare in Africa, the traditional communal intimacy between the artist and his audience is here a mere fiction of the plural voice. *Two Thousand Seasons* is the kind of "novel" that a griot would have written if he had had access to literary form; its interesting historical sleights-of-hand allow the author to grapple with the problems of artistic form confronted by Solo in the previous novel. He now artificially resolves the dilemma of the contemporary African artist by setting his tale in an indeterminate past when the artist was not yet alienated from his society but still immersed in a collective and egalitarian ethos, and then using the griot's voice vicariously to advocate communal commitment and popular revolution in a period of fragmentation and elitist privilege, when such conditions no longer prevail. This is, however, a deliberate polemical strategy: lacking a traditional audience, the book's message is aimed at those anglicized Africans who have ventured furthest from what

Armah hypothesizes as Africa's true self and there is thus no inconsistency between its form and its initial African publication. Neither does it matter much that the narrative, in its ideological urgency, draws not upon the tribal lore of any single community but upon the race-memory of a postulative continental fraternity. The migrations of the People of the Way suggest, primarily, the legendary origins of the Akan of Ghana in the medieval Sudanic kingdom of the same name, but their acephalous communalism seems to have more to do with the Igbo than the monarchical Akan and the concept of "reciprocity" would appear, in the light of the book's Tanzanian genesis, to owe something to the ethics of Tanzanian tribal cultures utilized by Nyerere's *Ujamaa*.

The basic problems created by *Two Thousand Seasons* are formal, aesthetic ones. The transmutation of oral literary forms into written ones is always an uncertain and unpredictable process and the survival of the styles and narrative techniques of the oral story-teller into the modern African novel is an especially haphazard affair. The graphic hyperbole of the griot is, for example, as pervasively in evidence and as much at home in novels with contemporary urban settings (such as Armah's first novel and Soyinka's *The Interpreters*), as are his other stock-in-trade in historical novels which deal with traditional cultures in an earlier period: for example, Achebe's *Things Fall Apart* and *Arrow of God*, where the idiomatic oral wisdoms which carry the main themes are encapsulated marginally in the proverbs, fables and folk-tales that punctuate the narrative. The experimentation with oral forms in *Two Thousand Seasons* — and in another visionary reconstruction of whole eras of African history with which it has been compared, Yambo Ouologuem's *Bound to Violence* — is generally more adventurous and risk-taking than in the historical novel proper, where it is usually more contained and pertains to the culture of a specific and limited period and place. It is impossible to legislate for oral transposition and the author's degree of success may depend upon whether he is content merely to reproduce selected oral features in a traditional novelistic context, as in Achebe's novels, or is simply out to capture the spirit and energy of the griot, as in Ouologuem's extravaganza, or whether, as in *Two Thousand Seasons*, he is making the more ambitious attempt to find precise written equivalents for oral stylistic devices. No matter how resourceful and inventive this latter labour is, the fact remains that the oral tale is designed to be said, not read, to be declaimed, not decoded. Thus, in practice, its greatest strengths seldom survive its transposition to written form and it may be seriously questioned how much justice is done in the execution of Armah's narrative to its oral prototypes.

In Armah's imitative version of griotature, oral in conception but literary in expression, the passage between forms is not assisted by an erratic and unhappy assortment of styles, ranging from the oracular and invocatory to the popular and idiomatically American: the harem women effect "the discombobulation of the askaris" (p. 31), and the two mad fugitives from the Arab "predators" have to be kept "from trying more homicide" (p. 47). Armah strains to reproduce an illusion of orality and, specifically, of vatic utterance through a formidable battery of rhetorical questions, lamentations and exclamations ("Hau!"), not to mention some frenzied alliteration — "This is no hurried hustle hot with sweaty anticipation" (p. 158) — and portentous-sounding adjectivally-sprung inversions: "Painful was the groping after lost reciprocity. Fertile had been the rule of women . . ." (p. 26). The attempt frequently overreaches itself, however, and produces a lugubrious, almost self-parodying rhetoric which is at home in neither the oral nor the literary form. Traditionally, the "backward scanning" techniques of oral narrative edit out errors and eliminate discrepancies by glossing over them or, as a very last resort, by self-correction.[5] Once something has been said, it exists ineradicably, so the option of omission is not open to the oral narrator and he is apt to convey emphasis by the frequency rather than the manner of expression. Oral expression favours repetition and, translated into written form, the results are a disastrous failure in economy and constitute some of Armah's most unreadable writing.[6]

Comparison with Armah's early prose might prove instructive at this point. The oracular narrative voice of *Two Thousand Seasons*, like that of the story "An African Fable" and the visionary passages of the first novel, has much to say about the moral and intellectual penetration of the "connected eye", which is here linked with "the soul's seeing", and the baleful effects of the dreaming "unconnected eye", which vaguely "finds beauty in death".[7] The "unconnected" or merely "beholding eye", a passive receiver of impressions that makes the first novel's gleam-worshippers prey to a deathly materialism, apprehends only material and human unconnectedness and fails to see beyond the short-term, selfish gains of the moment. In contrast, the more active and discriminating "connected" or "watching eye", in addition to being connected to other seeing eyes in the community, is integrated with "connected hearing" and "connected thinking" (the alert "listening ear" and "listening mind" of the man in the first novel), and, as in the case of the man, is attuned to a more far-sighted and cyclical conception of time. In *The Beautyful Ones Are Not Yet Born* the workings of the connected consciousness are perhaps most vividly presented in the wee-fellowship, where the later book's bald assertion that "There is no beauty but in relationships" is borne out by the expression, in moments of intensity, of the fullest individuality in community with other members of the group. The drug effects a simul-

taneous erosion of communications-barriers and time-
senses, linking "everything that was going on inside and
outside ourselves" and transporting its users "beyond the
pain of the moment" by letting each one "see the whole of
your life laid out in front of you" in a synchronic
continuum. But the trip is also a "frightening journey"
into the deeper connectedness of both the individual and
the group body. Fingertips observed under the drug's X-
ray intensity are a visceral flux of microscopic particles —
"thousands of little fluid bubbles in motion . . . And if a
fingertip could be so many loose bodies in so much
motion, what of the whole body when it felt that way?" —
and the image of the organic chain is translated into a
vision of a linked human community: "I see a long, long
way . . . so many people going so far into the distance that
I see them all like little bubbles joined together."[8] The
feeling of group intimacy and the shock of organic unity
are at once sensuously realized, as is the impact of the
sense of connectedness, of all things in space and time,
upon the reorientated human consciousness:

> I looked at the sea flowing toward and over the sand,
> and I no longer saw dead water hitting land in
> senseless waves of noise. The water and the sand
> were alive for me then; the water coming in long,
> slow movements stretching back into ages so very
> long ago, and the land always answering the move-
> ment, though in our dead moments we do not have
> eyes to see any of this. Sounds, the mild thunder of
> the night waves hitting calmer water and the sigh of
> retreating afterwaves, now joined together with what
> we saw. The land looked so beautiful then, so many
> little individual grains in the light of the night, giving
> the watcher the childhood feeling of infinite things
> finally understood, the humiliating feeling of the
> watcher's nothingness . . . There was nothing
> around me then that was not joined to everything
> else.[9]

Not only is time conceived here as a dynamic synchrony, in which everything that has existed is simultaneously apprehended, but sea and sand are revealed to be in a potent reciprocity of motion, each living grain minutely differentiated but connected in the flow of an unbroken cycle. This mystical cosmic connectedness is not quite of the same order as that which is wholeheartedly recommended by the narrator of *Two Thousand Seasons*, but it has at least been physically evoked, convincingly demonstrated and confronted in all of its exhilarating and frightening aspects. Here, by contrast, is the Way's crude racial codification of the earlier novel's subtle phenomenology of perception:

> The disease of death, the white road, is also unconnected sight, the fractured vision that sees only the immediate present, that follows only present gain and separates the present from the future, shutting each passing day in its own hustling greed.
>
> The disease of death, the white road, is also unconnected hearing, the shattered hearing that listens only to today's brazen cacophony, takes direction from that alone and stays deaf to the soft voices of those yet unborn.
>
> The disease of death, the white road, is also unconnected thinking, the broken reason that thinks only of the immediate paths to the moment's release, that takes no care to connect the present with past events, the present with future necessity. (p. 8)

The point laboured here is that a fractured vision cannot see the connectedness of two thousand seasons of fragmented racial memories and hopes, but it is principally a point about time and hardly at all about perception and community, which in the early novel are contingent upon and intimately associated with the proper experience of time. The familiar alignment of sensory and synchronic continuums with group consciousness is created with none of the imaginative force of the first book but has become a matter for doctrinal formulation. Moreover, the point is monotonously restated in the same form without any regard for the chosen vehicle: the narrator does not, after the fashion of the traditional griot, attempt to draw and elaborate upon the peculiar attributes of sight, hearing and thought, which might just as well have been taste, touch and smell.

The presentation of the ideology of the Way is similarly marked by a vagueness of definition and a disregard for concrete particulars and the quick of experience which are quite alien to the oral tradition. The interminable repetition of the Way's sacred trinity of neologisms — "reciprocity", "connectedness" and "creation" — is accompanied by so little explication of what they practically involve as a lived social pattern that they eventually become lifeless verbal tags, self-enclosed abstractions which fail to translate into anything beyond themselves. In *Two Thousand Seasons* the prose too often collapses into a lustreless demagogic jargon — "our way, the way", "the destruction of destruction", "the unconnected consciousness" — which is at its most stark in the formulation of the Law according to the Way, the ten commandments as handed down to Isanusi:

> Our way is reciprocity. The way is wholeness. Our way knows no oppression. The way destroys oppression. Our way is hospitable to guests. The way repels destroyers. Our way produces before it consumes. The way produces far more than it consumes. Our way creates. The way destroys only destruction.
> (p. 39)

The scriptural chant suffers from a kind of hermetic banality, a rhetorical stutter which repeats without revealing, exhorts without enlightening. Only in the Prologue, where thwarted racial destiny, frustrated generosity and failed reciprocity are powerfully realized in the imagery of springwaters flowing into the desert, do Armah's poetic powers appear to be at full stretch and do any real justice to his oral models. Paradoxically, the dazzling inventiveness and exuberant hyperbole of the griot are more in evidence in the scatology of the supposedly Western-oriented first novel than in the affected griotature of *Two Thousand Seasons*, where the literary compromise with oral form, far from being enriched by it, results in a comparatively restricted and impoverished verbal code.

The depiction of mass-mentalities, though it provides rousing racial propaganda, makes for dull, unengaging fiction, principally because of the deliberate thinness of characterization. The prophetic women Noliwe and Ningome are ethereal voices without physical presence; the superlative beauties Anoa and Idawa are negritudinous abstractions rather than human beings. These are not isolated stylistic failings but are bound up with more serious faults such as the literally black-and-white moral judgements, the crude differentiation of codes of conduct and an absence of dramatic tension. These latter reduce episodes like the raid on the castle at Poano and the destruction of the slave-ships to the level of a *Boy's Own* adventure yarn and, indeed, the juvenile pasteboard characterization, naiveties of style and occasional stilted dialogue are the usual limitations of this popular genre. At times Armah even appears to be writing a kind of African "Western": "From an Alari branch Kenia placed just one bullet dead between the second would-be killer's eyes" (p. 190). Behind all this, and the source of many of its moral and artistic problems, is the book's monotonous racial chauvinism. As Armah's writing heads off beyond the tensions and ambivalences of realist fiction into the unifying simplicities of mythology, the growing tendency to blame all Africa's woes upon the West, most pronounced in *Why Are We So Blest?*, stiffens, in *Two Thousand Seasons*, into an explicit racism which portrays whites as pathologically evil: "The white abomination: violence in its pure state, hatred unmixed", runs one of the narrator's undigested Fanonisms (p. 87). Robert Fraser has argued that the complexities, the openness to experience and the fundamental fairness of naturalistic narrative are not to be expected here because they have been side-stepped and transcended by the effort to provide modern Africa with a strong curative mythology as an antidote to its corrosive inferiority complex; and, further, that the true test of this kind of writing should therefore be its polemical persuasiveness and active efficacy rather than its purely artistic merit.[10] Though this explains Armah's strident racist simplicities, it does not necessarily justify them, however, for it does not show how a false and destructive myth can be a source of health, curing the sickness spread by colonial myths; how a wilful distortion of reality, serving African purposes, can be any more health-giving than the colonial distortions it counteracts. It is also hard for the Western critic to believe that efficacy and artistry are not bound up with one another and that persuasion does not rely on competent craftsmanship.

Two Thousand Seasons is essentially a therapeutic exorcism, at both the private and public levels. On the level of private penance, the alienated individuals of the early novels are implicitly reproved and outgrown in the harsh treatment of Dovi — "The selfish desire of the cut-off spirit was so strong in him" (p. 183) — and the selfless sacrifice of Abena: "There is no self to save apart from all of us. What would I have done with my life, alone, like a beast of prey?" (p. 111). At the public level the therapy is twofold. Firstly, the systematic direction of hatred at Arab and European whites is intended to exorcize the sensations of helplessness induced by colonialism and to clear the air of negative feeling so that the work of construction may begin: ideally, it is a catharsis which will prepare the mind for the creation of radical alternatives to the societies left behind by the imperialists. Secondly, the "destruction" which the whites inflict and which, to the narrator's delirious glee, they eventually draw upon themselves, provides the relief for the oppositional, mainly negative definition of the Way. Whatever the Way is in itself — and there are times when it seems no more than a convenience category for lost virtues — it is initially everything that "destruction" is not: "We are not a people to nurture kings and courtiers . . . We are not a trading people" (pp. 95, 98). "Leave the destroyers' spokesmen to cast contemptuous despair abroad. That is not our vocation. That will not be our utterance" (p. xvii). As far as political directions are concerned, the Way appears to amount to little more than resistance to oppression and the destruction of destroyers. In terms of socio-political models, it is not clear whether its indigenous communal spirit which runs across the centuries as a kind of racial destiny finds maximum fulfilment in the restricted village communalism of pre-colonial Africa or in the mass socialism of the post-colonial nation-state. Armah's notions of history and political systems are as imprecise in this work as the largely imaginary model of oral narrative which serves as their vehicle. Forgotten and not yet rediscovered, the Way is essentially an unknown quantity. Almost everything that happens in *Two Thousand Seasons* is a deviation from the Way unless its weaknesses are seen to be inherent in the Way itself, and the mystery of the precise character of the Way allows the author to blame at least half of the evils that befall it on outside forces. Armah has anticipated the problem of definition in his early essay on African socialism:

> Negative, anti-colonial feeling is relatively easy to come by. At any rate it does not demand any genius. The development of positive programmes and ideologies is a much more difficult proposition.[11]

In practice, this means that the rather drab and joyless communalism which the author, with at least part of his mind, wants to believe was the indigenous African way of life emerges as something that is more non-European, and anti-European, than specifically and recognizably African. In fact, certain features, such as the total rejection of family and kin urged upon Dovi in the name of a higher ideal and the overriding of territorial instincts by abstract ideological loyalties, would appear to be highly un-African, in the sense used by Achebe in his criticism of Armah's first novel.[12] If the early novels and essays question received ideas about "authentic" traditional values, *Two Thousand Seasons* fails to put anything positive in their place.

The continuities with the early books should not be lost sight of. The supreme archetype for the money-making, debased rites of the first two novels is to be found in the slave-king Koranche's ultimate ritual perversion of initiation ceremonies into the bitter rite of middle passage. In the more artificial device of the pluralized narrator who is not localized in place or time, the somewhat contrived notation of communal suffering in the early books — the inter-changing narrators at the fulcrum of the first novel, the village in *Fragments* whose name means "this is everywhere" — finds its culminating and most satisfying expression. In the light of the new orthodoxies of the Way, however, a corrective process is at work. The horror of isolation that dogs the careers of the man, Baako and Modin — "Nothing destroys the soul like its loneliness", runs the departure libation in *Fragments*[13] — is no less marked in the fourth book and, indeed, is the main impetus behind the doctrine of the Way, but this horror is now contained and overcome. Armah's familiar drugged, turgid prose evokes the usual circular notion of time, but with the differences that the circularity now takes the pattern of a progressive return, not entrapment in a cycle of futile repetitions. The recurring colonialisms of contemporary Africa become, on the larger canvas of *Two Thousand Seasons*, temporary aberrations in a wider "cycle of regeneration" (p. 2), which is destined to carry the continent back to indigenous roots. The "circle of regeneration" is momentarily "burst with the invading line of destruction" (p. 154), but this "white road" of linear fragmentation (roads are always destructive in Armah's novels) proves finally to be merely part of an immense curve on the circular "path" of the developing way. The completion of the cycle and the return to unitary beginnings is achieved, however, only by rewriting history. Armah does not so much record history as correct and reinvent it. The successful slave rebellion which realizes the Way's potential for victory is history as it might and should have been and as it might be yet if the conditions of the Way are adhered to. The principal aim is the remythologizing of history or what Soyinka has called "the visionary reconstruction of the past for the purposes of a social direction".[14] As Kofi Anyidoho has observed, there is never very much distance in the narrative between historical and present experience and never enough time in the present to absorb the meaning of the past: thus, Isanusi's recounting of the disastrous history of Anoa's people contains "immediate, urgent knowledge" which his disciples, in imminent danger of enslavement at the hands of their own leaders, fail to heed at their peril.[15] The words "vision" and "seer" occur in the narrative alongside, and as frequently as, the words "remembrance" and "rememberer", stressing the link between knowledge and foreknowledge and the importance of a usable version of the past which will provide guidance and goals, as well as warnings, for the future.

The egalitarian mini-Utopia erected around Isanusi's Way is essentially an imaginative construct, no less hypothetical and no more historical than Teacher's dream-past or Modin's *maji*. In each of these visions destruction and alienation are largely the preserve of the present whilst harmonious fulfilment belongs to the past. In the early novels, however, the vision is the subject of considerable irony whereas in the later ones it appears to be upheld and celebrated, which brings Armah's writing career to an ironic full circle. The concepts of "reciprocity" and "connectedness" and the ideal of an egalitarian non-ethnic African fraternity — a fiction that flies in the face of tribal, social and national divisions — are, finally, not very far from the decadent myths of pan-Africanism and the African Personality derided in the author's first polemical essay. In the terms of that essay, the socialism of the Way is "utopian", not "scientific"; a wish-fulfilment, not a rational ideology. Yet the germ of the later works' more positive outlook is also present:

> First, an analysis of the socialist tradition itself as a mytho-poetic system. The greatest source of power and influence available to the socialist tradition is its acceptance and imaginative use of the archetypal dream of total liberation, the end of all conflict and injustice . . . the thoroughgoing negation of all the repressive facts of real life.[16]

The socialism of the fifth grove (and of the healing enclaves of the next novel) is, self-consciously, a reality-negating mytho-poetic system and a powerful imaginative tool for the work of the future. It is an ideal projection yet to be realized, that must be believed in to be created, not an experienced life-form to be restored. The book's ethical manifestos belong to a higher, speculative order of reality and provide a frame of reference from which the prevailing destruction in the existing reality can be condemned and surmounted. Armah, as griot-like activist, joins in the struggle between creation and destruction depicted in his tale and paradoxically valorizes his new models for progress by inventing a mythical ancestry for them, thus urging the creation of what does not yet exist by insisting that it has always existed. These two orders of reality — the actual and the postulative — are evident in the naming of the characters in *Two Thousand Seasons*. The rogues' gallery boasts names and accompanying deeds which refer, directly or satirically, to historical personages (Kamuzu to Hastings Kamuzu Banda of modern Malawi, Koranche to the Portuguese-controlled puppet Kwamina Ansa, "the Golden" to Mansa Musa I of ancient Mali), whilst those who serve in the struggle for African freedom (Dedan Kimathi, Irele, Soyinka) are merely items in a list of names. Projected pan-African virtues are thus vaguely opposed to specific historical villainy.

One marked and perhaps surprising continuity between the earlier and later novels lies in Armah's fundamentally elitist outlook. The superman and superwoman skills which give the fifth-grove guerrillas their equality with one another render them superior in every way to the community at large. Armah's adoption of a communal narrative voice and promulgation of group-values do not successfully disguise the continuing polarization of his characters into benighted multitudes ruled by imbecile potentates and isolated sages and hermits banished, with their impotent wisdom, to the fringes of society. Isanusi's twenty are closer to the communal heart of their societies than the Western-educated intellectuals of the previous books but their literary precursors are, nevertheless, Teacher's wee-group and Ocran's artist-protégés. Like Baako and Modin before them, and Densu and Anan who come after in *The Healers*, they are natural winners, individual achievers and champions in any meritocracy but they choose, like both their forerunners and descendants, to opt out of an unfair competition and to renege on their superior talents before these can be manipulated and misused by corrupt powers. The radio song which so affects Teacher and the man in *The Beautyful Ones Are Not Yet Born* addresses itself to these exiled, fragmented fellowships: "A few people are seeing things and saying them," Teacher responds.[17] In *Two Thousand Seasons* the "We" of the text identifies not with the masses, except insofar as they are included in the spirit of the community and the race, but, most immediately, with the same superior few, the responsible intellectual elite which acts as the society's conscience:

> But among us the truly empathic have been few since the beginning of our exile from the Way. Among a people hustling into doom the feelingless are kings, and the thoughtless always follow kings . . . It was not their habit to see through his [Koranche's] protective social pomp and call it empty. And the few whose hearing, whose vision could penetrate its hollowness could not shout loud enough to be heard against the general noise of acquiescence. (pp. 63, 71)

The familiar opposition of these like-minds and kindred spirits to an errant mass-mentality is established on the first page of the Prologue: "You hearers, seers, imaginers, thinkers, rememberers, you prophets called to communicate truths of the living way to a people fascinated unto death . . ." (p. xi). The extra-sensory, almost telepathic powers of these "seers" and "hearers" are also enjoyed by the "keen, uncanny eyes and ears" of the "lunatic seers" who, in the first novel's famous staircase passage, apprehend the rot of contemporary history denied to the merely "beholding eye" of common mortal sight.[18] Only the "watching eyes" and "listening ears" of these enlightened few are alert to the elusive ambivalences of the Way, to its constancy of purpose and changing methods of execution and defence, and to its dynamism and its ability to remain unaffected by changing environmental influences and political developments during migrations from deserts to grasslands and forests: "We are not a people of stagnant waters. We are of the moving stream" (p. 192). The Way to which the few act as spiritual guardians never becomes the norm for the community: the latter, in reality, is always heedless of or opposed to the Way and, in its advancement towards the status-seeking materialism of

Armah's modern Ghana, isolates integrity and intelligence with such ease that the communal narrative-view and the validity of a responsible communal ethic are constantly undermined.

Two Thousand Seasons remains, however, an important turning point in Armah's career. The author's penitential submergence of his earlier isolated artists and visionaries in a communal vision is clearly an attempt to give his art a more democratic basis, and seems, on the surface, to move towards a more overt espousal of "authentic" African values. The rejection of despair and the rousing call for a halt to the further fragmentation of African society by the doubtful blessings of Western culture are positive gestures in a new direction. If the first novel approximates to the "assimilation phase" of Fanon's tripartite scheme for the decolonized writer, insofar as it is partly influenced by the literary techniques of the colonial power, and the next two novels fit into the second phase of disturbed liberation, in which the uprooted writer renegotiates the gulf which has grown between himself and his people, then *Two Thousand Seasons* clearly belongs to the "fighting phase", in which a polemical, future-oriented literature strives to revolutionize its African readership. Of course, the underlying message — that Africa's only hope for the future lies in breaking the paralysis of Western influence — is still the same, only bolder and louder, and the basic paradigms of Armah's fiction — exiled visionaries, healing creators, dictators who exist by the apathetic permission of their intellectual superiors, parasitical potentates who desire only to live in old slave-castles and cover their emptiness with material-ism — have not changed very much. Koranche is the historical prototype for Koomson and the Principal Secretaries, Kamuzu for the Nkrumah of the first novel. The freedom-fighters, and the healers of the next book, are now the collective carriers of the burden of corrupt leadership, the dead pollutive weight of parasitical power vividly characterized in the "ostentatious cripples". Still seminal to Armah's thought is the division between brute power and persecuted intelligence, idiot-kings and wise philosophers who, in one way or another, are always excluded from power. Here are Koranche's thoughts on the matter:

> Now life became clear again in his mind: a conflict between the unjustly intelligent, the experts with their skill and their intelligence on the one hand, and on the other hand those born mediocre, those born inferior through no fault of their own, the hollow ones, the stupid ones, the uncreative ones. Lucky arrangement indeed, that power in the present world was placed at the disposal of the latter . . . Lucky chance for kings, that power was pitted against intelligence. Lucky chance, that talent was suppressible by power. (p. 73–74)

"Our chiefs, our leaders," Juma confirms the cartoon contrasts, "they have bellies and they have tongues. Minds they do not have" (p. 146). "You have a fullness you need to bring out," Ocran tells Baako in *Fragments*. "It's not an emptiness you need to cover up with things."[19] The motif has resurfaced, with a monotonous predictability, in everything Armah has written since. Solo, in *Why Are We So Blest?*, speaks of Westernized Africans being lured towards "shiny things to waste lonely, useless time with".[20] Koranche, in due course, searches "in vain for ways to run from his inner emptiness" and cultivates "external pomp sufficient to cover him in the eyes of the world, and therefore in his own", whilst his courtiers "crave things to eke out their beings, things to fill holes in their spirits" (pp. 71, 202). The basic vision has survived the revolution in style and narrative strategies, but not unscathed, and if one has a deep and lingering reservation about the positive achievement of

Two Thousand Seasons it has not to do with its largely spurious simulated orality or even with its racist worldview but rather with the fact that some of these paradigms and metaphors, in their transposition to a more blatantly polemical context, have begun to wear thin and to sound stale and tired. The analysis surrounding them, instead of being sharpened and deepened by fresh insights, has been shorn of the detailed complexity which the reader has grown accustomed to expect from Armah's fiction.

IX

The Healing Vision

The historical myths of *Two Thousand Seasons* are fleshed out in Armah's next novel, in which Africa's destruction, localized to the tribulations of the Akan people in the previous book, is now narrowly refracted through a more precise historical prism: the single momentous event of the fall of the Asante empire at the hands of invading British forces during the second Asante War of 1873–74. *The Healers* is a more substantial work, with its own special kind of sombre beauty and haunting resonances, but its weaknesses lie in much the same areas as those of its predecessor and, as these have been discussed at length in the previous chapter, the novel will be dealt with summarily here.[1]

The griotarary narrator of the new book is no less intent than that of the old one upon both the reconstruction of African history in defiance of the received opinions of Western historians and the correction of its method of narration. Thus the Asante nation of *The Healers* ill fits its popular image of a helpless historical dinosaur stuck in the path of progress, a backward people irresistibly swept aside by a technologically superior civilization. It is, rather, an imperial power at the height of its expansion and yet rendered fatally vulnerable by a peculiar combination of historical circumstances: a succession of wasteful and enervating wars of conquest waged against its neighbours; the withdrawal of its army commander over a private grievance and the subsequent catastrophic decline of military morale; and the introduction into the political fabric of inner divisions and disharmonies by royal intriguers who, belatedly following the example of their smaller kindred societies, are finally induced to sell a kingdom in order to save a king. None of these events are located in the orthodox way on the European calendar; instead, a series of somewhat stagey, unedited interruptions of the narrative by the griotarary voice, correcting its own errors and invoking the spirits of past storytellers, maps the exact historical moments in the long oral memory of the Akan culture to which they belong. Moreover, into this web of history is woven, by dint of the griot's creative licence, the exemplary fictional narrative of the Fantse youth Densu, his wrongful arrest for the murder of a local prince, and his initiation into the persecuted healing enclaves of the novel's title. These latter illuminati devote their lives to the immediate curing of the physical and psychological casualties of court intrigue and, over a much longer term, to the repair of political divisions wrought by court manipulators like Ababio (the real murderer of the prince Appia) and of the broader tribal and national divisions which have fragmented the African people.

The Healers, however, does not burn with the polemical intensity of *Two Thousand Seasons*. The ideological hammer blows of the fourth book are apparently taken as satisfactorily received and their message absorbed by the reader, and the subsequent relaxation of the polemical thrust leaves more scope for the concrete particularization of historical reality. Tonally, *The Healers* is a mellower and saner book · than its predecessor. The solemn racial vituperation has been diluted to sardonic scorn, as in the satiric portraits of Wolseley and Glover — "No need for the searcher to tire himself searching. Glover was visible as the sun this Saturday morning" (p. 255) — and the dominant praise-word, encompassing the healing powers of men, rivers and forests alike, is now "gentle". Structurally, the novel moves from particulars to paradigms rather than the other way round, and its considerable wealth of documentary detail does at least manage to convey the sense of lived history which is missing from *Two Thousand Seasons*. The historical details do not always merge happily, however, with the visionary presentation of a timeless struggle between "manipulators" and "inspirers" or with the personal story of Densu, and this is the novel's main area of weakness. The Asante historical theme is not introduced until a third of the way through the novel, with the appearance of the Asante general Asamoa Nkwanta at Damfo's door, and remains a backdrop to the healers' activities, which are seen almost exclusively in relation to the intrigues of the Esuano world: significantly, the one crucial, historically decisive piece of Asante manipulation referred to in the novel — the sabotaging of Asamoa's battle plan — occurs off-stage and is reported. I have discussed at length elsewhere Robert Fraser's wholesale confusion of different ethnic groups and of history and fiction in the novel, and the resulting historical inaccuracy of his reading.[2] Fraser writes as if the Fantse society of Esuano, its dignitaries and ritual games, were not only similar to their Asante equivalents (which, in fact, they are not) but were one and the same; whereas for most of the novel Esuano stands not in alignment with Kumase but in contrast with and opposition to it, and Armah makes clear its separateness in the novel's first chapter. He is concerned to show that, long before the divisions sown by prospective white rulers, the ethnic splintering of the Akan world had caused its constituent groups to travel away from their common origin and to diversify into an unhealthy multiplicity of cultures. Thus it is important that the Fantse and Asante worlds, though traceable to a common ancestry, should be felt to be qualitatively different and distinct, each with its own finely-rendered ritual forms, folk-myths and superstitions, and peculiar modes of manipulation (secret murder in Fantse, open assassination in Asante), and thus for each to engender its own kind of oppositional conflicts (between instinctual drives and social convention in Araba's case, outraged filial feeling and ritual custom in Asamoa's).

Original source materials and Armah's historical re-invention are also mixed up in Fraser's reading of the novel. Fraser claims that Armah resists "simplistic notions of the Asante as a proud, warlike people" and "the popular impression of the tyrannical nature of traditional Asante", and, perhaps confusing the novelist's researches with his own, notes that Asamoa Nkwanta's "newly acquired pacifism" and "disaffection from the war interest" are well documented as historical facts.[3] This may well be the case but there is little evidence of them in Armah's fiction. "Is the army the court?" Asamoa is rebuked by his abandoned soldiers (p.179), and, though the former has become the "plaything" of the latter, the distinction between them is an important one. Asamoa's disaffection is with the Asante court alone; partly because of its exploitation of evil customs to settle private scores, as in the murder of his nephew, and partly because of its employment of armies in wasteful intertribal warfare designed only to sow division among and between neighbouring peoples in order to enhance its own power. "The royals of Asante do not wish the unity of black people all over this land," comments the healer Damfo, "since kings and chiefs suck their power from the divisions between our people" (pp. 267, 269).

The catastrophic expedition of the Asante army across the river Pra is testimony to this process:

> There the fiery flood stagnated, burning aimlessly, eating its own energy up, wasting itself utterly. The captain's story was a long dirge of disasters with no meaning, death for no reason, destruction with no end in sight . . . Now the army had gone down to the coast, but its commanders did not know what to do.

An army doing nothing rots: disease, not fighting,
had sickened the spirit of all the army's warriors.
(p. 187)

It is the anomy and aimless destruction wrought by such
wars of disunification with their mixture of inaction and
misdirected action that demoralizes the army and alienates its leader, not the military defence of the nation
against the British. Armah's Asamoa insists that he has
spent his life fighting to make Asante strong but now fears
that the result of all his work has been "simply to give
power to people who know only how to waste power and
waste life" (p. 180). Yet far from occupying, in Fraser's
words, "an opposite pole to the official militarist ideals",[4]
he retains an unsullied faith in the intrinsic virtues of the
warrior's life: "The army has been my life. I do not
remember a single unhappy day as a warrior. I wanted to
spend my life fighting for Asante . . . My spirit always
says the same thing . . . Fight, and teach men to fight.
Work for the army, the people" (pp. 180–81). Moreover,
Damfo, though reserving the doubt that devotion to
royalty is always divisive, endorses the general's senti-
ments on returning him, cured, to active service: "He is
whole again, and doing the work he loves . . . Asamoa
Nkwanta is a good man. He is also a valuable man, one of
those highly skilled in the pursuit of a vocation" (pp. 268–
69). Though Damfo leads Asamoa to question the moral
basis of the monarchical, slave-owning society which the
army serves, he never enquires into the *raison d'être* of
the army itself, as if the military was not originally
designed for war and conquest as well as defence and thus
part of the disease of division, and was not a ready-made
tool for the royals to use, with its own intrinsic potential
for evil (this begs the question of whether, in Damfo's
ideal world, armies would also disappear, along with
slaves and kings). Far from becoming, as Fraser claims,

chief spokesman for the opposition to the war interest and being ranked among those "who were sceptical of the value of resisting the British demands",[5] the fictional Asamoa "looks foward to fighting the whites" and conceives his most dearly-loved battle plan, fighting "not with guns but with the natural environment", to counter a white invasion (pp. 181–82). When asked by Damfo if it is impossible for him to follow his own spirit in some military action which is not wasteful, the general makes an exception in the case of tribes rallying together to fight the British: "If there was an invasion by whites, no. But these petty wars in which the army gets sent to fight other black people are a waste" (p. 183). Incidentally, it is in their terrorizing of other black people that Armah's Asante do indeed live up to their popular image of a proud, tyrannical and cruel nation, permanently at war, bent on aimless conquest and quick to sacrifice and enslave. Asamoa himself shrinks only from the Swamp of Death, where the corpses of executed prisoners and slaves are thrown, when one such death touches him personally for the first time (p. 177). Thus, although Glover is hard put to persuade the remoter eastern tribes to stop attacking their immediate neighbours and take up arms against the Asante, Wolseley is easily able to play on the southern chieftains' deep fear of Asante tyranny to rally black support for his invading white army since "the choice is between being slaves of the Asante kings and being slaves of the whites" (p. 267).

Fraser argues, on the strength of two fleeting impressions of the Asante Council of State in the last quarter of the book, that this commanding impression of the Asante as a merciless, warlike nation is "strongly countered" by "Armah's shrewd portrayal of a people sorely divided on the crucial issue as to whether or not to fight the British".[6] It is not merely that for most of the novel the Asante military viewpoint is represented not by the royals but by Asamoa Nkwanta and that fighting the British is the one issue on which he is *not* divided; it is also the case that the behaviour of the "peace interest" is always seen to be morally suspect. The hedging of the Asantehene and the "cold silence" with which the Queen Mother responds to Asamoa's battle plan of passive resistance give the first signs of their own devious ulterior motives for not wanting to fight the British and are not demonstrations either of uncertainty or pacifist commitment. Neither has the hypocritical breast-beating of the Queen Mother during the second Council of State — "We have done so many things to bring the curse of God on our heads, and God is punishing us" (p. 279) — much to do with the inner moral conflict and "crippling guilt" alleged by Fraser.[7] This carefully rehearsed rhetoric touches accidentally upon the futile military expeditions and the decimation of the army by disease and drowning witnessed earlier by Densu, but it is, first and foremost, a calculated ploy designed to give a spurious inevitability to the capitulation upon which the royals have already secretly decided. Fearing that the battle plan's extension of the war into Kumase itself will turn the general into the new national leader and advised by his mother that his choice is between being "king of a violated kingdom" and being "nothing in a virgin nation" (p. 291), the Asantehene is persuaded to sabotage Asamoa's plan and throw in his lot with the whites: thus he destroys his kingdom to keep his crown. Only at the eleventh hour, when they are dismayed by the demonstration of the Gatling gun into a sense of the unassailable odds stacked against them and wrongly imagine that Asamoa intends to use the British invasion to strip them of their power, do the Asante royals begin to negotiate for peace and to give out that "they have no quarrel with the whites, only other black people" (p. 201).

More seriously, Fraser confusingly takes the trials of

strength in the Fantse ritual games as evidence of the "crucial weaknesses of Asante society" and laments that "the original ideal of Akan 'wholeness' has been ditched in a surfeit of social competitiveness and a notion of purely individual advancement". He adds that at the heart of the healing code of Damfo "lies an attitude to the quality of life which cuts at the root of Asante political organization".[8] One does not have to read very far into the novel to be aware of the errors committed here. The Esuano world in which Appia, Anan and Densu compete for prestige is, of course, a Fantse society which, in the now divided Akan world, is quite separate from the Asante world centred on Kumase, as is made clear in the first pages:

> At Esuano the people, most of them, were content to know themselves as Fantse people. They knew of other people with ways and a language not really different from their own: Denchira, Wassa, Assen, Aowin, Nzema, Ekuapem, Asante. But they had not been brought up in the habit of thinking of all of these parts of a whole embracing themselves. (p. 6)

It is precisely because the essential oneness and wholeness of Akan culture have been ditched, not merely "in a surfeit of social competitiveness" but, more drastically, in favour of the petty nationalisms of tribe and territory, that the Fantse and the Asante have now become distinct enough not to be confused. Neither the trials of strength in the Fantse games nor their participants can therefore be successfully cited as signs of internal unease and division in the Asante world. The "inspiration" of Damfo's healing group does not, immediately, "cut at the root of Asante political organization" since it is opposed in the novel not to the Asante but, on a general level, to "manipulation" as practised by the whole Akan generic group and, on a specific level, to the local court intriguers Ababio and Esuman and the coterie of venal Fantse chieftains which they represent.

These criticisms purpose more than mere carping. If Damfo is to be believed, the Fantse and Asante societies that were once part of a single Akan culture will be unified again, once the damage of the diaspora is undone and the black peoples of *Ebibirman* reunited. Moreover, the means by which Ababio foments division in his own society are the same means by which the Asante royals sow dissension in the societies surrounding them. The manipulative power which thrives on divisiveness and fruitless competition and selfishly disregards all concern for cohesive unity is expressed equally well in ritual games, intertribal warfare and treacherous alliances with colonial powers. Armah's choice of Fantse society for the local, domestic story is significant because, as the marvellous burlesque of the Cape Coast durbar demonstrates, the Fantse chiefs were the ones to initiate the slow process of collusion with the British, into which the Asante kings were the last to be drawn. All local societies, it is assumed, were implicated in the fall of the mighty Asante empire and the white colonization of the Akan world — indeed, their rulers conspired to bring these about — and all were equally subject to and responsible for colonial rule and its legacies. At the same time, however, Armah is anxious to demonstrate that some time before the disruptions caused by the colonial powers, the splintering of the Akan world had carried its component parts a long way from their common source and into a divisive plethora of cultures and creeds. It is also part of his polemical point that, because of the "disease" of disintegration, the only common ground that these societies now have is the fragmentation that keeps them apart; they are alike only in being subject to a process of atomization that makes them unlike one another. Thus Esuano stands in close proximity to Kumase but in contrastive opposition to it. The former is initially destroyed by the ready, profitable compromise with white colonists by greedy royal advisers; the latter by the exhausting demands of aggressive colonial wars of its own and by its inability to administer justly — or, indeed, to do anything but enslave — its conquered peoples. Like the Fantse before them, the Asante royals finally sell their kingdom to keep the thrones which they imagine to be threatened, but they hold out and are the last to yield. In Armah's novel, as for a lengthy period of Akan history, their position in relation to the tribes they tyrannize is that of sole protector from, and last barrier against, total white rule.

Fraser's confusion of ethnic identities, of history and fiction, and of the novel's contrasts and continuities, is instructive insofar as it opens out into the troubled, problematic areas of the novel's own confused and divided vision. Such misreadings result from his over-strenuous attempt to dovetail the two halves of Armah's book — the domestic and the historical material — and the respective Fantse and Asante worlds in which they occur, when the text itself in fact evinces not so much a perfect fusion as a confusion of themes. Bernth Lindfors has noticed the suspicious smoothness with which the novel is unified by the imagery of disease: "Any manifestation of division in society is regarded as a symptom of the malady, a crippling indisposition requiring a cure."[9] Disease, as a metaphor for disintegration, becomes a symbolic catch-all accommodating many different kinds of personal and collective disunity, all of which are seen confusingly in terms of one another: the image ranges over the physical disease that rots the army, the psycho-somatic complications of Araba's traumatic illness, the spiritual suffering of Asamoa and the deeper moral sickness of Ababio and the court intriguers. Different kinds of pressure — political, marital, occupational — are exerted upon both healers and healed in their public and private lives under the name of "manipulation" and the victims are manipulated towards different ends — false and fruitless marriages, service as a tool of political corruption — quite apart from the manipulative practices of the healers themselves, such as Densu's disguises behind enemy lines and Damfo's subtle indoctrination of Asamoa. The result is that the concept threatens to become an intellectual vacuum into which almost anything can be put. Similarly, the different creative, anti-manipulative energies congregated under the umbrella concept of "Inspiration" — healing (Damfo), organizational (Asamoa), sexual (Araba), artistic (Kofi Entusa), all-round ability (Densu) — are taken as vaguely being aspects of one another without any effort being made to show how they might be concretely related and precisely what continuities exist between the domestic and historical realms. Araba, Asamoa and the Asante nation are, as Fraser claims, all alike at the level of analogy insofar as all have been deceived into betraying their deepest selves and are thus all part of a people in error,[10] but there seems to be no common reservoir of feeling and impulse from which their repressed drives and the various healing energies spring. At the beginning of the novel the two Fantse youths have underwater visions which allow Anan "to see what brings them [things] together so they make sense" and make Densu aware, in a scene reminiscent of the wee-smokers of the first novel, "of the skin joining him to the world", so that "it did not seem any more as if what was outside that skin was separate from the life within" (pp. 20, 22–23). This carries implications of a plunge into the social subconscious, where all things are still connected at source and the potential for harmony still exists, though divorced from the conscious will which is the weapon of manipulation — Damfo will later attempt a plunge into Araba's subconscious, asking her "to talk to him of something she had forgotten" (p. 70). But this evidently symbolic episode is not significantly linked with the narrative of healing activities and there is no reference back to it or metaphoric reverberation from it in the book. Sexual energy, for example, is neither condemned nor harnessed to the work of the healers, who are expected to keep to a rigorously ascetic and puritanical code (thus, the mutually joyous sexual experience of Ajoa and Densu appears to have no implications beyond itself), and it becomes possible to complain that in this novel, as in Armah's others, "creative sexuality and social or political power appear forever divorced from each other".[11]

At the more pedestrian level of the plot, the attempt to incorporate the historical material relating to the fall of Kumase into the personal story of Densu and the murder of Appia, and thus to achieve the "simultaneity of *bildung* and historicity" that Neil Lazarus takes as fully accomplished, is in fact responsible for some of the weakest episodes in the novel.[12] Chief among these are those scenes which carry the narrative into the realm of the historical novel of adventure. In this genre the hero not only enjoys exciting last-minute rescues from the brink of doom (Esuman's "drink of death") and undertakes dangerous river-journeys and missions, incognito, into the enemy camp, but also somehow manages to be magically and ubiquitously present at all the major historical events, a spectator with a charmed life, watching the violent scenes of history from a miraculously quiet corner. In Densu's case, the repertoire of epochal events covers the Asante expedition against the Fantse and the disastrous crossing of the Pra, the fall of Kumase, the re-education of the Asante military commander, the Cape Coast durbar of Fantse kings, and even the dealings of the white power-centres of Wolseley and Glover, which he infiltrates in the guise of the latter's personal servant (for this exercise in espionage Armah has to contrive a childhood flashback to contacts with a freelance white trader in order to give Densu some English). Far from merging the two into a single vision, these plot contrivances serve only to emphasize the separateness of the domestic and historical material and of their respective Fantse and Asante settings, and this is nowhere more in evidence than in the historical catastrophe at the novel's climax, when Densu calmly walks out of the burning Asante capital and returns to Esuano to give himself up for a crime he did not commit to the real perpetrator, the newly-crowned Ababio; he has, effectively, walked out of history and back into his personal story which, along with Damfo and his healers, has disappeared from view during the historical episodes. When Araba Jesiwa finally recovers the power of speech at Densu's trial, her restoration to health and the belated execution of justice signify a triumph for the healers, but this is only in respect of Densu's private ordeals and has no bearing upon the wider national collapse, which appears to have been forgotten in the general jubilation. History is brought back into the book only through the rather weak symbolic gesture of the sentimental conclusion which has West Indian slaves and their newly-colonized African counterparts dancing on the beach in token reconciliation and thus brings the historical wheel to a figurative full-circle by the enforced regathering of the black peoples of the world in white captivity. The grimness of the historical situation and the persistence of black puppet-rulers in the work of the whites give the wishful speculations of Ama Nkroma at the closing dance a nebulous and fanciful air:

> It's a new dance all right . . . and it's grotesque. But look at all the black people the whites have brought here. Here we healers have been wondering about ways to bring our people together again. And the whites want ways to drive us further apart. Does it not amuse you, that in their wish to drive us apart the whites are actually bringing us work for the future? Look! (p. 309)

In this way Armah's determined optimism strives to make a pan-African virtue out of the necessity of universal white conquest.

The Healers covers much the same ground as *Two Thousand Seasons*, only the failings are now writ large in the more substantial setting of a closely observed historical reality: a doctrinaire thinness of characterization, a conceptual vagueness about the practical applicability of the recommended ideology and the attainability of its goals, and a lingering elitism which oversimplifies and falsifies in the preference it gives to personalities over processes. Firstly, the characters of the novel are reduced to having a few fixed attitudes, mechanical thought-patterns and laboured catch-phrases, all strongly coloured by the prevailing ideological oppositions and seldom carrying an authentic ring of spontaneous utterance. Araba Jesiwa effuses about true and false selves and "the incredible joy of the rediscovery of the authentic self" to a fifteen-year-old boy (p. 68). Everything Ababio says is a variation on his cynical *realpolitik* about the sharers of secrets becoming friends or enemies until death and the need "to place yourself on the right side of changes as they come" (p. 29), whilst Asamoa Nkwanta's blind adherence to social custom and service of royalty reveals a psychology as inflexible as his battle plan, even to the extent of being fooled by the royals' pretended approval of that plan when he has already foreseen the grounds for their objection to it. Damfo's speech is an interminable jargon of contraries: manipulation and inspiration, power and understanding, the disease of division and "the bringing together again of the black people", the "smaller" and the "greater parts" of the individual cure and a broader social and racial healing. Meanwhile, the acolyte healers Ajoa and Densu mouth a variety of redundant Damfoisms, restating doctrinal orthodoxy on competition and cooperation, the individual and communal selves, the nature of royal power games and the future healing work of centuries. In the Socratic catechisms to which the latter two, and Asamoa, are subjected, the interlocutors do no more than keep up their end of the dialogue whilst Damfo delivers doctrine, and the irresistible impression is of the whole of human experience being manoeuvred into a few narrow ideological frames of reference, expressed in appropriately solemn, pontifical attitudes, and outside of which the characters have no lives of their own. Indeed, minor characters like the lapsed healer Esuman appear to exist only to prove true what Damfo says about them: in this case, that power corrupts healers into killers. The women are, once again, little more than abstractions of beauty, truth and wisdom — it has been suggested that Ajoa, Araba and Ama personify either these or the three ages of African womanhood in the closing scenes[13] — and Ajoa, in particular, is less a believable human child than a negritudinous presence: "She was then a small, fragile-looking child, but already her skin had that darkness that was a promise of inexhaustible depth, and her eyes were even then liquid, clear windows into the soul within. She was beautiful" (p. 63). This mystique of blackness is also present at the introduction of the hero. Significantly, Densu is perfectly and profoundly black — "His skin was black, with a suggestion of depth and coolness in its blackness" (p. 10) — whilst the imbecilic giant Buntui, whom Ababio uses in the service of his white masters, is "a sort of unfinished red . . . like a clay pot prematurely snatched out of the kiln that should have fired and darkened it" (p. 9), and Ababio himself, first referred to as "the intruder", is physically disproportioned, as if deformed by his conspiratorial practices. The racial polemics, subtle as they are when subdued to the level of symbolism as in the colour-reversals of the first novel, become obtrusive when crudely stated in the narrative as in these last two books. The relationship which the reader is invited to take up with the virtuous persecuted hero is not much more sophisticated. Basically, this is the simple, straightforward identification, without psychological complications or ironic reservations, of adolescent adventure-fiction: for all its tendentious philosophizing and remedial polemics, at the level of characterization *The Healers* is still, as Lindfors maintains, juvenile comic-strip history.[14]

A second problematic area of the novel concerns the nature of healing. Armah's priestly physicians and psychotherapists are apparently born with "a healer's nature", the source of which is obscure and indefinable:

"What gives the healer his nature?"
"The same that gives him life," the healer said.
"What is that?"
"I do not know," the healer said. (pp. 80–81)

They enjoy uncanny powers of intuition — the child Ajoa can distinguish a manipulator from an inspirer at a tender age — and their pharmacology has strongly supernatural and suprarational dimensions. The master healer derives his skills from an occult, magical discernment:

The healer sees not just a mass of leaves. He can recognize the different spirit in each kind of leaf. He can see the leaf that has a spirit opposite to, and stronger than the snake's poison . . . it is as if the spirits of all the leaves of the forest were talking to the healer, telling him what it is they each contain, what it is each can do, and what they cannot do . . . The healer learns the meaning of the river's sound, of the sounds of the forest animals. And when he needs the curing spirit from a plant, if his eyes are well prepared, he may see from a great distance some small sign of the leaf that is ready to be taken. (pp. 79–80)

The conditional "if", "as if" and "may" are imponderables. Damfo's traditional herbalism exists, of course, in the same historical world as the superstitious capers resorted to by the Asante priests to halt Wolseley's advance on Kumase and the mindless ju-ju exhumed by Esuman for Densu's sham trial, though how it is to be related to or distinguished from them is never wholly clear. It seems that we are again, as in *Two Thousand Seasons*, in the presence of dual orders of experience: the real and the ideal, the historical and hypothetical, the material and mystical, what exists and what is yet to be evolved. "A vague fear said the people in the seeker's mind did not exist," Densu begins to doubt. "His need was for relationships with people for whom the existing world was not perfect, not even reasonably satisfactory. These would be people whose place in the world was something yet to be created because their real world was not yet entirely present" (p. 229). Whether or not this projected reality can ever be made present is uncertain because it is undecided as to whether the true spirit of the healing code is a merely restorative or an activist one. Given the opportunity to influence political events through Asamoa Nkwanta, Damfo half accedes to the belief of his fellow healers that the general "could be the start of something new among our people" (p. 146), and proceeds to enlighten him with the healers' world-view. He is, moreover, himself prepared to use manipulative tactics for the greater good, notably propaganda (the campaign aimed at the carriers) and espionage (the use of Densu). But before long Damfo despairs of Asamoa's usefulness because "all his goodness has been spent in the service of Asante royalty", and his claim that "whoever serves royalty serves the disease, not the cure" and "works to divide our people, not to unite us, no matter what he hopes personally to do" (p. 269), is finally borne out by the royals' exploitation and betrayal of Asamoa to destroy the kingdom. Araba Jesiwa has commented earlier that Damfo's "real work is not the healing of sick individuals" (p. 78), but the restoration of

Akan society to its former wholeness as the first step towards the reunification of the whole black race, and Damfo himself has pronounced:

> The healing work that cures a whole people is the highest work, far higher than the cure of single individuals . . . A healer needs to see beyond the present and tomorrow. He needs to see years and decades ahead. Because healers work for results so firm they may not be wholly visible till centuries have flowed into millenia. (pp. 82, 84)

Collectives, however, are but the sum of their constituent individuals and, in the infirm Akan world of the present, the healing of powerful individuals like Asamoa Nkwanta is the only firm avenue of influence open to the healers; whatever its fatal tendency to undermine the ideals of those who seize it, this is the only power that exists. Damfo's fatalistic, Marxian-style faith in the ever-advancing communalist millenium lacks the usual accompaniments of such faiths: a belief in popular power, the critical analysis of power-structures and, crucially, the readiness to grasp what opportunities present themselves in the immediate future. Nyaneba protests that during her long lifetime "the hopes of healers have not moved one single step closer to realization" and another asks if "it is not possible we healers are suffering from a disease — the fear of power — that will keep us forever impotent", echoing Densu's earlier speculation that the healing of the disease of fragmentation is itself "a contrary disease, an urge to unite everything" (pp. 270, 230). Damfo's answer is not very persuasive:

> We healers do not fear power. We avoid power deliberately, as long as that power is manipulative power. There is a kind of power we would all embrace and help create. It is the power we use in our work. The power of inspiration. The power that respects the spirit in every being, in every thing, and

lets every being be true to the spirit within. Healers
should embrace that kind of power. Healers should
help create that kind of power. (p. 270)

The master healer seems to have retreated from constructive political action into a vague mysticism at this point.
The egalitarian, life-respecting power he theorizes about,
though perfectly at home in an ideal social order, is no
more immediately graspable or translatable into practical
actions and lived social realities in the existing order, than
the abstraction of racial reunification that Damfo proposes
to achieve with it. On the latter score, it should be said
that the existence of a black race (or any race) as a unitary,
altruistic entity, its subsequent scattering by "manipulation", and the possibility and desirability of its reunification, are all imponderable and unprovable notions. Yet
the idea of the regathering of the earth's black people, a
variant on the specious millenarian faith of the American
Black Muslims in an impending release from ordained
suffering at the end of the numbered days of white rule,[15]
appears to have graduated from mythical to full historical
status in its passage from *Two Thousand Seasons* to *The
Healers*. Indeed, the concept of this ultimate goal is
omnipresent in the individual and popular consciousness,
and is taken for granted by Asamoa, Densu, Ajoa and the
griotarary narrator. Although healing solutions are conceived as working over many centuries, the more precise
historical location and diagnosis of specific historical ills in
The Healers would seem to be grounds for the need for a
more closely-defined remedial ideology seen in terms of
the opportunities immediately available. But this pragmatic element is, finally, missing from the novel. The
healers' peculiar sanctification of the human spirit is more
exemplary than effectual, but emanating as it does from
such saintly illuminati, does not encourage emulation.
The sentimental denouement allows justice to catch up
with Ababio, but beside his calculated pragmatism — "A

man does himself harm when he puts a distance between himself and power" (p. 300) — the chiliastic dogma of social therapists who leave themselves immediately helpless by their avoidance of power looks weakly idealistic. The projected absolutes of Damfo's "Inspiration" are essentially no less theoretical than those of Isanusi's "Way" and the healers spend more time theorizing about causes and commitments than initiating them.

Finally, Armah's penchant for privilege and position in his choice of heroes remains unchanged. Little is seen or heard of those African people whose ultimate reunification Damfo tirelessly talks of, for Armah's desire to see monarchical power toppled does not lead him into alliances with a more popular, broadly-based power. Y.S. Boafo puts it succinctly:

> It looks as if a person has to have a certain social standing and to possess some uncommon personality to be able to stimulate any healing interest since only such individuals seem capable of influencing or appear to have the wherewithal to attract a sizeable following . . . Indeed, there must be an oddity, even a flaw, in a system which, in its operation, claims to exclude untalented, non-gifted individuals and yet at the same time, counts heavily on the cooperation of such individuals for any significant results.[16]

History is still seen not in terms of social processes and power-structures but in the light of superior individual personalities, polarized into heroes and villains and subject to the abstract forces of "Manipulation" and "Inspiration" that are assumed to motivate them. More blatantly than in the early novels, the salvation of society and the race is placed at the disposal of exceptional, privileged individuals and national ruin accounted for in terms of their personal decline or demise, which provokes the question of whether the whole Asante empire had no capable generals other than Asamoa Nkwanta or the

Fantse royal family any principled men other than the prince Appia. The reader is assured that Damfo's youthful protégés, aristocrats both by birth and talent, are natural champions who choose to relinquish their superior powers for the noblest of reasons: as Lindfors writes of Densu, "Armah lets us know that there is no prize, no merit badge that this paragon, born of noble blood, could not win if he really wanted to."[17] Meanwhile, Armah remembers, in the penultimate chapter of the novel, to arrange for the villainous Ababio to be an upstart of slave descent so as to highlight his fledgling healers' aristocratic virtue whilst simultaneously using him to expose the evil status quo of a monarchical slave society: "You don't get kings without slaves. You don't get slaves without kings. My family has been a part of this — at first the lower part, the slave part" (p. 300). The more solidly historical vision of *The Healers* notwithstanding, the truth is that Densu's priggish boy scout heroism, Anan's saintly virtue, and their common superman virtuosity are still uncomfortably close to the physically and ideologically flawless, beautiful creatures of the Way and about as far from identification with a genuinely communal spirit. Furthermore, as Boafo observes, the individuals whom these illuminati elect to heal seem always to be drawn from the higher echelons of society. Unwilling that seed should be sown in infertile ground, the aristocratic elite in charge of Armah's healing mission reserves its therapeutic energies for those of royal (Araba) and noble (Asamoa) birth. The healing of division is itself a divisive process.

X

Current Work and Conclusion

The essays that have trickled in a steady stream from Armah's pen since the publication of *The Healers* have pushed deeper into the polemics of the histories but in pursuit, principally, of their practical dimensions and potential for creative action. The mechanics of mental decolonization and the subsequent possibilities for the reindigenization of African cultural and political life are investigated in the specific areas of historical scholarship, language, publishing, translation, nomenclature, and political ideology, each of which has to be rescued from a disfiguring dependency upon Western concepts and controls.

"Dakar Hieroglyphs" applauds the "rehabilitation of African humanity in the context of world history" represented by the late Cheikh Anta Diop's development of palaeographic studies at the University of Dakar. Long frustrated by the neocolonial sycophancy of the pro-French Senghor regime, this endeavour has at last succeeded in providing for African scholars direct access to Egyptian hieroglyphic texts, without mediation by or interference from Western interpretation, and is pushing the academic study of the African past far beyond a few grudging Western concessions to oral history and the achievements of medieval Sudanic kingdoms.[1] Armah's group of essays devoted to the problem of language calls for the linguistic reunification of the African continent through the *lingua franca* of Kiswahili — a concern shared by other African writers such as Soyinka[2] — and itemizes the possible immediate gains. Firstly, according to "Our Language Problem", African writers working in their native micro-languages would also have a common African language in which to make their work available to other Africans (as Soviet ethnic groups have Russian), which need is not fulfilled by the continuing hegemony of the colonial language: "The vitality of individual ethnic and national languages depends on their organised connection to a central language that serves as an international universe. Unless organised around such a linguistic centre of their own, they invariably face an unpleasant choice: to be sucked into the orbit of some potent alien language, or to die."[3] Secondly, argues "The Oxygen of Translation", a common language would serve as the medium through which the world's entire intellectual and scientific knowledge might be transmitted to Africa's educational institutions and communications media and, conversely, from which the intellectual products of Africa's scientists, philosophers and artists might be translated into the world's major languages.[4] Thirdly, runs the argument of "Africa and the Francophone Dream", an African *lingua franca* would at least be a positive alternative to propping up declining colonial languages such as French, which now depends largely upon Africa for the maintenance of its international status and which, now that its hegemony is threatened, ironically looks to francophone African elites to help it resist the precise fate — a subordination tantamount to suppression — which the French them-selves have imposed on all African languages in their own colonial *espace*.[5] Taking up a point made in passing by "The Oxygen of Translation", the essay "Writers as Professionals" calls upon African authors, businessmen, publishers and distributors to form a continental cooperat-ive for the establishment of an entirely independent African publishing industry, devoted to the marketing of books, regular journals and literary translations produced by Africans (Armah, who must himself command at least four languages and who is currently adding Russian and Ancient Egyptian to his store,[6] has strong feelings about the importance of translation and traces the traditional hostility towards it in university English departments to ethnocentric prejudices which prevent a properly broad-minded approach to world literature).[7] Only a strong independent organization of this kind would be able to break the stranglehold of those multinational European and American publishing outfits which profit from the absence or fragility of indigenous publishing enterprises whilst refusing "to make the sort of investment necessary to lift African writing to professional plateaux of viability and performance" since the process of indigenization that normally follows from professionalization would drive them out of business.[8] In "The Third World Hoax" the derogatory appellation "Third World", interiorized by Africans who still lazily depend upon European definitions of their own realities, is seen as another fraudulent and obsolete Western export which its originators have long ceased to have any use for: in this case, a variant on the term "Third Estate", revived from the junkyard of European history. The African intellectual is exhorted to commence his own healing cure by breaking his addiction to "obsolete machinery, mildewed theories, unworkable development plans, structural adjustment programmes . . . shoddy goods and rotten ideas" dumped upon Africa by Europe.[9] "The View from PEN International" and "The Lazy School of Literary Criticism" fire off shafts at two latterday and diehard practitioners of "Larsony", Per Wästberg of the PEN presidency and an English research student chasing occult Faulknerian connections with Armah's work; both of whom persist in bygone colonial assumptions about African history and literature which reduce Africa to an historical and cultural zero, and neither of whom, ludicrously unaware as they are of the present state of research in these subjects, deserve the intelligent refutation with which Armah compliments them.[10] "One Writer's Education" corrects some mistaken impressions concerning the writer's educational career, provides some valuable insights into both this and the breakdown that led to his American hospitalization, and insists upon the irrelevance to the African writer of concepts of creativity which do not incorporate the changing of Africa's social and political realities.[11]

The most substantial of this batch of writings is, however, the long article, "Masks and Marx: The Marxist Ethos vis-á-vis African Revolutionary Theory and Praxis". Armah is concerned here to rescue the universal occurrences of revolution and communism, and of systematic thinking about them, from those Marxist monopolies which have recently become a significant variant on Western intellectual proprietorship in African ideological circles. His argument is that Marxism is, demonstrably, as colonial-imperialist, assimilationist-Eurocentric, and racist-evolutionist as its capitalist counterpart, and is equally unhistorical in its thinking about non-Western peoples and its unexamined assumption that the world and civilization are coterminous with the West. One by one, Marxist myths are stripped of their mystifying jargon and universalist pretensions by their subjection to the scrutiny of "Third World" revolutionary theory and practice. Firstly, there are the dogmas of peasant stupidity and proletarian rationality which respectively dismiss peasant communism as merely primitive or fanatical and suppose machine processes to rationalize the proletarian consciousness rather than regimentalize it into a series of automatic reflexes. Then there is the fallacious doctrine of abundance as a precondition for communism, with its assumption that wealth and power must first be accumulated and concentrated before they can be shared,

when the Western historical example more often suggests
that greed and power know no upper limits and frustrate
demands for democracy, and the African one suggests
that scarcity is more likely to foster sacrifice and democratic sharing than plenty. Finally, there are the myopic
evolutionist mystifications that societies must first
be industrialized and capitalized before they can be
communized, property privatized before it can be com-
munalized, and human beings sieved through a "natural"
phase of egotistical individualism in order to reach a
more "advanced" socialized condition, when the evidence
argues that the supposedly primitive Asian and African
societies which resisted Western invasion were in fact
fighting for a way of life that was already fundamentally
communistic. Marxist contempt for peasant societies and
for the non-European world in general, together with the
myth of linear evolution, has ensured that only Europe's
brand of revolution, manufactured and exported by itself,
has been declared ideologically valid: thus, whilst Irish
emancipation was allowed by Marx and Engels to predate
English proletarian power and so become an exception to
the doctrinal rule, non-white colonies could not be
expected to liberate themselves but could only imitate the
revolutionary example of the European proletariat once
the latter had succeeded in abolishing capitalism. "When
Westerners invade China, killing and looting, they are
preparing the way for the ultimate revolution. But when
the Chinese people organize and fight wars of national
liberation, they are guilty of fanaticism."[12] Armah looks
away from mere material realities for his revolutionary
incentives and towards more African and ideational
factors such as religion, culture and social ethics, all
thought ephemeral by Marx:

> The guarantee of democratic economics and social
> organization is not material abundance but human
> consciousness . . . Any society whose members are

intelligent enough to plan the democratic sharing of
power and resources (scarce or abundant) and committed enough to work out practical methods for
implementing such plans, is ready for communism,
no matter how poor that society is. Any society
whose members are bent each on maximising his
private property and minimizing his personal sacrifices is not ready for communism, no matter how
gross its national product may be.[13]

The essay, inevitably, rehashes a number of stale Fanonisms. Its addition of Marxism to the African elite's
repertoire of lazily-consumed, ready-made intellectual
products packaged in the West gives a new twist to the
adoption of neocolonial values; but that elite's continued
sabotaging of re-Africanization programmes, the acquisitive psychology of urban proletariats, and the latter's poor
achievement record in revolution and the maintenance of
international justice are all standard Fanon. The same is
true of the presentation of the Western educational
experience which, as already demonstrated by Armah's
portrait of Westernized, would-be revolutionaries in *Why
Are We So Blest?*, does not teach solidarity with the poor
but is "tacitly structured to make the elite African
incapable of democratic cooperation" and consequently "a
lousy comrade".[14] The West's technological superiority
notwithstanding, its entire history is seen as "a series of
lessons in how *not* to be human", recalling Fanon's
farewell to Eurocentrism at the end of *The Wretched of the
Earth*: "Let us try to create the whole man, whom Europe
has been incapable of bringing to triumphant birth . . .
Leave this Europe where they are never done talking of
Man, yet murder men everywhere they find them, at the
corner of every one of their own streets, in all corners of
the globe."[15]

But there are some interesting post-Fanonian developments and an important and positive new input from the

pragmatism of Cabral and his return to African sources for revolutionary inspiration in the essays. African Marxism, Armah concludes, is in part a mere social fad and, insofar as it has become a mark of elitist snob-status in neocolonial urban power-centres, a variant on Christianity:

> Marxism is an excellent half-way house for anyone previously addicted to Christianity . . . The young Christian, who used to hate African religions as superstitious antitheses to his civilized Eurocentric religion, becomes an adult Marxist who still hates African worldviews and calls them mysticism and unscientific antitheses to his new-found Marxism.[16]

More seriously, it is an opportunistic and diversionary form of "lipservice to the struggle of our people", a mask for guilty inertia, and a line of least resistance since it seldom develops into anything beyond academic talk:

> The problem for us, then, is how to find some formula that enables us to integrate into Western life-styles but at the same time enables us to hide our ideopractical identity behind an abstract revolutionary facade . . . For the elite African, Marxism has saving qualities. It enables him to acquire a reputation as a revolutionary while, in fact, he is busily building up a life of unproductive consumerism for himself and elitist privilege for his children, thus expanding the human base of Eurocentrism. Marxism enables a person to do all this at the slight cost of the energy invested in talking. Cold betrayal in practice; fiery revolution in words.[17]

Meanwhile, as the writings of Cabral make clear, practising revolutionaries express their commitment not through words but through an active community of sacrifice, in which they live at the level of those they fight for and share their hunger and danger along with their food and medicine.[18] Their business is not talkative or even demonstrative but active:

The revolutionary, according to Fanon, inserts himself quietly among his people. This is a pivotal formulation, but because it is so understated, its myriad implications escape casual readers. Cabral adds that, in the revolutionary process, the desire for visibility is a teething disease and that massive crowds, gathered together to make demonstrations of insurrectionary yearning before the enemy, make no sense. Quiet, selective, effective, efficient initiatives do. Cabral is on ancestral ground here: the meliorative secret society is nothing new in Africa.[19]

The meliorative secret society's gradual, invisible revolutionary activities, sharply contrasted with the sudden, putschist seizure of power which characterizes urban proletarian revolutions in the Marxist model, is seen as a return to a valuable African source and Armah implicitly views the struggles of his healing enclaves and fifth grove guerrillas, as well as his own role as a writer, in these terms and as part of the same protracted creative task.

These essays, like the conclusions to the two historical novels, issue calls to action, make positive probes towards an alternative vision of Africa's future, and are written in a dauntless, determinedly optimistic mood. The polemic is resolutely forward looking and when the past is called to the aid of the argument, as in the restatement of the ancient professional pedigrees of oral literature and translation in Africa, its use is constructive, not consolatory: "for our purpose, knowledge of our past is a springboard, not a mattress to doze on."[20] To a hopeful long-term view is added the recommendation of immediate action. Linguistic unity, though frustrated by events in the present, "is both immediately sensible and ultimately achievable" and writers, though unable to accomplish the task alone, may begin by making "a concerted effort to bring the principle down to earth" and setting themselves to "examine the most promising attempts now being made to find exits from the language trap".[21] Once a possible other case for the future has been established and a radical alternative to the present imaginatively entertained, the possibilities are boundless:

> If at some point in the near or distant future Africans became sufficiently conscious of our own interests to intelligently organise the immense cultural and linguistic resources we do have . . . that one African *lingua franca* would become a potent instrument of cultural advancement, a trunk language ensuring simultaneous, permanent contact with roots and a confident flowering into the great wide universe.[22]

This buoyancy is, however, earthed by a hard-headed realism as regards the probabilities of short-term success. All of this "presupposes a new generation of African decision-makers . . . no longer willing to have the continent's people, languages and culture serve as cannon fodder in wars between rival imperialists", and always, compared to the alternative of drifting along with a neocolonial tide of ready-made, second-hand ideas, "the liberatory option is unattractively hard".[23] Armah's appeal is to the Africans themselves and his target, as always, is the Westernized elite:

> Marx has become a functional, philosophical, ancestral mentor-surrogate for intellectuals either ignorant of, or simply deprived of, their own philosophical lineages — they are intellectual orphans. The non-Western world in these neo-colonial times is a breeding ground of young intellectuals who never had their own ideational family trees revealed to them . . . The majority of non-Western intellectuals educated in colonial or neo-colonial institutions are trained to be ignorant of their own philosophical antecedents while struggling to assimilate data, theories and father-figures from the Western arsenal . . . As for those who do, in fact, have their own lineages but have been trained not to recognize them,

> some will cling with combative desperation to the
> *ersatz* fathers they have found, thinking them even
> better than the real ones they might have had. But the
> most intelligent will keep searching for the truth until
> they find their lost ancestors and selves.[24]

Thus it seems that Armah's faith in Africa's future,
restated with uncompromising integrity and a wry humour
that has mellowed over the years, is still placed principally
in a few superior specimens of the intelligentsia and their
kindred spirits and potential followers among the masses:
"One lucky fact remains: most Africans do not refer to
themselves as Third World people. Only certain African
intellectuals do."[25] It is up to the enlightened few to rally
together — "If we are to be the antenna probing the way to
the future unity, we ourselves will have to bring our
minds together first"[26] — and to persuade and convince
the rest of their class. Armah does not waste time blaming
Europeans for dumping third-rate goods, ideas and
definitions upon Africa, for the real question to be
answered is why Africans themselves are so receptive,
indeed addicted, to these things and therefore deserving
of the contempt implied by the intellectual lassitude of the
West in its recourse to Third World identity tags. Similarly,
the good or ill will of foreign publishers towards Africa is
irrelevant since the kind of commitment that can short-
circuit them can come only from within the culture itself:
"As long as major African writers are happy to depend on
Western publishers or their local placemen, we shall
remain blocked at pre-professional levels", and it makes
no sense for such writers to "attack African politicians for
their chronic dependence on foreign patrons" whilst
remaining "heroically mute about our own dependence on
publishers in those same imperial centres".[27] Armah's
appeal to African intellectual elites — writers, scholars,
businessmen and politicians — is consistently coupled
with the sceptical fear that this hand-picked group has so

deeply internalized Western habits of thought that it will not be able to respond to the call: "Meanwhile it is clear that the French authorities have picked the right elite to promote *la francophonie* . . . African leaders eager to sacrifice the development of a viable African language to the development of *anglophonie, francophonie* or any other *phonie* . . ."[28] The emancipation of African publishing houses "will have to wait until our rulers and businessmen are hit by a near-fatal attack of intelligence".[29] On the broader issue of mental and moral decolonization Armah entertains no illusions about the difficulties of the task ahead:

> Against the minority of the African elite with enough intelligence and initiative to seek re-Africanization, the barriers are formidable. Among the strongest intellectual barriers is the Manichaean stigmatization of African values. It is impossible for anyone, African or foreigner, to co-operate harmoniously with Africans if that person has been trained to think of Africans as primitive, savage, barbarous or what have you — in other words, if culturally the person is a Westerner.[30]

This, as Cabral argues,[31] is the fundamental problem and source of all others, and must be returned to and resolved before the others can be confronted.

Armah's recent essays have explored the practical implications of the polemics contained in the last two novels but have suggested no new areas of artistic development and, since *The Healers*, he has published only one minor piece of fiction. This is the short story "Halfway to Nirvana", a poignant satire on the lives of United Nations conferees who spend their lives wining and dining on Africa's catastrophic drought and hunger. Its ironic hero, Christian Mohamed Tumbo (the ecumenical symmetry of his name suggests the degree of foreign incursion), graduates from the life of a starving school-teacher, via a Swedish foundation and "Anti-Drought

Organization", to the earthly "Nirvana" of the UN system: "European salaries diplomatic status tax exemption duty free goodies travel galore clean paperwork cool hotels, per diems in dollars."[32] Tumbo fatalistically accepts that "drought and floods have been part of Africa's history for thousands of years" and announces with cynical frankness that "it will be a sad day for some of us when this catastrophic drought is over. Fortunately . . . it will go on. And on".[33] Finally, at one of the conferences which he regularly sleeps through, Tumbo's cynicism catches both himself and his colleagues out. At the point where delegates are theorizing about "the implementational modalities for achieving the objective of the total eradication of poverty and injustice in Africa by, at the latest, the year Plus 4000", he embarrasses the whole conference with what is most likely an expression of its own unstated feeling by crying out in his drunken sleep "Vive la Sécheresse!", thus carrying to its logical conclusion what he has earlier referred to as "the technique of the griot" — the adoption of "a bantering attitude to truths others prefer to bury under taciturn official masks".[34] Western aid-systems, the tale alleges, suck into their orbit mainly opportunists and frustrated careerists who have nowhere to go except deeper into mindless hedonism or cynical self-loathing. "Halfway to Nirvana" is biting, and sometimes bitter, satire, reverting to the tone of the early novels and demonstrating that Armah has lost none of his sureness of touch.

In the absence of further major works, however, the state of debate about the novels has advanced hardly at all beyond the discussion of the problematic value of polemical fiction in the conclusion to Robert Fraser's book, published in 1980. Fraser perceives the stylistic and narrative experiments of the later work to be dictated by an increased awareness of the social and political context in which the professional artist in Africa must operate, a deepening sense of obligation towards an African audience, and a growing need to question the purpose of the anglophone African novel in the setting of a post-colonial state and a suffering continent, in which all issues at some stage assume a political form.[35] The African writer may be unable to do anything about the catastrophic facts of poverty and drought but he can apply his healing art to the poverty of the imagination and the spiritual drought responsible for modern Africa's colossal failure of national and racial self-confidence, preparatory to the task of reconstruction — provided that he first cures himself of the bacillus of self-distrust infecting all Africans. Most of this, especially the latter preoccupation, is borne out by Armah's recent writing. "One Writer's Education" informs us that, after recovering from his breakdown, Armah finally opted for writing,

> not indeed as the most desired creative option, but as the least parasitic option open to me . . . I was in the position of a spore which, having finally accepted its destiny as a fungus, still wonders if it might produce penicillin.[36]

Armah makes it clear that, from a very early stage in his studies, this personal creative task was conceived in the context of a much wider creativity; that his problem as a writer has always been "how to work up some semblance of motivation for living in a world dying for change, but which I couldn't help to change". In his first year at Harvard, Armah tells us, his "centre of interest shifted from the contemplation of arrangements of symbols, images and words, to a scrutiny of the arrangements of the social realities buried under those words, images and symbols" and his respect was transferred from writers to those "involved in creativity of a more difficult and necessary type . . . to persons and groups that had worked to create new, better social realities".[37] For the young African student who felt a compelling need to bring his literary studies into the same world as, and into relationship with, the enormity of the crime committed against Lumumba in the Congo (a matter further complicated by the benevolence of Armah's Western hosts), the traditional study of literature could only be an aestheticist retreat. Hence Armah's own studies in the Social Sciences and his recommendation to the aspiring literary critic to be involved in comprehensive multidisciplinary studies that clarify the "interconnections between the economics of continents, the politics of nations and the sociology and culture of peoples".[38] The importance, in Armah's credo, of these interconnections as a context for the writer's search for value, and for a sense of his own value, cannot be overstressed, and the opening of the "Masks and Marx" essay leaves the reader in no doubt that there is a long tradition behind what he is doing:

> As far back as our written and unwritten records go, it has been the prime destiny of the serious African artist to combine the craft of creativity with the search for regenerative values . . . Kagemni, Ani, Neferti — all in their works were concerned with philosophy, with values.[39]

For Armah, the traditional relationship between men of art and men of power is a symbiotic one: "The connection of art and politics yields great potency because in this worldview . . . the artist is a serious craftsman who draws his inspiration from his people's history. In return the more active members who help shape this history look to the artist for inspiration in difficult times, and for edification in easier times."[40] Robert Fraser points out, in defence of Armah's polemics, that even modern African writers as fair-minded, impartial and as little given to invective as Achebe have formulated some concept of the relation of literature to social and political reality, and the relevant passage from Achebe is worth requoting:

Here, then, is an adequate revolution for me to espouse — to help my society regain its belief in itself and put away the complexes of the years of denigration and self-denigration. And it is essentially a question of education in the best sense of that word . . . You have all heard of the African Personality; of African democracy, of the African way of socialism, of negritude, and so on. They are all props we have fashioned at different times to help us get on our feet again. Once we are up we shall not need any of them any more.[41]

The important difference, however, is that, in Armah's more pessimistic vision, the period of self-abasement and dependency complexes is not yet over and the struggle goes on: "For I saw and still see the neocolonial order we're all living with as profoundly destructive, its ruling arrangements incurably parasitic," he writes in 1985.[42] The re-education of modern Africans is therefore conceived in a more crusading and partisan spirit and as a collective mission, in contrast with Achebe's essentially individualistic approach, and Fraser concedes as much. But there remains the vexed question of whether the concepts of the African Personality, African Democracy and the Way to African Socialism are merely mythical props and polemical devices in Armah's last two books (significantly, Achebe has avoided them himself) or are perceived as attainable historical realities. Fraser has argued that if these novels can be seen as "active, efficient social instruments", then the persuasiveness of their arguments and their practical efficacy, not abstract excellence, become the correct criteria for judgement, and he infers as follows: "As a whole both these books are indubitably powerful and persuasive: the cogency of the case they make is undeniable. As instruments of persuasion, popular yet with a certain gravity of utterance, they are certainly effective."[43] There seems to be more assertion than argument here and certain important questions are left unanswered. Are diatribe, dogma and invective ultimately persuasive and how is it proposed to measure their "effectiveness" and "efficiency", both unproven and unprovable qualities? In what, exactly, does the intellectual strength and the supposedly argumentative power of these works consist? Earlier in his book Fraser claims that the communal reformist purposes of *Two Thousand Seasons* carry its racist polemic beyond the "individualistic, humanist strain" of Western literature and "the domain of realist art".[44] Does this mean that communalist bigotry and polemical chauvinism are more defensible than the ordinary individual, realistic kind? The doctrine of art for the sake of political reconstruction may pose a healthy challenge to the orthodox pieties of Western aestheticism, but does it justify bad art? Fraser concludes by asking if Armah might have paid too high a qualitative price for the dogmatic thrust of the last two books and partly concedes this, but with the proviso that "we are here in great danger of letting our quibbles about the minutiae of the text interfere with the powerful sense that we must have of the cumulative dramatic power of both these books, their drive and momentum, together with the remarkable refurbishing of the novelist's craft that they represent."[45] But are not the text and its minutiae the final realities against which all general allegations about the novel must be measured and is it not the case that the turgidity of these two texts — too great to be reduced to minutiae and dismissed as a ground for quibbles — actually detracts from their dramatic power and clogs their momentum? Is not Fraser, finally, exalting a theory and a polemic of fiction over the realities of creative practice, giving what is merely "represented" by Armah's experimentation priority over what is successfully realized? There is much cogency in his claims for the critical irrelevance of the canons of Western taste to Armah's histories and for the Western critic's failure, when faced with the shift from purist to functionalist art, to cope with the "acute problem of critical readjustment", but Fraser's retreat behind the defence that "the critical resistance to Armah's books to date has been part and parcel of the cultural dislocation which they portray" anticipates and disarms criticism so unilaterally as to render them virtually unassailable.[46] The writer escapes too easily when the critic and his cultural assumptions are always to blame.

Few would deny the flamboyant originality of the histories but there seems to be a consensus of opinion among all but his most polemically-minded critics that they show signs of flagging inspiration and waning artistic execution.[47] Fraser himself admits that Armah's later style is often laboured, repetitious, and overburdened with adjectives and high-sounding phrases which sometimes conceal illogicalities of thought,[48] and the opening of *The Healers* is a case at hand:

> In the twentieth year of his life, a young man found himself at the centre of strange, extraordinary events. Someone was murdered — a youth exactly the same age as himself. The killing was done in a particularly bloody, brutal way. Those who saw the victim's butchered body agreed on one thing: the murderer acted from a fierce, passionate motive springing out of jealousy made hotter by pure, vindictive hate.[49]

Do the overt storytelling techniques of the oral artist quite justify the supererogatory adjectival insistence in these sentences or the novel's many other stylistic redundancies, such as "the uncertain, confusing, unpleasant but intense feelings" Ababio inspires in Densu, and the all-purpose use of "gentle" for light, vegetation and motion, sometimes three or more times on the same page, during Densu's river journey?[50] What rescues *The Beautyful Ones Are Not Yet Born* from the bareness of its plot and the cartoon-like banality of its political vision is not only its labyrinthine ritual subtext but the formidable performance of the novel's language — its sheer imaginative penetration and metaphoric richness, unsurpassed in African fiction except, perhaps, by Soyinka's two novels. In the histories, however, a parallel textural sparseness in narrative and characterization receives little help from the language, which often seems to be straining after vocabulary and which generally lacks energy and power.

Another crucial difference between the early and late novels is in the nature of their ethno-historical visions and the manner of their realization. The "Africanness" fabricated by the last two books has very little to do with the ritual undercurrents running through the first two, though their effort, through recourse to vernacular oral traditions, to recapture the broad egalitarian appeal of the griot would appear on the surface to be a step towards more "authentic" African values. The historical outlook of these last books constitutes a largely negative departure rather than a positive development from early practice, and it is arguable that after *Fragments* there is, in fact, a notable diminution of authentic African source-material in Armah's fiction that coincides with the multiplication of its formal failings. In the American-influenced *Why Are We So Blest?* Africa is only a distant presence and *Two Thousand Seasons* is concerned with the creation of an explicitly ideological "Africanness" which, arguably, is really least authentic where it is most insistent and which is certainly less subtle and closely-textured than its subtextual counterpart in the first two books. In both histories the fictive richness which arose in the early work from the imaginative engagement between myth, ritual and historical realism is lost as a result of the substitution of ideological for historical imagination and, at the level of characterization, of type for complex consciousness. Hence it is perhaps no accident that the most intricate and incisive critical writing on Armah — notably the articles of

Izevbaye, Griffiths and Priebe — has concentrated on the early novels. In the complex shifting vision of *Fragments* and *The Beautyful Ones Are Not Yet Born* the past is by turns a moral yardstick, a betrayed ideal, a lost alternative and a mine of potential corruption. In *Two Thousand Seasons*, however, its vanished cultures have been narrowly regimented into the simplistic dogma of a pristine African "Way". Since they deliberately mix realism and fantasy in a fictional mode which has its eye as much on the future as on the past, it would be unfair to fault the histories for being "unhistorical". But the remoteness of their setting from the experience of both reader and writer results in faults which are often the lot of historical fantasy: unreal dialogue, thinness of characterization and a general failure to create a convincing world. Naana's gnomic utterances, in *Fragments*, give her a numinous quality which makes her a stranger to the new world she finds herself in, but she remains a creature of a solidly historical past with its own finely delineated customs, rituals and faiths, and her reality is never in doubt. Isanusi, Densu and Damfo, by contrast, are ethereal, other-worldly creatures, beings of another order entirely. Paradoxically, the African focus that Armah has so strenuously sought for his later writing is probably most profound and authentic where it is least insistent — camouflaged yet immanent in a fabric of ritual and mythological allusion, as in the first two books — and least convincing when overtly formulated into ideology.

Dogma and diatribe are not without precedent in African literature, but the very different achievements of the two historical works built upon them are as mixed as their critical reception has been. Some will continue to wonder whether their polemics, ill-suited as they are to the form of the novel, are not better expressed in the accompanying essays, whilst others question the method and manner by which the beautiful ones are finally born in Armah's fiction and doubt whether the histories' radical line of departure can be convincingly bent into an arc of continuous development and achievement from the early novels. The last two books have been hailed, by some African critics as well as by Fraser, as evolving what promises to be a major new style for African fiction. Significantly, they have not given birth to further published novels by Armah himself.[51] Two recent essays, which stress the little creative time available to the writer earning his living as a freelance translator and lament the lack of an independent African publishing industry, suggest some possible explanations.[52] Even then, a decade-long silence following the publication of five novels in the previous decade is a puzzling affair and it is tempting to look for the reasons within the novels themselves. Could it be, for example, that the forced conclusions of the histories, confidently envisaging victorious struggle and ultimate reunification, have left nothing to be said or that their author has run himself into some kind of formal cul-de-sac? Whether there is any truth in either of these contentions, or any real possibility that the two fictional worlds of the early and late novels might yet be brought into a more organic relationship by the evolution of another new narrative mode, can only be matters of speculation until the appearance of some more major fiction by this most unpredictable and enigmatic of African writers.

Notes

Chapter I

1. Ben Obumselu, "Marx, Politics and the African Novel", *Twentieth Century Studies* 10 (1973), pp. 114–15.

2. Charles Nnolim, "Dialectic as Form: Pejorism in the Novels of Armah", *African Literature Today* 10 (1979), p. 209.

3. Chinua Achebe, *Morning Yet On Creation Day* (London: Heinemann, 1975), pp. 25–26; Kofi Awoonor, "Africa's Literature Beyond Politics", *Worldview* 15, 3 (1972), p. 23.

4. S. A. Gakwandi, *The Novel and Contemporary Experience in Africa* (London: Heinemann, 1977), pp. 88, 94.

5. Charles Larson alleged mysteriously that there were "few Africanisms" in the first two novels and made the following, equally mysterious, claim: "Armah tends to regard himself . . . as a novelist only incidentally African. On occasion Armah has gone to rather great pains to make it clear that he is writing literature first, and that the Africanness of his writing is something of less great importance." Taking this for truth, John Povey repeated it: "Certainly Armah has declared that the Africanness of his writing is something of lesser importance." In the face of these impetuous fabrications one can only state that there is no record of the novelist going to any pains to make any such declaration and that Armah himself, in his "Larsony" essay (see note 13), vehemently refuted these allegations. See: Charles Larson, *The Emergence of African Fiction* (London: Macmillan, 1978), 2nd edition, p. 258; John Povey, review of Larson, *ASA Review of Books* 2 (1975), p. 64.

6. Nnolim, p. 109.

7. Ayi Kwei Armah, *The Beautyful Ones Are Not Yet Born* (London: Heinemann, 1969), reset Heinemann edition 1975, p. 174.

8. Emmanuel Obiechina, *Culture, Tradition and Society in the*

West African Novel (Cambridge: Cambridge University Press, 1975), p. 192.

9. For a more detailed discussion of the novel's relevance to historical reality, see: Derek Wright, "Armah's Ghana Revisited: History and Fiction", *International Fiction Review* 12, 1 (1985), pp. 23–27.

10. Basil Davidson, *Black Star: A View of the Life and Times of Kwame Nkrumah* (London: Allen Lane, 1973), p. 133.

11. Armah, *The Beautyful Ones.* . ., p. 66.

12. Achebe, *Morning Yet*, p. 26.

13. Ayi Kwei Armah, "Larsony, or Fiction as Criticism of Fiction", *New Classic* 4 (November 1977), pp. 33–45.

14. Armah, *The Beautyful Ones.* . ., p. 44.

15. Ibid., p. 67.

16. Ama Ata Aidoo, "No Saviours", *African Writers on African Writing*, ed. G. D. Killam (London: Heinemann, 1973), p. 15.

17. Sunday Anozie, "Le Nouveau Roman Africain", *The Conch* 2, 1 (1970), p. 29.

18. Wole Soyinka, *Myth, Literature and the African World* (Cambridge: Cambridge University Press, 1976), p. 116.

19. Kofi Awoonor, "Voyager and the Earth", *New Letters* 40, 1 (1973), p. 88.

20. Obiechina, *Culture, Tradition and Society*, pp. 104–08.

21. S.O.Iyasere, "Cultural Formalism and the Criticism of Modern African Literature", *Journal of Modern African Studies* 14, 2 (1976), p. 327.

22. D.S.Izevbaye, "Time in the African Novel", *Journal of Commonwealth Literature* 17, 1 (1982), p. 74.

23. E.M.W.Tillyard,*Shakespeare's History Plays* (Harmondsworth: Peregrine, 1962), pp. 240–318.

24. Robert Fraser, *The Novels of Ayi Kwei Armah: A Study in Polemical Fiction* (London: Heinemann, 1980), pp. 29, 62.

25. Ibid., pp. 12–13.

26. Ayi Kwei Armah, *Fragments* (London: Heinemann, 1974), p. 285.

27. Fraser, *The Novels of Ayi Kwei Armah*, p. 13.

Chapter II

1. Ayi Kwei Armah, "Asemka", *Okyeame* 3, 1 (December 1966), pp. 28–32.
2. Ibid., p. 32.
3. Ayi Kwei Armah, "Yaw Manu's Charm", *Atlantic Monthly* (May 1968), pp. 89–95.
4. Ibid., p. 89.
5. Ibid., pp. 93–94.
6. Ibid., p. 90.
7. Ayi Kwei Armah, "A Mystification: African Independence Revalued", *Pan-African Journal* 2, 2 (1969), p. 149.
8. Ayi Kwei Armah, "The Offal Kind", *Harper's Magazine* 1424 (January 1969), pp. 79–84.
9. Ibid., p. 84.
10. Ayi Kwei Armah, "Contact", *The New African* 4, 10 (December 1965), pp. 244–48.
11. Ibid., p. 246.
12. Ibid., p. 248.
13. Ibid., p. 248.
14. Ibid., p. 245.
15. Ibid., p. 246.
16. Ibid., p. 246.
17. Ayi Kwei Armah, "An African Fable", *Présence Africaine* 68 (1968), p. 193.
18. D.S.Izevbaye, "Ayi Kwei Armah and the 'I' of the Beholder", in *A Celebration of Black and African Writing*, eds. B. King and K.Ogungbesan (Oxford: Oxford University Press, 1975), p. 232.
19. Ayi Kwei Armah, *The Beautyful Ones Are Not Yet Born* (London: Heinemann, 1969), reset Heinemann edition, 1975, p. 148.
20. Armah, "An African Fable", p. 192.
21. Ibid., p. 194.
22. Ibid., p. 193.
23. Ibid., p. 192.
24. Ayi Kwei Armah, *Why Are We So Blest?* (London: Heinemann, 1974), p. 231.
25. Armah, "A Mystification. . .", p. 143.

26. Ayi Kwei Armah, "African Socialism: Utopian or Scientific?", *Présence Africaine* 64 (1967), p. 28.

27. Armah, "An African Fable", p. 196.

28. Ibid., p. 196.

29. Ibid., p. 196.

30. Ibid., p. 193.

31. Ayi Kwei Armah, "Aftermath", in *Messages: Poems from Ghana*, eds. K. Awoonor and G.Adali-Mortty (London: Heinemann, 1971), p. 89.

32. Ibid., p. 91.

Chapter III

1. Ayi Kwei Armah, *Why Are We So Blest?* (London: Heinemann, 1974), pp. 33, 100–03; "Fanon: The Awakener", *Negro Digest* 18, 12 (1969), p. 7.

2. Frantz Fanon, *The Wretched of the Earth*, trans. Constance Farrington (Harmondsworth: Penguin, 1967), pp. 46, 65, 118; Ayi Kwei Armah, "African Socialism: Utopian or Scientific?", *Présence Africaine* 64 (1967), pp. 26, 28.

3. Ayi Kwei Armah, "A Mystification: African Independence Revalued", *Pan-African Journal* 2, 2 (1969), p. 143.

4. Fanon, *The Wretched of the Earth*, pp. 138–39.

5. Ibid., pp. 120–45.

6. Armah, "A Mystification. . .", p. 146.

7. Armah, "African Socialism. . .", p. 15.

8. Ayi Kwei Armah, *Fragments* (London: Heinemann, 1974), p. 284.

9. Ibid., p. 116.

10. Fanon, *The Wretched of the Earth*, pp. 121, 125.

11. Armah, *Why Are We So Blest?* p. 163.

12. Fanon, *The Wretched of the Earth*, p. 142.

13. Armah, "African Socialism. . .", p. 29.

14. Fanon, *The Wretched of the Earth*, pp. 42, 74, 105–06, 127.

15. Armah, "African Socialism. . .", pp. 21–26; Fanon, *The Wretched of the Earth*, p. 132.

16. Armah, "A Mystification. . .", pp. 148, 151.

17. Fanon, *The Wretched of the Earth*, p. 137.

18. Armah, *Why Are We So Blest?*, p. 26.

19. Ibid., p. 243.

20. Frantz Fanon, *Toward the African Revolution*, trans. Haakon Chevalier (Harmondsworth: Penguin, 1970), p. 116; *The Wretched of the Earth*, p. 199.

21. Fanon, *The Wretched of the Earth*, p. 182.

22. Ibid., p. 48.

23. Ayi Kwei Armah, "Larsony, or Fiction as Criticism of Fiction", *New Classic* 4 (November 1977), p. 33.

24. Frantz Fanon, *Black Skin, White Masks*, trans. Charles Lam Markmann (New York: Grove Press, 1967), pp. 188, 191; *Toward the African Revolution* p. 30.

25. Frantz Fanon, *A Dying Colonialism*, trans. Haakon Chevalier (New York: Grove Press, 1967), p. 47.

26. Ibid., p. 63.

27. Fanon, *Black Skin, White Masks*, p. 69; Armah, *Why Are We So Blest?*, p. 101.

28. Armah, "African Socialism. . .", p. 16.

29. Fanon, *Black Skin, White Masks*, p. 116.

30. Armah, *Why Are We So Blest?*, pp. 127, 159.

31. Armah, "Fanon. . .", p. 42.

32. Armah, *Why Are We So Blest?*, pp. 231–32.

33. Fanon, *The Wretched of the Earth*, pp. 79, 134.

34. Armah, "A Mystification. . .", pp. 147–49.

35. Ibid., pp. 149, 151; Fanon, *The Wretched of the Earth*, pp. 135, 156.

36. Armah, "Larsony. . .", p. 44.

37. Fanon, *Black Skin, White Masks*, p. 129.

38. Armah, "Larsony. . .", pp. 43–44.

39. Armah, "African Socialism. . .", p. 29.

40. Armah, "Fanon. . .", p. 6.

41. Roger Barnard, "Frantz Fanon", *New Society* 11, 275 (January 4th, 1968), p. 13.

42. Fanon, *The Wretched of the Earth*, p. 192.

43. Ibid., p. 159.

44. Ayi Kwei Armah, "Pour les ibos, le régime de la haine silencieuse", *Jeune Afrique* 355 (October 29th, 1967), p. 20.

45. Fanon, *Toward the African Revolution*, p. 196.

46. Armah, "African Socialism. . .", p. 15.

47. Fanon, *The Wretched of the Earth*, pp. 168–70.

48. The critics who have commented on Armah's debts to Fanon are too numerous to mention here, but see in particular the following: Frederick I. Case, "The African Bourgeois in West African Literature", *Canadian Journal of African Studies* 7 (1973), pp. 262–65; Gareth Griffiths, "Structure and Image in Kwei Armah's *The Beautyful Ones Are Not Yet Born*", *Studies in Black Literature* 2, 2 (1971), pp. 5–6; Edward Lobb, "Personal and Political Fate in *Why Are We So Blest?*, *World Literature Written in English* 19 (1980), pp. 7, 14–16; Kirsten Holst Petersen, "Loss and Frustration: An Analysis of Armah's *Fragments*", *Kunapipi* 1, 1 (1979), p. 62; Emmanuel Obiechina, "Post-Independence Disillusionment in Three African Novels" in *Neo-African Literature and Culture*, eds. B. Lindfors and U. Schild (Wiesbaden: Heymann, 1976), pp. 143–46; Ben Obumselu, "Marx, Politics and the African Novel", *Twentieth Century Studies* 10 (1973), pp. 110–12.

49. Fanon, *The Wretched of the Earth*, p. 179.

50. Gwendolyn Brooks, *Report From Part One* (Detroit: Broadside Press, 1972), p. 127.

51. Ayi Kwei Armah, "Chaka", *Black World* 26, 4 (February 1975), pp. 87–88. Prototypical bloodthirsty polygamists and sorcerer-kings are also in plentiful supply in the medieval oral epic *Sundiata*, reviewed by Armah: see Ayi Kwei Armah, "Sundiata, An Epic of Old Mali", *Black World* 23, 7 (May 1974), p. 93.

52. Wole Soyinka, *Myth, Literature and the African World* (Cambridge: Cambridge University Press, 1976), p. 106.

53. Fanon, *The Wretched of the Earth*, pp. 171, 193.

54. Ibid., pp. 107–08.

Chapter IV

1. Ayi Kwei Armah, *Fragments* (London: Heinemann, 1974), p. 1.

2. Ibid., p. 223.

3. Arnold van Gennep, *The Rites of Passage*. 1906, trans. S. T. Kimball (London: Routledge & Kegan Paul, 1960), pp. 52–53.

4. Ayi Kwei Armah, *Why Are We So Blest?* (London: Heinemann, 1974), p. 263.

5. Armah, *Fragments*, pp. 138–39.

6. Kofi Awoonor, *This Earth, My Brother. . .* (London: Heinemann, 1972) p. 13.

7. Christie C. Achebe, "Literary Insights into the Ogbanje Phenomenon", *Journal of African Studies* 7, 1 (1980), p. 36.

8. Armah, *Fragments*, p. 284.

9. John S. Mbiti, *African Religions and Philosophy* (London: Heinemann, 1969), pp. 24–26, 82–84.

10. Geoffrey Parrinder, *West African Religion* (London: Epworth Press, 1969), 3rd edition, p. 115.

11. Ayi Kwei Armah, *The Beautyful Ones Are Not Yet Born* (London: Heinemann, 1969), reset edition, 1975, p. 145.

12. Joan Solomon, "A Commentary on Ayi Kwei Armah's *The Beautyful Ones Are Not Yet Born*", *English in Africa* 1, 2 (1974), p. 28.

13. Henry Chakava, "Ayi Kwei Armah and a Commonwealth of Souls", *Standpoints on African Literature*, ed. C. Wanjala (Nairobi: East African Literature Bureau, 1973), pp. 205, 207.

14. Armah, *The Beautyful Ones*, p. 88.

15. K. Ogungbesan, "Symbol and Meaning in *The Beautyful Ones Are Not Yet Born*", *African Literature Today* 7 (1975), p. 97; Eustace Palmer, *An Introduction to the African Novel* (London: Heinemann, 1972), pp. 132, 138.

16. Armah, *The Beautyful Ones*, pp. 46–49.

17. Armah, *Fragments*, p. 5.

18. Ibid., p. 280.

19. Daniéle Stewart, "Disillusionment Among Anglophone and Francophone African Writers", *Studies in Black Literature* 7, 1 (1976), p. 8.

20. Armah, *Fragments*, p. 6.

21. J. B. Danquah, *The Akan Doctrine of God* (London: Lutterworth Press, 1944), pp. 82–83.

22. Armah, *Fragments*, pp. 5, 7, 9.

23. Ibid., p. 213.

24. Ibid., p. 88.

25. Ibid., p. 139.

26. Ibid., pp. 1–2, 138.

27. Mbiti, *African Religions and Philosophy*, p. 25.

28. Armah, *Fragments*, pp. 282–83.

29. Armah, *The Beautyful Ones*, p. 98.

30. Armah, *Why Are We So Blest?*, pp. 31–32.

31. Ibid., pp. 222–23..

32. Armah, *Fragments*, p. 112.

33. Ibid., p. 122.

34. See Richard Priebe: "Escaping the Nightmare of History: The Development of a Mythic Consciousness in West African Literature", *Ariel* 4, 1 (1973), pp. 55–67; "Demonic Imagery and the Apocalyptic Vision in the Novels of Ayi Kwei Armah", *Yale French Studies* 53 (1976), pp. 102–36; "Popular Writing in Ghana: A Sociology and Rhetoric", *Research in African Literatures* 9, 3 (1978), pp. 395–422.

35. Victor Turner, *The Ritual Process* (Harmondsworth: Pelican, 1974), p. 114.

36. Mary Douglas, *Purity and Danger* (London: Routledge & Kegan Paul, 1969), pp. 35–40; Armah, *The Beautyful Ones*, pp. 101–02, 119, 178.

37. Victor Turner, *The Forest of Symbols* (Ithaca: Cornell University Press, 1970), p. 95.

38. Ayi Kwei Armah, "A Mystification: African Independence Revalued", *Pan-African Journal* 2, 2 (1969), p. 146.

39. See note 34 for a list of Priebe's articles.

40. Priebe, "Demonic Imagery. . .", p. 115. See my response to Priebe's argument in Derek Wright, "Ritual Modes and Social Models in African Fiction: The Case of Ayi Kwei Armah", *World Literature Written in English* 27, 2 (1987), pp. 195–207.

41. Harold Collins has dealt at length with Armah's ironic vision in "The Ironic Imagery of Armah's *The Beautyful Ones Are Not Yet Born*: The Putrescent Vision", *World Literature Written in English* 10 (1971), pp. 37–50.

42. The presence of a pattern of ritual purification in the first novel has been noticed by a number of critics, but see in particular: Leslie Fenton, "Symbolism and Theme in Peter's *The Second Round* and Armah's *The Beautyful Ones Are Not Yet Born*", *Pan-African Journal* 6 (1973), pp. 86–89; Emile Snyder, "New Directions in African Writings", *Pan-African Journal* 5 (1972), pp. 257–60; Solomon, "A Commentary. . .", p. 31. Priebe, to be

accurate, does speak of "carrying" ("Demonic Imagery. . .",
pp. 116, 121, 128) and at one point mentions the carrier
("Escaping the Nightmare. . .", p. 64), but he either confuses
him with the more properly transitional figure of the scapegoat,
who is more relevant to Baako in the second novel than to the
man in the first, or he uses the term in a general sense, without
reference to the rite's peculiar character and status, as part of his
ritual model of communitas-regenerated-structures taken from
Turner.

43. See, for example, Robin Horton, "New Year in the Delta",
Nigeria Magazine 67 (1960), pp. 256–74.

44. van Gennep, pp. 11, 21.

45. Turner, *The Forest of Symbols*, p. 102.

46. Wole Soyinka, Interview by Louis S. Gates, *Black World* 24,
10 (1975), pp. 40–41.

47. Ibid., pp. 40–41.

48. Soyinka has insisted upon the ordinariness of carriers,
who "are not artists, or teachers, or any of these special
classifications of society; they are just ordinary human beings
like you and me . . . The individual who acts as a carrier . . . is
doing nothing special, from other members of society who build
society and who guarantee survival of society in their own
way." Interview by Gates, p. 41.

49. Armah, *Fragments*, p. 145.

50. Soyinka, Gates Interview, p. 41. See also Kofi Awoonor,
Interview in *Palaver*, ed. B. Lindfors (Austin: African Research
Institute, University of Texas, 1972), p. 62, and Interview by
John Goldblatt, *Transition* 41 (1972), p. 44; J. O. Awolalu, *Yoruba
Beliefs and Sacrificial Rites* (Harlow: Longman, 1979), pp. 179–80;
Horton, "New Year in the Delta", pp. 260, 267.

51. Wole Soyinka, *Collected Plays, Vol.1* (Oxford: Oxford
University Press, 1973), pp. 113–46; Kofi Awoonor, *This Earth,
My Brother. . .* (London: Heinemann, 1972), pp. 17–23, 175–79.
See also Awoonor, Goldblatt Interview, p. 44; Horton, "New
Year in the Delta", pp. 272–73.

52. Gerald Moore argues that "redemption can only be the
reward of collective struggle, not a boon — a sort of golden
apple — delivered to us by a lone questing hero who searches
and suffers for an indifferent community". See his "Death,

Convergence and Rebirth in Two Black Novels", *Nigerian Journal of the Humanities* 2 (1978), p. 16. Chidi Amuta considers it to be "the paradox of Armah's art that he opts for a society based on community while confining the heroic functions to single individuals who are incapable of championing the communal cause", and charges the author with "creating visionary protagonists who do nothing physically about their decadent societies". See, respectively, his "Ayi Kwei Armah and the Mythopoesis of Mental Decolonization", *Ufahamu* 10, 3 (1981), p. 54, and "The Contemporary African Artist in Armah's Novels", *World Literature Written in English* 21, 3 (1982), p. 473.

53. Armah, *Why Are We So Blest?*, p. 101.

54. Mircea Eliade, *The Myth of the Eternal Return* (Princeton: Princeton University Press, 1974), 2nd edition, pp. 62–73.

Chapter V

1. Ayi Kwei Armah, *The Beautyful Ones Are Not Yet Born* (London: Heinemann, 1969). All page references are taken from the 1975 reset Heinemann edition and are given in parentheses in the text of the chapter.

2. Harold Collins, "The Ironic Imagery of Armah's *The Beautyful Ones Are Not Yet Born*: The Putrescent Vision", *World Literature Written in English* 20 (1971), p. 42.

3. Henry Chakava, "Ayi Kwei Armah and a Commonwealth of Souls", *Standpoints on African Literature*, ed. C. Wanjala (Nairobi: East African Literature Bureau, 1973), p. 198.

4. Robin Horton, "African Traditional Thought and Western Science", *Africa* 37 (1967), pp. 176–81. Dennis Duerden, however, has taken the contrary view that opposition to memorial retention of time is not designed to deny evidence of change but is instead intended to prevent the slavish imitation of inherited models that stops change from taking place, and that the destructiveness of historical time is, in fact, accepted by traditional African societies. Dennis Duerden, *African Art and Literature: The Invisible Present* (London: Heinemann, 1977), pp. 3–24.

5. Mircea Eliade, *The Myth of the Eternal Return*, trans. Willard. R. Trask (Princeton: Princeton University Press, 1974), 2nd edition.

6. John S. Mbiti, *African Religions and Philosophy* (London: Heinemann, 1969), pp. 22–28.

7. Sunday Anozie, *Structural Models and African Poetics* (London: Routledge & Kegan Paul, 1981), pp. 50–61.

8. D. S. Izevbaye, "Time in the African Novel", *Journal of Commonwealth Literature* 17, 1 (1982), pp. 78–85.

9. Time in traditional Africa, argue the theorists, is not an abstract, autonomous sequence existing in its own right but is measured and characterized by what is done in it and has no existence apart from events and immediately imaginable events, so that the remote future and forgotten past do not constitute time. Gerald Moore speaks of "a projection from living experience" in which "the activity itself is paramount, the time sequence relative and adaptable"; Mbiti of the traditional society's "phenomenon calendars" which, in the place of numeral calendars, register time as a composition of events. "Time has to be experienced in order to make sense or to become real," says Mbiti, "and is meaningful at the point of the event and not at the mathematical moment." Okot p'Bitek's Lawino would seem to be in full agreement with this: "In the wisdom of the Acoli/Time is not stupidly split up/Into seconds and minutes/It does not flow/Like beer in a pot/That is sucked/Until it is finished/. . .A person's age/Is shown by what he or she does/It depends on what he or she is." Walter Ong has demonstrated, moreover, that the perception of time in terms of occurrences is a feature common to all oral cultures and therefore not limited to African ones.

See, respectively: Gerald Moore, "Time and Experience in African Poetry", *Transition* 26 (1966), p. 18; Mbiti, pp. 17, 19; Okot p'Bitek, *Song of Lawino* (Nairobi: East African Publishing House, 1966), pp. 97, 105; Walter Ong, *Orality and Literacy* (London: Methuen, 1982), pp. 31–33, 46–49, 66–67, 76–77.

10. Mbiti conceives of time in traditional Africa as a rhythmical, seasonal continuum, endlessly returning: "Outside the reckoning of the year, African time concept is silent and indifferent. People . . . expect the events of the rain season, planting, harvesting, dry season, rain season again, planting again, and so on to continue for ever. Each year comes and goes, adding to the time dimension of the past." Mbiti, p. 21.

11. Among the many commentators who have noticed Western influences on Armah's first novel, Shelby Steele has traced imagistic and stylistic features to the existentialist novels of Sartre and Camus, *Nausea* and *The Stranger*, and Sandra Barkan to the works of Celine and Rabelais, whilst Sunday Anozie has linked the spatial, descriptive treatment of time in this and other African novels with Robbe-Grillet's "mental architecture of time" and "mental structures denuded of time".

See, respectively: Shelby Steele, "Existentialism in the Novels of Ayi Kwei Armah", *Obsidian* 3, 1 (1977), pp. 10–11; Sandra Barkan, "Beyond 'Larsony': On the Possibility of Understanding Texts Across Cultures", *World Literature Today* 57, 1 (1983), p. 37; Anozie, pp. 66–75; Alain Robbe-Grillet, *Pour un nouveau roman* (Paris: Gallimard, 1963), p. 164.

12. Horton, "African Traditional Thought. . .", p. 177.

13. Kofi Awoonor, *This Earth, My Brother. . .* (London: Heinemann, 1972), pp. 28, 179.

14. Anozie, p. 61. The idea of the synchronic continuum is favoured by a number of writers and theorists of traditional time in Africa. "Since whatever has happened or will happen to the living man exists within him at the present moment," argues Gerald Moore, "there is a sense in which all experience enjoys a simultaneous reality." Moore views time in traditional communities as a flux of "past, present and future which all exist simultaneously in the continuum of space-time". The idea that all events contain the possibility of other past or future events informs some religious conceptualizations of time as a cyclic reality in which, as in Soyinka's Yoruba cosmology, "present life contains within it manifestations of the ancestral, the living and the unborn".

See, respectively: Gerald Moore, "Time and Experience in African Poetry", p. 19, and "The Imagery of Death in African Poetry", *Africa* 38 (1968), p. 63; Wole Soyinka, *Myth, Literature and the African World* (Cambridge: Cambridge University Press, 1976), p. 144.

15. Mbiti, p. 23.

16. Eliade, p. 90.

17. Ibid., pp. 134–36.

18. Ibid., p. 118.

19. Eva Meyerowitz, *The Sacred State of the Akan* (London: Faber, 1951), p. 153.

20. Kofi Awoonor, Interview in *Palaver: Interviews with Five African Writers*, ed. B. Lindfors (Austin: African Research Institute, University of Texas, 1972), p. 62.

21. J. G. Frazer, *The Golden Bough*, 1922 (London: Macmillan, 1967), abridged version, p. 756.

22. Wole Soyinka, Interview by Louis S.Gates, *Black World* 24, 10 (1975), pp. 40–41.

23. R. N. Henderson, *The King in Everyman: Evolutionary Trends in Onitsha Ibo Society and Culture* (New Haven: Yale University Press, 1972), p. 407.

24. J. O. Awolalu, *Yoruba Beliefs and Sacrificial Rites* (Harlow: Longman, 1979), p. 180.

25. Awoonor, *This Earth, My Brother. . .*, p. 122.

26. Richard Priebe, "Demonic Imagery and the Apocalyptic Vision in the Novels of Ayi Kwei Armah", *Yale French Studies* 53 (1976), p. 110; Kofi Awoonor, Interview by John Goldblatt, *Transition* 41 (1972), p. 44.

27. Awolalu, pp. 155, 179–80; Robin Horton, "New Year in the Delta", *Nigeria Magazine* 67 (1960), p. 259; Henderson. p. 402.

28. Terry Goldie, "A Connection of Images: The Structure of Symbols in *The Beautyful Ones Are Not Yet Born*", *Kunapipi* 1, 1 (1979), p. 104.

29. Horton, "New Year in the Delta", p. 273.

30. Ibid., pp. 273–74.

31. Margaret Folarin, "An Additional Comment on Ayi Kwei Armah's *The Beautyful Ones Are Not Yet Born*", *African Literature Today* 5 (1971), p. 122.

32. Leonard Kibera, "Pessimism and the African Novelist: Ayi Kwei Armah's *The Beautyful Ones Are Not Yet Born*", *Journal of Commonwealth Literature* 14, 1 (1979), p. 69.

33. Richard Niemi, "Will the Beautiful Ones ever be Born?" *Pan-Africanist* 3 (1971), p. 22.

34. D. S. Izevbaye, "Ayi Kwei Armah and the 'I' of the Beholder", in *A Celebration of Black and African Writing*, eds. B.King and K. Ogungbesan (Oxford: Oxford University Press, 1975), p. 234.

35. Horton, "New Year in the Delta", p. 273; E. O. James,

Sacrifice and Sacrament (London: Thames & Hudson, 1962), pp. 105–08.

36. S. K. Panter-Brick, "Fiction and Politics: The African Writer's Abdication", *Journal of Commonwealth and Comparative Politics* 13 (1975), p. 80.

37. Frazer, p. 738.

38. E. O. James, *Origins of Sacrifice* (New York & London: Kennikat Press, 1933), p. 25.

39. L. Levy-Bruhl, *Primitives and the Supernatural* (London: Allen & Unwin, 1936), pp. 242–43.

40. S.O. Iyasere, "Cultural Formalism and the Criticism of Modern African Literature", *Journal of Modern African Studies* 14, 2 (1976), p. 327.

41. R. S. Rattray, *Ashanti* (Oxford: Clarendon Press, 1923), p. 167.

42. Horton, "New Year in the Delta", p. 274.

43. Awoonor, *Palaver*, p. 62.

44. Awoonor, Goldblatt Interview, p. 44.

45. Awoonor, *This Earth, My Brother. . .*, p. 179.

46. Awoonor, Goldblatt Interview, p. 44.

47. R. S. Rattray, *Religion and Art in Ashanti* (Oxford: Clarendon Press, 1927), p. 136, and *Ashanti*, pp. 153, 165; Meyerowitz, *Sacred State*, pp. 153–54, 161, 174–75.

48. Rattray, *Ashanti*, pp. 165–66, 210, and *Religion and Art*, pp. 128, 138; Eva Meyerowitz *The Akan of Ghana* (London: Faber, 1958), p. 39, and *Sacred State*, pp. 155–56.

49. Rattray, *Ashanti*, pp. 209, 211, and *Religion and Art*, p. 126; Meyerowitz, *Sacred State*, p. 155.

50. Rattray, *Ashanti*, pp. 165, 167, and *Religion and Art*, pp. 128, 139, 143; Meyerowitz, *Akan of Ghana*, p. 69.

51. Gabriel Okara, *The Voice* (London: Heinemann, 1970). See my article, "Ritual and Reality in the Novels of Wole Soyinka, Gabriel Okara and Kofi Awoonor", *Kunapipi* 9, 1 (1987), pp. 65–74.

52. The Ijaw carrier removes the sicknesses of the recent past by re-enacting the conquest of smallpox by the rite's founder in the ancestral past, and the Onitsha king, in his "dreaming", communes with figures from the mythical past whilst the past year's "hunger time" is symbolically swept from kitchens.

Horton, "New Year in the Delta", p. 259; Henderson, pp. 391–92, 407.

53. Awoonor, *This Earth, My Brother. . .*, p. 29.

54. Derek Wright, "The Ritual Context of Two Plays by Soyinka", *Theatre Research International* 12, 1 (1987), pp. 51–61.

55. Wole Soyinka, *The Strong Breed* and *The Bacchae of Euripides, Collected Plays Vol.1* (Oxford: Oxford University Press, 1973), pp. 113–46, 233–307.

56. Appropriately, the disease-awakening and slowly-refertilizing flood tides which determine the nature of purification rituals in West African delta communities characterize the year's death as a slow wasting or sluggish entropy, and have little in common with the apocalyptic deluge which heralds the re-creation of the world in Eliade's account of New Year ceremonies. Eliade, pp. 62–68.

57. Horton, "New Year in the Delta", p. 274.

58. In transition rites proper, blood may connote purification or revived blood-bonds of communal solidarity, menstrual exhaustion or the quickening potency of sacrifice; palm-fronds figure both as punitive instruments and as fertility wands; and dirt, which Mary Douglas regards as unstructured matter ambiguously between states and so "unclean" because unclear, acquires a special and dangerous energy. "Undoing, dissolution, decomposition," writes Victor Turner, "are accompanied by processes of growth, transformation, and the reformulation of old elements in new patterns."

See, respectively: Mary Douglas, *Purity and Danger* (London: Routledge & Kegan Paul, 1969), pp. 35–40, 94–97, 114–28; Victor Turner, *The Forest of Symbols* (Ithaca: Cornell University Press, 1970), p. 95.

59. Blood in the Ijaw *Amagba*, and in the Ashanti *Odwira* in Rattray's account, signifies menstrual pollution and purification, and palm-fronds have no fertility potential: protecting the carrier-figure in these rites as the tyre tube does the man in Armah's novel, they are the standard material for insulating dangerous and polluting objects, and in the Yoruba *Bòábù*, where they are sacred to Ogun, they are used for the purification of house-sweeping and mock-scourging.

See, respectively: R. S. Rattray, *Religion and Art*, pp. 136-37;

Horton, "New Year in the Delta", p. 260; Awolalu, pp. 155, 169.

60. Dirt as it figures in the carrier rite would therefore, in Mary Douglas's classifications, be safe from the "pollutive danger" which issues from the ambiguous, anarchic half-identities of viscously active, rotting and excremental material. Douglas, p. 160.

61. Douglas, pp. 7–58, 94–129, 159–79; Victor Turner, *The Ritual Process* (Harmondsworth: Penguin, 1974), pp. 80–118.

62. Horton, "New Year in the Delta", p. 274.

63. Awoonor, Goldblatt Interview, p. 44; Interview in *Palaver*, p. 60.

64. Awoonor, Goldblatt Interview, p. 44.

65. Robert Fraser, *The Novels of Ayi Kwei Armah* (London: Heinemann, 1980), p. 25.

66. Awoonor, Goldblatt Interview, p. 44.

Chapter VI

1. Ayi Kwei Armah, *Fragments* (London: Heinemann, 1974). All page references are taken from this edition and are given in parentheses in the text of the chapter.

2. S. G. Williamson, *Akan Religion and the Christian Faith* (Accra: Ghana Universities Press, 1965), pp. 56–57.

3. Ayi Kwei Armah, *The Beautyful Ones Are Not Yet Born* (London: Heinemann, 1969), reset Heinemann edition 1975, pp. 124–25.

4. Ibid., p. 106.

5. Robert Fraser has detected in the novel's pivotal infanticide an attempt to exorcize a general, communal impotence. See Robert Fraser, *The Novels of Ayi Kwei Armah* (London: Heinemann, 1980), pp. 41–42.

6. Northrop Frye, "The Archetypes of Literature", *Kenyon Review* 13, 1 (1951), p. 103. The relevance of Frye's remarks about ritual to *Fragments* has been noticed by William Lawson, *The Western Scar* (Athens: Ohio University Press, 1982), p. 84. B. J. Barthold sees Naana as the "Keeper of Time" in the novel. See B. J. Barthold, *Black Time: Fiction of Africa, the Caribbean and the U.S.A.* (New Haven: Yale University Press, 1981), pp. 32–33.

7. Kenelm Burridge, *New Heaven, New Earth* (Oxford: Black-well, 1969), p. 52. The conditions for cargoism laid down by Burridge comprise an oppressed or dissatisfied population awaiting a miraculous deliverance as a reaction to unequal access to newly-acquired power, privilege and the material comforts of European-style prosperity; a readiness in the popular consciousness to believe in America as an "ultimum bonum", a land "far away and beyond the sea where everything could be learned and the good things of this world obtained"; and a post-colonial black-white reversal which produces "a new man, a black man with European abilities and capacities of understanding, a black man enjoying European conditions of being" (Burridge, pp. 48, 57, 69). The situation of the Ghanaians in *Fragments* approximates to cargo-conditions in each of these particulars. For a fuller treatment of the novel's cargoist themes, see my article, *Fragments*: The Cargo Connection", *Kunapipi* 7, 1 (1985), pp. 45–58.

8. Ibid., pp. 32, 52.

9. W. E. Abraham, *The Mind of Africa* (London: Wiedenfeld & Nicolson, 1962), p. 62.

10. Burridge, p. 50.

11. J. S. Mbiti, *African Religions and Philosophy* (London: Heinemann, 1969), p. 70.

12. J. H. Nketia, *Funeral Dirges of the Akan People* (New York: Negro Universities Press, 1969), p. 120.

13. Abraham, p. 52; Kofi Opoku, "The World-View of the Akan", in *Akan History and Culture*, ed. J. K. Fynn (Harlow: Longman, 1982), p. 62.

14. A. van Gennep, *The Rites of Passage* (London: Routledge & Kegan Paul, 1960), p. 168.

15. Abraham, p. 62; Mbiti, p. 161; Gerald Moore, "The Debate on Existence in African Literature", *Présence Africaine* 81 (1972), p. 46.

16. Nketia, pp. 189, 48–49; Mbiti, pp. 26, 82–84; Richard Priebe, "Demonic Imagery and the Apocalyptic Vision in the Novels of Ayi Kwei Armah", *Yale French Studies* 53 (1976), p. 126.

17. Mbiti, p. 70; Nketia, p. 25.

18. Nketia, pp. 200–03.

19. Ron Rassner, "Fragments: The Cargo Mentality", *Ba Shiru* 5, 2 (1974), p. 60.

20. Abraham, p. 73.

21. Ibid., p. 75.

22. Williamson, pp. 127, 129.

23. Mbiti, p. 110.

24. Eva Meyerowitz, *The Akan of Ghana* (London: Faber, 1958), p. 112.

25. Mbiti, p. 162.

26. Ibid., p. 27.

27. Madelaine Manoukian, *Akan and Ga-Adangme Peoples* (London: Africa Institute, 1950), p. 89.

28. van Gennep, pp. 51–53; Geoffrey Parrinder, *West African Religion* (London: Epworth Press, 1969), p. 96.

29. Parrinder, p. 98.

30. Manoukian, p. 51.

31. Mbiti, p. 84.

32. Parrinder, p. 106; Mbiti, p. 90.

33. Eva Meyerowitz, *The Sacred State of the Akan* (London: Faber, 1951), p. 86.

34. Ibid., p. 142.

35. van Gennep, p. 179.

36. Meyerowitz, *The Sacred State of the Akan*, pp. 76–77.

37. Williamson, p. 88; Mbiti, p. 45; Meyerowitz, *The Sacred State of the Akan*, p. 77.

38. Meyerowitz, *The Sacred State of the Akan*, p. 174; R. S. Rattray, *Religion and Art in Ashanti* (Oxford: Clarendon Press, 1927), p. 135.

39. Abraham, p. 60; Meyerowtiz, *The Akan of Ghana*, p. 123; Manoukian, p. 58; Robert Fraser, *The Novels of Ayi Kwei Armah* (London: Heinemann, 1980), p. 39.

40. Williamson, pp. 105–06; Nketia, p. 27; Opoku, p. 72.

41. Manoukian, pp. 26–27.

42. Meyerowitz, *The Sacred State of the Akan*, p. 197.

43. Nketia, pp. 6, 121–23; Parrinder, p. 106.

44. Nketia, pp. 139, 200–03; Meyerowitz, *The Akan of Ghana*, p. 69.

Chapter VII

1. Ayi Kwei Armah, *Why Are We So Blest?* (London: Heinemann, 1974), p. 70. Further page references are given in parentheses in the text of the chapter.

2. Robert Scholes, *The Fabulators* (New York: Oxford University Press, 1967), p. 171.

3. Northrop Frye, "The Archetypes of Literature", *Kenyon Review* 13, 1 (1951), p. 103.

4. Mircea Eliade, *The Myth of the Eternal Return* (Princeton: Princeton University Press, 1974), 2nd edition, pp. 12–21, 36.

5. Ayi Kwei Armah, *Fragments* (London: Heinemann, 1974), pp. 111, 13. Further page references are given in parentheses in the text of the chapter.

6. Robert Fraser, *The Novels of Ayi Kwei Armah* (London: Heinemann, 1980), p. 56.

7. Malcolm X, with the assistance of Alex Haley, *The Autobiography of Malcolm X* (Harmondsworth: Penguin, 1968), p. 371.

8. Stokely Carmichael and Charles V. Hamilton, *Black Power* (Harmondsworth: Pelican, 1969), p. 68.

9. Angela Davis, *If They Come in the Morning* (London: Orbach & Chambers, 1971), pp. 188–90; Carmichael and Hamilton, pp. 47, 54–55, 72; Malcolm X, pp. 343, 479, 487.

10. LeRoi Jones, "A Black Value System", in *Black Poets and Prophets*, eds. W. King and E. Anthony (New York: New American Library, 1972), pp. 141, 146; Carmichael and Hamilton, p. 72; Malcolm X, p. 352.

11. Carmichael and Hamilton, p. 95.

12. Ayi Kwei Armah, "Fanon: The Awakener", *Negro Digest* 18, 12 (October 1969), pp. 6, 37.

13. Eldridge Cleaver, *Post-Prison Writings and Speeches*, ed. Robert Scheer (London: Jonathan Cape, 1969), p. 61; Carmichael and Hamilton, pp. 26–31, 46–47.

14. James Baldwin, *The Fire Next Time* (Harmondsworth: Penguin, 1964), p. 43.

15. Ayi Kwei Armah, "African Socialism: Utopian or Scientific?", *Présence Africaine* 64 (1967), p. 12.

16. Carmichael and Hamilton, p. 184.

17. James Baldwin, *Nobody Knows My Name* (London: Corgi, 1965), p. 151.

18. Malcolm X, pp. 112, 183–84, 210–11.

19. Robert Fraser, "The American Background in *Why Are We So Blest?*", *African Literature Today* 9 (1978), p. 40.

20. James Booth has drawn attention to these aspects of sexuality in the novel in his trenchant article,"*Why Are We So Blest?* and the Limits of Metaphor", *Journal of Commonwealth Literature* 15, 1 (1980), p. 60.

Chapter VIII

1. Ayi Kwei Armah, *Why Are We So Blest?* (London: Heinemann, 1974), p. 231.

2. Ayi Kwei Armah, *Two Thousand Seasons* (London: Heinemann, 1979). All page references are taken from this edition and are given in parentheses in the text of the article.

3. Isidore Okpewho, "Myth and Modern Fiction: Armah's *Two Thousand Seasons*", *African Literature Today* 13 (1983), pp. 4–12.

4. Wole Soyinka, *Myth, Literature and the African World* (Cambridge: Cambridge University Press, 1976), pp. 107–08.

5. Walter J. Ong, *Orality and Literacy: The Technologizing of the Word* (London & New York: Methuen, 1982), p. 104; Jack Goody, *The Domestication of the Savage Mind* (Cambridge: Cambridge University Press, 1977), pp. 49–50; D. S. Izevbaye, "Time in the African Novel", *Journal of Commonwealth Literature* 17, 1 (1982), p. 74.

6. Ong, pp. 40–41.

7. See my Chapter 2, pp. 28–31, and Chapter 5, p. 93–94.

8. Ayi Kwei Armah, *The Beautyful Ones Are Not Yet Born* (London: Heinemann, 1969; reset edition, 1975), pp. 70, 71, 72, 74.

9. Ibid., pp. 72, 75.

10. Robert Fraser, *The Novels of Ayi Kwei Armah* (London: Heinemann, 1980), pp. 72–73, 105.

11. Ayi Kwei Armah, "African Socialism: Utopian or Scientific?", *Présence Africaine* 64 (1967), p. 15.

12. Chinua Achebe, *Morning Yet on Creation Day* (London: Heinemann, 1975), pp. 25–26.

13. Ayi Kwei Armah, *Fragments* (London: Heinemann, 1974), p. 6.

14. Soyinka, p. 106.

15. Kofi Anyidoho, "Historical Realism and the Visionary Ideal: Ayi Kwei Armah's *Two Thousand Seasons*", *Ufahamu* 11, 2 (1981–82), p. 114.

16. Armah, "African Socialism. . .", p. 8.

17. Armah, *The Beautyful Ones. . .*", p. 52.

18. Ibid., p. 12.

19. Armah, *Fragments*, p. 275.

20. Armah, *Why Are We So Blest?*, p. 208.

Chapter IX

1. Ayi Kwei Armah, *The Healers* (London: Heinemann, 1979). All page references are taken from this edition and are given in parentheses in the text of the chapter.

2. Derek Wright, "Critical and Historical Fictions: Robert Fraser's Reading of *The Healers*", *English In Africa* 15, 1 (1988), pp. 71–82.

3. Robert Fraser, *The Novels of Ayi Kwei Armah* (London: Heinemann, 1980), pp. 88–90.

4. Ibid., p. 89.

5. Ibid., p. 88.

6. Ibid., p. 88.

7. Ibid., p. 97.

8. Ibid., p. 91.

9. Bernth Lindfors, "Armah's Histories", *African Literature Today* 11 (1980), p. 91.

10. Fraser, pp. 91–92.

11. Abena P. A. Busia, "Parasites and Prophets: The Use of Women in Ayi Kwei Armah's Novels" in *Ngambika: Studies of Women in African Literature*, eds.Carole Boyce Davies and Anne Adams Graves (Trenton: Africa World Press, 1986), p. 111.

12. Neil Lazarus, "Implications of Technique in Ayi Kwei Armah's *The Healers*", *Research in African Literatures* 13, 4 (1982), p. 490.

13. Jennifer Evans, "Women of 'The Way': *Two Thousand Seasons*, Female Images and Black Identity", *ACLALS* 6, 1 (1982), p. 26.

14. Lindfors, p. 95.

15. Malcolm X, *Autobiography of Malcolm X* (Harmondsworth: Penguin, 1968), pp. 261, 347. The rhetoric of "white devilry" was also adopted by the Black Muslim preachers: the "white devils" of *Two Thousand Seasons* are the colonial counterparts of those who populate the pages of Malcolm X.

As regards the unitary origins of the earth's black people, Armah claims, in his review of *Sundiata*, that the griot is no mere tribal artist but "a historian of the black people" and refers to the knowledge, passed on by the oral memory, of "how the black people divided into tribes". He has earlier in the essay, however, described *Sundiata* as "the prime stuff of legends and archetypal myths", not an objective historical record. Ayi Kwei Armah, "Sundiata, An Epic of Old Mali", *Black World* 23, 7 (May 1974), pp. 94–95.

16. Y. S. Boafo, "The Nature of Healing in Ayi Kwei Armah's *The Healers*", *Komparatistische Hefte* 13 (1986), pp. 99–102.

17. Lindfors, p. 93.

Chapter X

1. Ayi Kwei Armah, "Dakar Hieroglyphs", *West Africa* 19 May 1986, pp. 1043–44. Armah has also taken Senghor and his Catholic-Islamic hegemony to task for the banning of *Ceddo*, Sembene Ousmane's iconoclastic film about the struggles of traditional Senegalese communities and their religions against the incursions of Islam and Christianity. Ayi Kwei Armah, "Islam and *Ceddo*", *West Africa* 8 October 1984, p. 2031.

2. Wole Soyinka, "We Africans must speak in one language", *Afrika* 20, 9 (1979), pp. 22–23.

3. Ayi Kwei Armah, "Our Language Problem", *West Africa* 29 April 1985, p. 832.

4. Ayi Kwei Armah, "The Oxygen of Translation", *West Africa* 11 February 1985, p. 263.

5. Ayi Kwei Armah, "Africa and the Francophone Dream", *West Africa* 28 April 1986, pp. 884–85.

6. Ayi Kwei Armah, "The Lazy School of Literary Criticism", *West Africa* 25 February 1985, p. 355.

7. Armah, "The Oxygen of Translation", p. 263.

8. Ayi Kwei Armah, "Writers as Professionals", *West Africa* 11 August 1986, p. 1680.

9. Ayi Kwei Armah, "The Third World Hoax", *West Africa* 25 August 1986, p. 1782.

10. Ayi Kwei Armah, "The View from PEN International", *West Africa* 26 November 1984, pp. 2384–85; "The Lazy School of Literary Criticism", p. 356.

11. Ayi Kwei Armah, "One Writer's Education", *West Africa* 26 August 1985, pp. 1752–53.

12. Ayi Kwei Armah, "Masks and Marx: The Marxist Ethos vis-à-vis African Revolutionary Theory and Praxis", *Présence Africaine* 131 (1984), p. 53.

13. Ibid., p. 55.

14. Ibid., p. 62.

15. Frantz Fanon, *The Wretched of the Earth*, trans. Constance Farrington (Harmondsworth: Penguin, 1967), pp. 251–52.

16. Armah, "Masks and Marx", p. 59.

17. Ibid., p. 63.

18. Amilcar Cabral, *Return to the Source* (New York: Monthly Review, 1973), pp. 45, 54–55; *Revolution in Guinea* (New York: Monthly Review, 1972), p. 37.

19. Armah, "Masks and Marx", pp. 63–64.

20. Armah, "Writers as Professionals", p. 1680.

21. Armah, "Our Language Problem", pp. 831–32.

22. Armah, "Africa and the Francophone Dream", p. 885.

23. Ibid., p. 885.

24. Armah, "Masks and Marx", p. 58.

25. Armah, "The Third World Hoax", p. 1782.

26. Armah, "Our Language Problem", p. 832.

27. Armah, "Writers as Professionals", p. 1680.

28. Armah, "Africa and the Francophone Dream", p. 885.

29. Armah, "The Oxygen of Translation", p. 263.

30. Armah, "Masks and Marx", p. 62.

31. Cabral, *Return to the Source*, p. 49.

32. Ayi Kwei Armah, "Halfway to Nirvana", *West Africa* 24 September 1984, p. 1948.

33. Ibid., pp. 1947–48.

34. Ibid., p. 1947.

35. Robert Fraser, *The Novels of Ayi Kwei Armah* (London: Heinemann, 1980), pp. 101–06.

36. Armah, "One Writer's Education", p. 1753.

37. Ibid., pp. 1752–53.

38. Ibid., p. 1753; "The Lazy School of Literary Criticism", p. 356.

39. Armah, "Masks and Marx", pp. 35–36.

40. Ayi Kwei Armah, "Sundiata, an Epic of Old Mali", *Black World* 23, 7 (1974), p. 96.

41. Chinua Achebe, "The Novelist as Teacher", in John Press ed. *Commonwealth Literature* (London: Heinemann, 1965), p. 204.

42. Armah, "One Writer's Education", p. 1753.

43. Fraser, pp. 105–06.

44. Ibid., pp. xii, 72.

45. Ibid., p. 106.

46. Ibid., pp. 105, xii.

47. A number of critics have complained of a decline in quality since *Fragments*. See: Gerald Moore, *Wole Soyinka*, 2nd edition (London: Evans Bros., 1978), p. 164; Peter Sabor, "Palm-Wine and Drinkards: African Literature and its Critics", *Ariel* 12, 3 (1981), p. 123.

48. Fraser, p. 106.

49. Ayi Kwei Armah, *The Healers* (London: Heinemann, 1979), p. 1.

50. Ibid., pp. 27, 148.

51. It is widely rumoured that Armah has produced two more novels since *The Healers* but, for one reason or another, has not seen fit to publish them. One of his recent essays refers to "work on notes for several novels, short stories and essays". Armah, "The Lazy School of Literary Criticism", p. 355.

52. Ibid., p. 355; Armah, "Writers as Professionals", p. 1680.

Bibliography

Primary Works

Works by Ayi Kwei Armah

Novels

The Beautyful Ones Are Not Yet Born. Boston: Houghton Mifflin, 1968; London: Heinemann Educational Books, 1969, reset 1975. Translated into Swahili as *Wema Hawajazaliwa*. Nairobi: Heinemann, 1976.

Fragments. Boston: Houghton Mifflin, 1970; London: Heinemann Educational Books, 1974; Nairobi: East African Publishing House, 1974.

Why Are We So Blest? New York: Doubleday, 1972; London: Heinemann Educational Books, 1974; Nairobi: East African Publishing House, 1974.

Two Thousand Seasons. Nairobi: East African Publishing House, 1973; London: Heinemann Educational Books, 1979; Chicago: Third World Press, 1980.

The Healers. Nairobi: East African Publishing House, 1978; London: Heinemann Educational Books, 1979.

Short Stories

"Contact". *The New African*, 4, 10 (December 1965), 244–46, 248.

"Asemka". *Okyeame*, 3, 1 (December 1966), 28–32.

"Yaw Manu's Charm". *Atlantic* (May 1968), 89–95.

"An African Fable". *Présence Africaine*, 68 (1968), 192–96.

"The Offal Kind". *Harper's Magazine*, 1424 (January 1969), 79–84.

"Halfway to Nirvana". *West Africa*, 24 September 1984, 1947–48.

Poem

"Aftermath". In *Messages: Poems from Ghana*. Eds. Kofi Awoonor and G. Adali Mortty. London: Heinemann Educational Books, 1970. pp. 89–91.

Essays

"La mort passe sous les blancs". *L'Afrique Littéraire et Artistique*, 3 (February 1960), 21–28.

"Pour les ibos, le régime de la haine silencieuse". *Jeune Afrique*, 355 (29 October 1967), 18–20.

"African Socialism: Utopian or Scientific?" *Présence Africaine*, 64 (1967), 6–30.

"A Mystification: African Independence Revalued". *Pan-African Journal*, 2, 2 (Spring 1969), 141–51.

"Fanon: The Awakener". *Negro Digest*, 18, 12 (October 1969), 4–9, 29–43.

"Sundiata, An Epic of Old Mali". *Black World*, 23, 7 (1974), 51–52, 93–96.

"Chaka". *Black World*, 24, 4 (1975), 51–52, 84–90. Reprinted as "The Definitive Chaka". *Transition*, 50 (1976), 10–15.

"Larsony, or Fiction as Criticism of Fiction". *Asemka*, 4 (September 1976), 1–14. Reprinted in *New Classic*, 4 (November 1977), 33–45.

"Masks and Marx: The Marxist Ethos vis-à-vis African Revolutionary Theory and Praxis". *Présence Africaine*, 131 (1984), 35–65.

"Islam and 'Ceddo'". *West Africa*, 8 October 1984, 2031.

"The View from PEN International". *West Africa*, 26 November 1984, 2384–85.

"The Oxygen of Translation". *West Africa*, 11 February 1985, 262–63.

"The Lazy School of Literary Criticism". *West Africa*, 25 February 1985, 355–56.

"The Caliban Complex". *West Africa*, 18 & 25 March 1985, 521–22, 570–71.

"Our Language Problem". *West Africa*, 29 April 1985, 831–32.

"The Teaching of Creative Writing". *West Africa*, 20 May 1985, 994–95.

"One Writer's Education". *West Africa*, 26 August 1985, 1752–53.
"Flood and Famine, Drought and Glut". *West Africa*, 30 September 1985, 2011–12.
"Africa and the Francophone Dream". *West Africa*, 28 April 1986, 884–85.
"Dakar Hieroglyphs". *West Africa*, 19 May 1986, 1043–44.
"Writers as Professionals". *West Africa*, 11 August 1986, 1680.
"The Third World Hoax". *West Africa*, 25 August 1986, 1781-82.

Works by other Authors

Achebe, Chinua. *Things Fall Apart*. London: Heinemann, 1958.
—— *No Longer At Ease*. London: Heinemann, 1960.
Aidoo, Ama Ata. *The Dilemma of a Ghost*. Harlow: Longman, 1965.
—— *No Sweetness Here*. Harlow: Longman, 1970.
Awoonor, Kofi. *This Earth, My Brother. . .* London: Heinemann, 1972.
—— "Comes the Voyager at Last". *Okike*, 7 (April 1975), 31–57.
Baldwin, James. *The Fire Next Time*. Harmondsworth: Penguin, 1964.
—— *Nobody Knows My Name*. London: Corgi, 1965.
Mofolo, Thomas. *Chaka*. 1925. Trans. Daniel P. Kunene. London: Heinemann, 1981.
Okara, Gabriel. *The Voice*. London: Heinemann, 1970.
Ouologuem, Yambo. *Bound To Violence*. Trans. Ralph Manheim. London: Heinemann, 1971.
p'Bitek, Okot. *Song of Lawino*. Nairobi: East African Publishing House, 1966.
Schwartz-Bart, André. *The Last of the Just*. Trans. Stephen Becker. Harmondsworth: Penguin, 1977.
Soyinka, Wole. *The Interpreters*. London: Heinemann, 1970.
—— *Season of Anomy*. London: Rex Collings, 1973.
—— *Collected Plays*. Vol. 1. Oxford: Oxford University Press, 1973.
—— *The Bacchae of Euripides*. London: Eyre Methuen, 1973.

Secondary Works

Books

Abraham, W.E. *The Mind of Africa*. London: Weidenfeld & Nicolson, 1962.

Achebe, Chinua. *Morning Yet On Creation Day*. London: Heinemann, 1975.

Anozie, Sunday. *Structural Models and African Poetics*. London: Routledge & Kegan Paul, 1981.

Awolalu, J. Omosade. *Yoruba Beliefs and Sacrificial Rites*. Harlow: Longman, 1979.

Awoonor, Kofi. *The Breast of the Earth*. New York: NOK, 1975.

Balmer, W.T. *A History of the Akan Peoples of the Gold Coast*. Repr. New York: Negro Universities Press, 1969.

Barthold, Bonnie Jo. *Black Time: Fiction of Africa, the Caribbean and the U.S.A.* New Haven: Yale University Press, 1981.

Booth, James. *Writers and Politics in Nigeria*. London: Hodder & Stoughton, 1981.

Brooks, Gwendolyn. *Report From Part One*. Detroit: Broadside Press, 1972.

Brown, Lloyd W. Ed. *The Black Writer in Africa and the Americas*. Los Angeles: Hennessey & Ingalls, 1973.

Burke, Kenneth. *A Grammar of Motives*. New York: Prentice Hall, 1945.

Burness, Donald. *Shaka, King of the Zulus in African Literature*. Washington D.C.: Three Continents Press, 1976.

Burridge, Kenelm. *Mambu: A Melanesian Millenium*. London: Methuen, 1960.

_____ *New Heaven, New Earth: A Study of Millenarian Activities*. Oxford: Basil Blackwell, 1969.

Cabral, Amilcar. *Revolution in Guinea*. New York: Monthly Review, 1972.

_____ *Return to the Source*. New York: Monthly Review, 1973.

Carmichael, Stokely and Charles V. Hamilton. *Black Power: The Politics of Liberation in America*. Harmondsworth: Pelican, 1969.

Caute, David. *Fanon*. London: Fontana, 1970.

Cleaver, Eldridge. *Post-Prison Writings and Speeches*. Ed. Robert Scheer, London: Jonathan Cape, 1969.

Cook, David. *African Literature: A Critical View*. Harlow: Longman, 1977.

Cook, Mercer and Stephen Henderson. *The Militant Black Writer in Africa and the United States*. Madison: University of Wisconsin Press, 1969.

Danquah, J.B. *The Akan Doctrine of God*. London: Lutterworth Press, 1944.

Dathorne, O.R. *African Literature in the Twentieth Century*. London: Heinemann, 1976.

Davidson, Basil. *Black Star: A View of the Life and Times of Kwame Nkrumah*. London: Allen Lane, 1973.

——— *Africa in History*. Revised Ed. St Albans: Paladin, 1974.

——— *Africa in Modern History*. Harmondsworth: Pelican, 1978.

Davis, Angela. *If They Come In the Morning*. London: Orbach & Chambers, 1971.

Diop, Cheikh Anta. *The African Origin of Civilisation: Myth or Reality*. Trans. Mercer Cook. Westport: Laurence Hill, 1974.

Douglas, Mary. *Purity and Danger: An Analysis of the Concepts of Pollution and Taboo*. Revised Ed. London: Routledge & Kegan Paul, 1969.

Du Bois, W.E.B. *The World and Africa*. Revised Ed. New York: International Publishers, 1965.

Duerden, Dennis. *African Art and Literature: The Invisible Present*. London: Heinemann, 1975.

Eliade, Mircea. *The Myth of the Eternal Return, or Cosmos and History*. 2nd Ed. Princeton: Princeton University Press, 1971.

Etherton, Michael. *The Development of African Drama*. London: Hutchinson, 1982.

Fage, J.D. *A History of West Africa*. 4th Ed. Cambridge: Cambridge University Press, 1969.

Fanon, Frantz. *A Dying Colonialism*. Trans. Haakon Chevalier. New York: Grove Press, 1967.

——— *Black Skin, White Masks*. Trans. Charles Lam Markmann. New York: Grove Press, 1967.

——— *The Wretched of the Earth*. Trans. Constance Farrington. Harmondsworth: Penguin, 1967.

——— *Toward the African Revolution*. Trans. Haakon Chevalier. Harmondsworth: Pelican, 1970.

Fraser, Robert. *The Novels of Ayi Kwei Armah: A Study in Polemical Fiction*. London: Heinemann, 1980.

Frazer, J.G. *The Golden Bough*. Abridged Version. London: Macmillan, 1967.

Freud, Sigmund. *Totem and Taboo*. London: Routledge & Kegan Paul, 1950.

Frye, Northrop. *An Anatomy of Criticism*. Princeton: Princeton University Press, 1957.

Gakwandi, Shatto Arthur. *The Novel and Contemporary Experience in Africa*. London: Heinemann, 1977.

Goody, Jack. *The Domestication of the Savage Mind*. Cambridge: Cambridge University Press, 1977.

Griffiths, Gareth. *A Double Exile: African and West Indian Writing Between Two Cultures*. London: Marion Boyars, 1978.

Henderson, R.N. *The King in Everyman: Evolutionary Trends in Onitsha Ibo Society and Culture*. New Haven: Yale University Press, 1972.

Irele, Abiola. *The African Experience in Literature and Ideology*. London: Heinemann, 1981.

James, E.O. *Origins of Sacrifice*. New York/London: Kennikat Press, 1933.

——— *Sacrifice and Sacrament*. London: Thames and Hudson, 1962.

Larson, Charles. *The Emergence of African Fiction*. 2nd Ed. London: Macmillan, 1978.

Lawson, William. *The Western Scar: The Theme of the Been-to in West African Fiction*. Athens: Ohio University Press, 1982.

Levi-Strauss, C. *The Savage Mind*. London: Weidenfeld & Nicolson, 1966.

Levy-Bruhl, L. *Primitives and the Supernatural*. London: Allen & Unwin, 1936.

Lloyd, P.C. *Africa in Social Change*. Revised Ed. Harmondsworth: Penguin, 1972.

Malcolm X, with the assistance of Alex Haley. *The Autobiography of Malcolm X*. Harmondsworth: Penguin, 1968.

Manoukian, Madelaine. *Akan and Ga-Adangme Peoples*. London: Africa Institute, 1950.

Mbiti, John S. *African Religions and Philosophy*. London: Heinemann, 1969.

McEwan, Neil. *Africa and the Novel*. London: Macmillan, 1983.

Meyerowitz, Eva. *The Sacred State of the Akan*. London: Faber, 1951.

—— *The Akan of Ghana: Their Ancient Beliefs*. London: Faber, 1958.

Moore, Gerald. *The Chosen Tongue*. Harlow: Longman, 1969.

—— *Wole Soyinka*. 2nd Ed. London: Evans Brothers, 1978.

—— *Twelve African Writers*. London: Hutchinson, 1980.

Ngara, Emmanuel. *Stylistic Criticism and the African Novel*. London: Heinemann, 1982.

Nketia, J.H. *Funeral Dirges of the Akan People*. New York: Negro Universities Press, 1969.

Nkosi, Lewis. *Tasks and Masks: Themes and Styles of African Literature*. Harlow: Longman, 1981.

Obiechina, Emmanuel. *Culture, Tradition and Society in the West African Novel*. Cambridge: Cambridge University Press, 1975.

Ong, Walter J. *Orality and Literacy*. London: Methuen, 1982.

Palmer, Eustace. *An Introduction to the African Novel*. London: Heinemann, 1972.

—— *The Growth of the African Novel*. London: Heinemann, 1979.

Parrinder, Geoffrey. *Religion in Africa*. Harmondsworth: Penguin, 1969.

—— *West African Religion*. London: Epworth Press, 1969.

Peters, Jonathan A. *A Dance of Masks: Senghor, Achebe, Soyinka*. Washington D.C.: Three Continents Press, 1978.

Rattray, R.S. *Ashanti*. Oxford: Clarendon Press, 1923.

—— *Religion and Art in Ashanti*. Oxford: Clarendon Press, 1927.

Robbe-Grillet, Alain. *Pour un nouveau roman*. Paris: Gallimard, 1963.

Roscoe, Adrian. *Mother is Gold: A Study in West African Literature*. Cambridge: Cambridge University Press, 1971.

Scholes, Robert *The Fabulators*. New York: Oxford University Press, 1967.

Soyinka, Wole. *Myth, Literature and the African World*. Cambridge: Cambridge University Press, 1976.

Steiner, Franz. *Taboo*. Harmondsworth: Penguin, 1967.

Todd, Jan. *Notes on "The Beautyful Ones Are Not Yet Born"*. Harlow: Longman, York Press, 1982.

Turner, Victor. *The Forest of Symbols*. Ithaca: Cornell University Press, 1970.

_____ *The Ritual Process*. Harmondsworth: Pelican, 1974.

van Gennep, Arnold. *The Rites of Passage*. 1906. Trans. S.T. Kimball. London: Routledge & Kegan Paul, 1960.

Vincent, Theo, Ed. *The Novel and Reality in Africa and America*. Lagos: University of Lagos Press, 1973.

Williams, Chancellor. *The Destruction of Black Civilization*. Dubuque: Kendall/Hunt Publishing Company, 1971.

Williamson, S. G. *Akan Religion and the Christian Faith*. Accra: Ghana Universities Press, 1965.

Zell, Hans, Carol Bundy and Virginia Coulon, Eds. *A New Reader's Guide to African Literature*. London: Heinemann; New York: Africana, 1983.

Articles

Achebe, Chinua. "The Novelist as Teacher". In *Commonwealth Literature*. Ed. John Press. London: Heinemann, 1965, pp. 202–05.

_____ "Africa and Her Writers". In *In Person: Achebe, Awoonor, and Soyinka at the University of Washington*. Ed. Karen Morell. Washington: University of Washington Press, 1975, pp. 1–59.

_____ Discussion with Kofi Awoonor, Ali Mazrui and others. *Issue*, 6, 1(1976), 37.

Achebe, Christie C. "Literary Insights into the Ogbanje Phenomenon". *Journal of African Studies*, 7, 1(1980), 31–38.

Aidoo, Ama Ata. "No Saviours". In *African Writers on African Writing*. Ed. G.D. Killam. London: Heinemann, 1973, pp. 14–18.

Amuta, Chidi. "Ayi Kwei Armah, History and 'The Way': The Importance of *Two Thousand Seasons*". *Komparatistische Hefte*, 3 (1981), 79–86.

_____ "Ayi Kwei Armah and the Mythopoesis of Mental Decolonisation". *Ufahamu*, 10, 3 (Spring 1981), 44–56.

_____ "The Contemporary African Artist in Armah's Novels". *World Literature Written in English*, 21, 3 (Autumn 1982), 467–76.

Anon. Biographical Note on Ayi Kwei Armah. *Cultural Events in Africa*, 40 (March 1968), 5.

Anon. "What Does Ghana Really Owe?". *West Africa* 28 January 1972, 87.

Anozie, Sunday. "Le Nouveau Roman Africain". *The Conch*, 2, 1 (1970), 29–32.

Anyidoho, Kofi. "Historical Realism and the Visionary Ideal: Ayi Kwei Armah's *Two Thousand Seasons*". *Ufahamu*, 11, 2(1981–82), 108–30.

____ "African Creative Fiction and a Poetics of Social Change". *Komparatistische Hefte*, 13(1986), 67–82.

Awoonor, Kofi. "Nationalism: Masks and Consciousness". *Books Abroad*, 45 (1971), 207–11.

____ "Kwame Nkrumah: Symbol of Emergent Africa". *Africa Report* (June 1972), 22–25.

____ "Africa's Literature Beyond Politics". *Worldview*, 15, 3 (1972), 21–25.

____ Interview by John Goldblatt. *Transition*, 41, (1972), 42–44.

____ Interview in *Palaver*. Eds.Bernth Lindfors, Ian Munro, and Richard Priebe. Austin: African and Afro-American Research Institute, University of Texas, 1972, pp. 47–64.

____ Interview by Robert Serumaga. In *African Writers Talking*. Eds.Dennis Duerden and Cosmos Pieterse. London: Heinemann, 1973, pp. 29–50.

____ "Voyager and the Earth". *New Letters*, 40, 1 (1973), 85–93.

____ "Tradition and Continuity in African Literature". In *In Person: Achebe, Awoonor and Soyinka at the University of Washington*. Washington: University of Washington Press, 1975, pp. 133–60.

____ Discussion in *Issue*, 6, 1 (1976), 5–13, 22–40.

Barkan, Sandra. "Beyond Larsony: On the Possibility of Understanding Texts Across Cultures". *World Literature Today*, 57, 1 (1983), 35–38.

Barnard, Roger. "Frantz Fanon". *New Society* 11,275(4 Jan 1968), 11–13.

Bishop, Rand. "The Beautyful Ones Are Born: Armah's First Five Novels". *World Literature Written in English*, 21, 3 (1982), 531–37.

Boafo, Y.S. "The Nature of Healing in Ayi Kwei Armah's *The Healers*". *Komparatistische Hefte*, 13 (1986), 95–104.

Booth, James. "*Why Are We So Blest?* and the Limits of Metaphor". *Journal of Commonwealth Literature*, 15, 1 (1980), 50–64.

Britwum, Atta. "Hero-Worshipping in the African Novel". *Asemka*, 3 (1975), 1–18.

Busia, Abena. "Parasites and Prophets: The Use of Women in Ayi Kwei Armah's Novels". In *Ngambika: Studies of Women In African Literature*. Ed.C.B.Davies and A.A.Graves. Trenton: African World Press, 1986, pp. 89–114.

Case, Frederick I. "The African Bourgeois in West African Literature". *Canadian Journal of African Studies* 7 (1973), 257–66.

Chakava, Henry. "Ayi Kwei Armah and a Commonwealth of Souls". In *Standpoints on African Literature*. Ed.C.Wanjala. Nairobi: East African Literature Bureau, 1973, pp. 197–208.

Chetin, Sarah. "Armah's Women". *Kunapipi*, 6, 3 (1974), 47–57.

Chinweizu. "Surfaces of Disillusion". *Okike*, 6, 3 (1974), 88–96.

Collins, Harold. "The Ironic Imagery of Armah's *The Beautyful Ones Are Not Yet Born*: The Putrescent Vision". *World Literature Written in English*, 20 (November 1971), 37–50.

Colmer, Rosemary. "The Human and the Divine: *Fragments* and *Why Are We So Blest?*". *Kunapipi*, 2, 2 (1980), 77–90.

Echeruo, Michael. Interview in *Dem-Say*. Ed.Bernth Lindfors. Austin; African and Afro-American Research Institute, University of Texas, 1973, pp. 12–15.

Evans, Jennifer. "Women of 'The Way'", *ACLALS*, 6, 1 (November 1982), 17–26.

Fenton, Leslie. "Symbolism and Theme in Peters' *The Second Round* and Armah's *The Beautyful Ones Are Not Yet Born*". *Pan-African Journal*, 6 (1973), 83–90.

Fernandez, James W. "The Shaka Complex". *Transition*, 29 (1967), 11–15.

Feuser, Willfried. "Reflections of History in African Literature". *World Literature Written in English*, 24, 1 (1984), 52–64.

Folarin, Margaret. "An Additional Comment on Ayi Kwei Armah's *The Beautyful Ones Are Not Yet Born*". *African Literature Today*, 5 (1971), 116–29.

Fraser, Robert. "The American Background in *Why Are We So Blest?*". *African Literature Today* 9, (1978), 39–46.

Frye, Northrop. "The Archetypes of Literature". *Kenyon Review*, 13, 1 (1951), 92–110.

Goldie, Terry. "A Connection of Images: The Structure of

Symbols in *The Beautyful Ones Are Not Yet Born"*. *Kunapipi*, 1, 1 (1979), 94–107.

Goody, Jack. "Ethnohistory and the Akan of Ghana". *Africa*, 29 (1959), 67–81.

Griffiths, Gareth. "Structure and Image in Armah's *The Beautyful Ones Are Not Yet Born"*. *Studies in Black Literature*, 2, 2 (1971), 1–9.

——— "The Language of Disillusion in the African Novel". In *Commonwealth*. Ed. Anna Rutherford. Aarhus: University of Aarhus Press, 1971, pp. 62–72.

Horton, Robin. "New Year in the Delta". *Nigeria Magazine*, 67 (1960), 256–74.

——— "African Traditional Thought and Western Science". *Africa*, 37 (1967), 176–81.

Ikonne, Chidi. "Purpose versus Plot: The Double Vision of Thomas Mofolo's Narrator" In *Aspects of South African Literature*. Ed.Christopher Heywood. London: Heinemann, 1976, pp. 54–65.

Irele, Abiola. Review of *The Beautyful Ones Are Not Yet Born*. *Okyeame*, 4, 2 (June 1969), 125–27.

Izevbaye, D.S. "Ayi Kwei Armah and the 'I' of the Beholder". In *A Celebration of Black and African Writing*. Eds.Bruce King and Kolawole Ogungbesan. Oxford: Oxford University Press, 1975, pp. 232–44.

——— "Naming and the Character of African Fiction". *Research in African Literatures*, 12, 2 (1981), 162–84.

——— "Time in the African Novel". *Journal of Commonwealth Literature*, 17, 1 (1982), 74–89.

Iyasere, Solomon O. "Oral Tradition in the Criticism of African Literature". *Journal of Modern African Studies*, 13, 1 (1975), 107–19.

——— "Cultural Formalism and the Criticism of Modern African Literature". *Journal of Modern African Studies*, 14, 2 (1976), 322–30.

Johnson, Lemuel A. "Ideology, Art and Community: African Literature and the Issues". In *African Literature as a Shared Experience*. Eds.Richard Priebe and Thomas Hale. Washington D.C.: Three Continents Press, 1979, pp. 181–203.

——— "The Middle Passage in African Literature: Soyinka,

Ouologuem, Armah". *African Literature Today*, 11 (1980), 62–84.

Johnson, Joyce. "The Transitional Gulf: A Discussion of Wole Soyinka's *Season of Anomy*". *World Literature Written in English*, 18, 2 (1979), 287–302.

——— "The Promethean 'Factor' in Ayi Kwei Armah's *Fragments* and *Why Are We So Blest?*". *World Literature Written in English*, 21, 3 (1982), 497–510.

Jones, Eldred. Review of *The Beautyful Ones Are Not Yet Born*. *African Literature Today*, 3 (1969), 55–57.

Jones, LeRoi (Imamu Amiri Baraka). "A Black Value System". In *Black Poets and Prophets: The Theory, Practice and Esthetics of the Pan-Africanist Revolution*. Eds.Woodie King and Earl Anthony. New York: New American Library, 1972, pp. 137–47.

Kibera, Leonard. "Pessimism and the African Novelist: Ayi Kwei Armah's *The Beautyful Ones Are Not Yet Born*". *Journal of Commonwealth Literature*, 14, 1 (1979), 64–72.

Kilson, Martin. "African Political Change and the Modernisation Process". *Journal of Modern African Studies*, 1, 4 (1962), 425–40.

Kronenfeld, J.Z. "The 'Communistic' African and the 'Individualistic' Westerner". In *Critical Perspectives on Nigerian Literatures*. Ed. Bernth Lindfors. London: Heinemann, 1979, pp. 237–64.

Larson, Charles, "Ayi Kwei Armah's Vision of African Reciprocity". *Africa Today*, 21, 2 (1974), 117–19.

Lazarus, Neil. "The Implications of Technique in *The Healers*". *Research in African Literatures*, 13, 4 (1982), 488–98.

——— Review of the *The Novels of Ayi Kwei Armah* by Robert Fraser. *Research in African Literatures*, 15, 3 (1984), 444–47.

——— "Pessimism of the Intellect, Optimism of the Will: A Reading of Ayi Kwei Armah's *The Beautyful Ones Are Not Yet Born*". *Research in African Literatures*, 18, 2 (1987), 137–175.

Lindfors, Bernth. "Armah's Histories". *African Literature Today* 11 (1980), 85–96.

Lobb, Edward. "Armah's *Fragments* and the Vision of the Whole". *Ariel*, 10, 1 (1979), 25–38.

——— "Personal and Political Fate in Armah's *Why Are We So Blest?*". *World Literature Written in English*, 19, 1 (1980), 5–18.

Lurie, Joseph. "*Fragments*: Between the Loved Ones and the Community". *Ba Shiru*, 5, 1 (1973), 31–41.

Maugham-Brown, David. "Interpreting and *The Interpreters*". *English in Africa*, 6, 2 (September 1978), 54–60.

____ "Review of *The Emergence of African Fiction* by Charles Larson. *English in Africa*, 6, 1 (March 1979), 91–96.

Mensah, A.N. "The Crisis of the Sensitive Ghanaian: A Review of the First Two Novels of Ayi Kwei Armah". *Universitas*, 2, 2 (1973), 3–17.

Meredith, Martin. "The Broken Dream". *The Sunday Times Magazine*, 7 March 1982, 21–30.

Meyerowitz, Eva. "A Note on the Origins of Ghana". *African Affairs*, 51 (1952), 319–22.

Moore, Gerald. "Time and Experience in African Poetry". *Transition*, 26 (1966), 18–22.

____ "The Imagery of Death in African Poetry". *Africa*, 38 (1968), 57–70.

____ "The Writer and the Cargo Cult". In *Commonwealth*. Ed.Anna Rutherford. Aarhus: University of Aarhus Press, 1971, pp. 73–84.

____ "The Debate on Existence in African Literature". *Présence Africaine*, 81 (1972), 18–48.

____ "Reintegration with the Lost Self". *Revue de Littérature Comparée*, 48 (1974), 488–503.

____ "Armah's Second Novel". *Journal of Commonwealth Literature*, 9, 1 (August 1974), 69–71.

____ "Death, Convergence and Rebirth in Two Black Novels". *Nigerian Journal of the Humanities*, 2 (1978), 6–17.

Mutiso, G.C.M. "African Socio-Political Process: A Model from Literature". In *Black Aesthetics*. Eds. A. Gurr and E. Zirimu. Nairobi: East African Literature Bureau, 1973, pp. 143–68.

Nicholson, Mary. "The Organization of Symbols in Ayi Kwei Armah's *The Beautyful Ones Are Not Yet Born*". *Asemka*, 1, 2 (December 1974), 7–16.

Niemi, Richard. "Will the Beautiful Ones ever be Born?". *Pan-Africanist*, 3 (1971), 18–23.

Niven, Alastair. "Exile and Expatriation in African Literature". *Literary Half-Yearly*, 21, 1 (1980), 167–80.

____ "Wars, Skirmishes and Strategies in the Criticism of

Modern African Literature". *World Literature Written in English*, 19, 2 (1980), 144–51.

_____ "The Family in African Literature". *Ariel*, 12, 3 (1981), 81–91.

Nnolim, Charles. "Dialectic as Form: Pejorism in the Novels of Armah". *African Literature Today*, 10 (1979), 207–23.

_____ Letter to the Editor. *Research in African Literatures*, 14, 4 (1983), 567–70.

Noble, R.W. "A Beautyful Novel". *Journal of Commonwealth Literature*, 9, 2 (1970), 117–19.

Nwoga, Donatus I. "Alienation in Modern African Fiction". *Muse*, 5 (1973), 23–27.

Obiechina, Emmanuel. Review of *The Beautyful Ones Are Not Yet Born*. *Okike*, 1, 1 (1971), 49–53.

_____ "Post-Independence Disillusionment in Three African Novels". In *Neo-African Literature and Culture: Essays in Memory of Jahnheinz Jahn*. Eds.Bernth Lindfors and Ulla Schild. Wiesbaden: B.Heyman, 1976, pp. 119–46.

Obumselu, Ben. "Marx, Politics and the African Novel". *Twentieth Century Studies*, 10 (1973), 107–27.

Ogunba, Oyin. "The Traditional Content of the Plays of Wole Soyinka". *African Literature Today*, 4 (1970), 2–18.

_____ "The Politics of Poverty: Two Novels on Political Independence In West Africa". *Oduma*, 2, 1 (1974), 24–27, 30–33.

Ogungbesan, K. "A King for All Seasons: Chaka in African Literature". *Black Orpheus*, 3, 2/3 (October 1974-June 1975), 86–95.

_____ "Symbol and Meaning in *The Beautyful Ones Are Not Yet Born*". *African Literature Today*, 7 (1975), 93–110.

_____ "Simple Novels and Simplistic Criticism". *Umoja*, 1, 3 (Fall 1977), 31–42.

Ojong, Ayuk G. "The Lust for Material Well-Being in *The Beautyful Ones Are Not Yet Born* and *Fragments* by Ayi Kwei Armah". *Présence Africaine* 132 (1984), 33–43.

Ola, V.U. "The Feminine Principle and the Search for Wholeness in *The Healers*". *Ufahamu*, 14, 3 (1985), 73–82.

Okai, Atukwei. "Vision, Image and Symbol in Ghanaian Literature". *Pacific Quarterly*, 6, 3–4 (1981), 51–61.

Okpewho, Isidore. "Myth and Modern Fiction: Armah's *Two*

Thousand Seasons". *African Literature Today*, 13 (1983), 1–23.

Omotoso, Kole. "Trans-Saharan Views: Mutually Negative Portrayals". *African Literature Today*, 14 (1984), 111–17.

Opoku, Kofi Asare. "The World View of the Akan". In *Akan History and Culture*. Ed.J.K.Fynn. Harlow: Longman, 1982, pp. 61–73.

Owusu, Kofi. Review of *The Novels of Ayi Kwei Armah* by Robert Fraser. *African Literature Today*, 13 (1983), 237–39.

Palmer, Eustace. "Social Comment in the West African Novel". *Studies in the Novel*, 4, 2 (1972), 218–30.

_____ "Negritude Rediscovered: A Reading of the Recent Novels of Armah, Ngugi and Soyinka". *International Fiction Review*, 8, 1 (1981), 1–11.

Panter-Brick, S.K. "Fiction and Politics: The African Writer's Abdication". *Journal of Commonwealth and Comparative Politics*, 13 (1975), 79–86.

Peplow, Michael W. "The 'Black White Man' in African Protest Literature". *Lock Haven Review*, 13 (1972), 3–14.

Petersen, Kirsten Holst. "The New Way: Armah's *Two Thousand Seasons"*. *World Literature Written in English*, 15 (1976), 330–35.

_____ "Loss and Frustration: An Analysis of A.K. Armah's *Fragments"*. *Kunapipi*, 1, 1 (1979), 53–65.

Povey, John. "Bartered Birthrite: A Comment on the Attitudes to the Past in West African Poetry". In *National Identity*. Ed.K.L.Goodwin. London/Melbourne: Heinemann, 1970, pp. 38–50.

_____ Review of *The Emergence of African Fiction* by Charles Larson. *ASA Review of Books*, 2 (1975), 62–65.

_____ "Africa through African Eyes". *Intellect*, 104 (1976), 323–26.

Priebe, Richard. "Escaping the Nightmare of History". *Ariel*, 4, 2 (1973), 55–67.

_____ "Kofi Awoonor's *This Earth, My Brother. . .* as an African Dirge". *Benin Review*, 1 (1974), 95–106.

_____ "Demonic Imagery and the Apocalyptic Vision in the Novels of Ayi Kwei Armah". *Yale French Studies*, 53 (1976), 102–36.

_____ "Popular Writing in Ghana: a Sociology and Rhetoric". *Research in African Literatures*, 9, 3 (1978), 395–422.

Rassner, Ron. "*Fragments*: The Cargo Mentality". *Ba Shiru*, 5, 2 (1974), 55–64.

Ravenscroft, Arthur. "Novels of Disillusionment". *Journal of Commonwealth Literature*, 6 (January 1969), 120–37.

Rohdie, Samuel. "Liberation and Violence in Algeria". *Studies on the Left*, 6, 3 (May-June 1966), 83–88.

Sabor, Peter. "Palm-Wine and Drinkards: African Literature and its Critics". *Ariel*, 12, 3 (1981), 113–25.

Sekyi-Otu, Ato. "Towards Anoa. . .Not Back to Anoa: The Grammar of Revolutionary Homecoming in *Two Thousand Seasons*". *Research in African Literatures* 18, 2 (1987), 192–214.

Shehu, Emman Usman. "A Blessing of Contradictions: A Reading of *Why Are We So Blest?*". *Kakaki*, 1 (1980), 25–52.

Simonse, Simon. "African Literature Between Nostalgia and Utopia". *Research in African Literatures*, 13, 4 (Winter 1982), 451–87.

Smith, Edwin W. "Religious Beliefs of the Akan". *Africa*, 15 (1945), 23–29.

Snyder, Emile. "New Directions in African Writings". *Pan-African Journal*, 5 (1972), 253–61.

Solomon, Joan. "A Commentary on Ayi Kwei Armah's *The Beautyful Ones Are Not Yet Born*". *English in Africa*, 1, 2 (September 1974), 25–31.

Soyinka, Wole. "And After the Narcissist?". *African Forum*, 1, 4 (1966), 53–64.

_____ "The Writer in an African State". *Transition*, 31 (June-July 1967), 11–13.

_____ "*The Writer in a Modern African State*". In *The Writer in Modern Africa*. Ed.P.Wästberg. Uppsala: Almquist & Wiksell, 1968, pp. 14–21.

_____ Interview. *The Militant*, 2, 1 (December 1972), 3–7.

_____ Interview by Ezekiel Mphalele, Lewis Nkosi and Dennis Duerden. In *African Writers Talking*. Eds.Dennis Duerden and Cosmo Pieterse. London: Heinemann, 1972, pp. 169–80.

_____ Interview by B. Jeyifo. *Transition*, 8, 5 (1973), 62–64.

_____ Interview by Louis S. Gates. *Black World*, 24, 10 (1975), 30–48.

_____ "We Africans Must Speak in One Language". *Afrika*, 20, 9 (1979), 22–23.

Staniland, Martin. "Frantz Fanon and the African Political Class". *African Affairs*, 68 (1969), 4–25.

Staudt, Kathleen. "The Characterisation of Women in Soyinka and Armah". *Ba Shiru*, 8, 2 (1977), 63–69.

Steele, Shelby. "Existentialism in the Novels of Ayi Kwei Armah'. *Obsidian*, 3, 1 (1977), 5–13.

Stewart, Danièle. "L'être et le monde dans les premiers romans d'Ayi Kwei Armah". *Présence Africaine*, 85 (1973), 192–208.

_____ "Ghanaian Writing in Prose: A Critical Survey". *Présence Africaine*, 91 (1974), 73–105.

_____ "Disillusionment among Anglophone and Francophone African Writers". *Studies in Black Literature*, 7, 1 (1976), 6–9.

Thomas, Peter. Review of *Why Are We So Blest?*. *African Arts*, 6, 3 (1973), 81–82.

Tucker, Martin. "Tragedy of a Been-to". *The New Republic*, 162 (31 January 1970), 24–26.

Urena, C.P. Letter to the Editor. *Research in African Literatures*, 14, 2 (1983), 269–73.

van der Geest, Sjaak. "The Image of Death in Akan Highlife Songs of Ghana". *Research in African Literatures*, 11, 3 (1980), 146–74.

Webb, Hugh. "The African Historical Novel and The Way Forward". *African Literature Today*, 11 (1980), 24–38.

Williams, Denis. "The Mbari Publications". *Nigeria Magazine*, 75 (1962), 69–74.

Wright, Derek. "Armah's Ghana Revisited: History and Fiction". *International Fiction Review*, 12, 1 (1985), 23–27.

_____ "Fragments: The Cargo Connection". *Kunapipi*, 7, 1 (1985), 45–58.

_____ "Love and Politics in the African Novel". *ACLALS Bulletin*, 7, 1 (1985), 13–27.

_____ "The Metaphysical and Material Worlds: Armah's Ritual Cycle". *World Literature Today*, 59, 3 (1985), 337–42.

_____ "Tradition and the Vision of the Past in the Early Novels of Ayi Kwei Armah". *English in Africa*, 12, 2 (1985), 83–97.

_____ "Motivation and Motif: The Carrier Rite in Ayi Kwei Armah's *The Beautyful Ones Are Not Yet Born*". *English Studies in Africa*, 28, 2 (1985), 119–33.

_____ "Saviors and Survivors: The Disappearing Community in

the Novels of Ayi Kwei Armah". *Ufahamu*, 14, 2 (1985), 134–56.

_____ "Method and Metaphor: A Note on Armah's First Novel". *New Literature Review*, 14 (1985), 42–46.

_____ "The Early Writings of Ayi Kwei Armah". *Research in African Literatures*, 16, 4 (1985), 487–513.

_____ "The Chaka Syndrome: Armah and Mofolo". *Literary Criterion*, 20, 2 (1985), 42–47.

_____ "Flux and Form: The Geography of Time in *The Beautyful Ones Are Not Yet Born*". *Ariel*, 17, 2 (1986), 63–77.

_____ "The Ritual Context of Two Plays by Soyinka'. *Theatre Research International*, 12, 1 (1987), 51–61.

_____ "Ritual Modes and Social Models in African Fiction". *World Literature Written in English*, 27, 2 (1987), pp. 195–207.

_____ "Fragments: The Akan Background". *Research in African Literatures*, 18, 2 (1987), pp. 176–191.

_____ "Ritual and Reality in the Novels of Wole Soyinka, Gabriel Okara and Kofi Awoonor". *Kunapipi* 9, 1 (1987), 65–74.

_____ "Scapegoats and Carriers: New Year Festivals in History and Literature". *Journal of African Studies*, 14, 4 (1987), 183–89.

_____ "Critical and Historical Fictions: Robert Fraser's Reading of *The Healers*". *English in Africa*, 15, 1 (1988), pp. 71–82.

_____ "Orality in the African Historical Novel". *Journal of Commonwealth Literature*, 23, 1 (1988), pp. 99–101.

Wright, Edgar. "The Bilingual, Bicultural African Writer". In *The Commonwealth Writer Overseas: Themes of Exile and Expatriation*. Ed. Alastair Niven. Brussels: Didier, 1976, pp. 107–19.

Yankson, Kofi. "*Fragments*: The Eagle that Refused to Soar". *Asemka*, 1, 1 (1974), 53–59.

Theses

Barthold, Bonnie Jo. "Three West African Novelists; Achebe, Soyinka, Armah". Ph.D. University of Arizona, 1976.

Colmer, Rosemary. "The Development of the Sub-Saharan Black African Novel". Ph.D. Macquarie University, Sydney, 1979.

Crewe, Adrian. "Ayi Kwei Armah and the Mirage of African Socialism: Problems of ideology and literary production in post-colonial Africa". M.A. University of Sussex, 1976.

Davenport, Randall Louis. "The Bourgeois Rebel: A Study of the Been-To in Selected West African Novels". Ph.D. Northwestern University, Illinois, 1978.

Lawson, William Vincent. "The Western Scar: The Theme of the Been-To in West African Fiction". Ph.D. Stanford University, 1976.

Lurie, Joseph. "Neo-Colonialism, the Individual and Conflict: a study of thematic development in the novels of Ayi Kwei Armah". M.A. University of Wisconsin, Madison, 1973.

Priebe, Richard. "The Development of Mythic Consciousness in West African Literature". Ph.D. University of Texas, Austin, 1973.

Walker, William A. "Major Ghanaian Fiction in English: a study of the novels of Ayi Kwei Armah and Kofi Awoonor". Ph.D. University of Texas, Austin, 1976.

Index